To have made the Carry On series is not an achievement –
it's a bloody liberty.
(Peter Rogers, Producer of the Carry Ons)

THE CARRY-ON BOOK

KENNETH EASTAUGH

David & Charles
Newton Abbot · London · North Pomfret (Vt)
Vancouver

To Mum and Robert

ISBN 0 7153 7403 6

© Kenneth Eastaugh 1978

Typeset by HBM Typesetting Limited,
Standish Street, Chorley, Lancashire
and printed in Great Britain
by Redwood Burn Limited,
Trowbridge & Esher
for David & Charles (Publishers) Limited
Brunel House, Newton Abbot, Devon

Published in the United States of America
by David & Charles Inc
North Pomfret, Vermont 05053, USA

Published in Canada
by Douglas David & Charles Limited
1875 Welch Street North, Vancouver BC

Contents

Part One
The Story

Sid James wasn't in the last Carry On.
He was sick on the morning they made it.

(Film industry joke)

*Carry On Abroad . . . or What a Package . . .
or It's All In . . . or Swiss Hols In The Snow*
It's Barbara Windsor covered in embarrassment—
and very little else! What Barbara has seen is Sid
James walking into what she thought was her
private bathroom. But look what Sid saw! Though
not for as long as you're seeing it! The scene
featured Barbara, as Miss Sadie Tomkins, and
Sid, as Vic Flange, among a party of unfortunates
spending a long weekend in a half-finished hotel on
'The Paradise Island of Elsbels'. In fact, the name
of the island is what Barbara is saying in this
picture!

Carry On Sergeant When the NCO yelled 'Get fell in'—he didn't mean here, you drip! You've heard of the Grenadier Guards? Well these are the mud guards. They are members of Britain's stream lying . . . sorry . . . streamlined army. Despite appearances they are not taking to soldiering like ducks to water. Indeed, in more ways than one, they are scraping the bottom with this lot! The obvious earth-loving type is recruit Peter Golightly (Charles Hawtrey). His wet nurse is recruit Andy Galloway (Gerald Campion). Golightly was supposed to go lightly across the stream on a rope, but he couldn't get in the swing of it. His expression is almost certainly caused by two fish up his trousers saying: 'What are you doing round these parts?'

In *Carry On Sergeant*, Kenneth Williams, Charles Hawtrey, Bob Monkhouse and others, playing Army recruits, had to swing on a rope across a wide, mud-filled ditch which was part of an assault course. The object of the scene was for Charles Hawtrey to fall in. Bob Monkhouse, in line to follow Hawtrey across the ditch, did not really have to make the swing. The wanted shot was in the can. But he decided to go.

Almost as soon as he grabbed the rope and pushed off from the bank, however, he began to lose his hold and did not know why. The more feverishly he tried to hang on the more he slid, inch by inch, down the rope which was now suspended, almost motionless, above the centre of the ditch.

Whadya mean, am I bumming a lift? Here's a star in stripes pretending not to know whether he's coming or going, though we can all guess where he's been! It's Kenneth Williams putting his back into what can only be called a stripe-tease—but not, as it might appear, for *Carry On Behind*. In that sense the picture is a bum steer.

For Kenny's 'This-is-the-end-of-me!' pose was done as a lark while making *Carry On Abroad*, in which he plays a super-efficient holiday tours' courier—who, at the moment, is just a little behind! His trunks look well packed, but he has still to pick up his bags!

For a few action-packed seconds Monkhouse worked, in a lightning hand-over hand flurry, to hold on, watched now by jubilant actors and camera crew. His efforts were useless. The end was gleefully obvious to everyone. The rope slipped through Monkhouse's hands and he plunged into the waiting mud. The cameraman, Alan Hume, was laughing so much that he forgot to work the camera and the shot was lost.

The cause of Bob's slide from grace was Kenneth Williams who, in typical mischievous mood, had smeared the rope with half-a-pound of butter while everybody else's attention was on the fallen Hawtrey. 'A gnat could not have clung on there, I promise you!', says Bob.

As he crawled out of the ditch, dripping slime and mud, somebody yelled: 'Ah well, butter late than never!' And Williams started calling him Bob Mudhouse.

For a scene in *Carry On Abroad*, Sid James had to arrive at a travel agency, put his suitcase down, collect some tickets, pick up the suitcase and board a coach. In reality the suitcase was empty, but by the time the second part of the scene was filmed, and Sid had to pick it up, one of the camera crew had filled it with weights. Sid, expecting an empty suitcase, nearly wrenched every muscle in his body and was almost pulled flat on his back . . . while everybody on the set, primed about the joke, exploded in laughter. After some mock anger, Sid joined in.

In *Carry On Spying*, a night scene, supposedly taking place in a menacing warehouse, was shot in the property storeroom at Pinewood Studios at 3 o'clock in the morning. In the scene, Kenneth Williams, Bernard Cribbins, Charles Hawtrey and Barbara Windsor, as bungling British spies, are trying to cross-question a knifed and dying foreign agent (played by Victor Maddern) who answers only in groaning 'oooh's and 'aaah's.

Alan Hume, the film's director of photography, found it all so funny that every now and then he had to crawl behind some large packing cases, with a handkerchief stuffed in his mouth, to prevent disrupting the scene with guffaws and being sent off the set by director Gerald Thomas. Towards the end of the scene, feeling another bout of laughter coming on, Hume quickly stuffed the handkerchief back into his mouth and crawled behind the cases, only to come face to face with somebody else, also with a handkerchief stuffed in his mouth, crawling round the cases from the other side. It was director Gerald Thomas.

Kenneth Connor, playing a school's new science master in *Carry On Teacher*, had a scene in which he went into his laboratory for the first time and slowly walked round it, looking this way and that, taking it all in. At one point he had to sniff with curiosity at an open jar. But, unbeknown to him, the camera crew had put a stink bomb in the jar. Slowly Connor moved towards the jar, bent, sniffed . . . and staggered back, pulling an agonised face. 'Corrr!' he yelled, bursting into laughter. 'You dirty, rotten so-and-so's!'

'Cut', called director Thomas, himself in on the gag, and laughing.

While taking part in a scene for *Carry On Constable* being made in a street at West Ealing, London, Kenneth Williams was approaching by a woman passer-by who said: 'Here, don't I know you?'

'I'm sorry, not just now dear if you don't mind', said Williams kindly, pointing at director Gerald Thomas. 'I'm being directed.'

The woman looked puzzled. 'What?' she said.

Williams again pointed at Gerald Thomas. 'That man is directing me', he said.

The woman looked concerned. 'Oh, I didn't realise you were lost', she said. 'Can I help?'

For a lark, during the making of the same film, Leslie Phillips and Kenneth Williams, dressed for their roles as policemen, held up the traffic in the centre of Ealing. 'We just walked into the road, stuck our hands up and everything stopped', said Phillips. 'Then we looked at each other, and waved them all on again. The drivers certainly thought we were real coppers, but it was such an obviously pointless thing to do I expected a great uproar, but not a single motorist even asked what it was all about—thank God!'

These sort of things happen all the time during the making of a Carry On film. Actors agree that, even without the prankish presence of Kenneth Williams, there are more laughs, more outrageous and comical happenings while working on a Carry On film than on any other type of show in any medium in any other country.

Leslie Phillips, who has acted in many parts of the world, including Hollywood, and has starred in three Carry Ons, says: 'The director, Gerald Thomas, is a hustler. He really pushes everything along. But he has a great sense of fun. He knows when to take off the pressure. Though you're rushed from one scene to the next, you're enjoying yourself so much, you don't notice the speed at which you're working. Some of my happiest times in show business were spent making Carry On films.'

Part Two of this book is devoted almost entirely to the funny things that happen on the way to completing a Carry On film. Such events occur not only despite the no-nonsense, high-speed work schedule (which can turn out a Carry On in five weeks), the ruthlessly pruned resources, conditions, amenities, locations and pay, but, to some extent, *because* of these things.

Making *Carry On Camping*, for example, in slushy autumn, with girls in bikinis and wellington boots, then filming them only from the knees up because the action is supposed to be taking place in sweltering, lush summer, sets the scene for more laughs, outraged dignity and ego-shattering, mud-spattering slapstick than just that which reaches the screen.

Then there is the thrift which makes a French Foreign Legion film (*Carry On . . . Follow That Camel*) on Camber Sands, Sussex, instead of Morocco, shoots adventure on the high seas (*Carry on Jack*) on Frensham village pond, Surrey, and creates the wide, open spaces of the Old West (*Carry On Cowboy*) on Chobham Common, Surrey. The three weeks spent at Camber Sands is the longest the Carry On team have worked away from Pinewood Studios. Beddgelert in North Wales, at the foot of Mount Snowdon, is the furthest they have ever been—for *Carry On Up The Khyber*.

Anybody who believes that the camera never lies should watch director Gerald Thomas and his merry men shooting a Carry On film and making familiar bits of the Home Counties look like romantic, sunny lands across the seas. 'But that's what show business is about', says Thomas with a grin. 'Make believe!' It is also about keeping the cost of a film to the minimum so that it will be easier to borrow the money to make it and profits will begin sooner once it is made. 'And what does it matter where you shoot the film as long as it looks right, as long as the illusion is maintained, as long as you are producing a professional saleable commodity?' says Thomas.

For the stars the illusion connected with a Carry On can begin months before it is made. Despite experiences to the contrary, most have continued to believe the rumours or the nudge-nudge, wink-wink 'cast-iron certainty' before a more exotic Carry On, that this time, for the very first time, the location was going to be the real, luxurious thing. They were at last going to experience what it was like to be proper film stars. No ingeniously disguised field behind Pinewood Studios for them this time. They were going to have the respect befitting their art, perhaps even proper dressing rooms and a bit of awed civility. They were going to be stars on location abroad.

When shooting eventually begins in an ingeniously-disguised field behind Pinewood Studios there are shrugs and jokes and laughter and everybody says they never believed it anyway about going abroad. For one thing, producer Peter Rogers would not leave his three dogs—not for five weeks. He is devoted to those dogs— and, anyway, he does not like going abroad. Besides, Pinewood is much handier for the M4 than Arizona.

Before *Carry On . . . Follow That Camel* some stars were contemplating buying suntan oil and lightweight underwear in anticipation of the three weeks' filming in Morocco which they had heard was scheduled. Even American comedy actor Phil Silvers, who starred in the film, arrived from Hollywood half-expecting to be bound for North Africa. Instead of warm breezes from the Mediterranean, they got icy blasts from the English Channel, shivering on a Sussex beach.

It has been suggested that producer Peter Rogers combines his sense of humour and his sense of business on these occasions and mischievously uses such exotic bait to hook his stars at bargain rates with the least amount of bartering. He denies it with a grin, adding: 'These rumours about exotic foreign trips are dreamed up and spread by the actors themselves. They sit around between scenes and twitter away and decide that if the next film is about the French Foreign Legion then it can't help but be made in Morocco.

'But that's not how we work. Anybody can spend a million pounds and shoot a film in Morocco or the South of France. That's easy. What we do is sit down and work out ways of doing it so that it will look just as good on the screen, but will be a lot cheaper to make.'

Kenneth Williams, however, tells a tale about the exciting promises connected with the making of the sixth film in the series, *Carry On Cruising*.

At the time, Williams was angling for more money. Rogers' response to an actor trying to increase his fee is very often to laugh. Sometimes he finds a loophole in the actor's argument and goes on to show, at least to his own satisfaction, that the actor is extremely well off on the money he is getting for the amount of time he is putting in.

Tales of how actors have been dropped from the series or had their fees reduced

This caps everything! A rare picture of Carry-On producer Peter Rogers larking about during the making of a Carry On. Happily lying in the bed he has made for himself, as it were. The film was *Carry On Regardless*. Rogers, a shy man, hates having his photograph taken and has said he will never appear on television. 'Sometimes I pick up a book and think I will read it. Then I see the picture of the author on the back and I'm put off. The same principle applies as to why I won't appear on television,' he says. 'I don't want to put people off the films!'

because they wanted more money, are rife. One said: 'In a way Peter Rogers is odd about money. If I were in financial difficulties he, or Gerald Thomas, would be the first person I would go to and I'm confident either would help, without pushing me for the money later. In fact, I'd like to bet they would never mention it again. They would trust me to return it when I could. But if I'm asking Peter for a pay rise, for work I am going to do for him, for something, in fact, which I am immediately giving back in return, I'm not a tenth as confident that I will get it. Peter is remote, yet he can be very good on human terms. He's tough as nails, though, on financial terms.'

Rogers has loaned money to several people who have worked for the Carry On series. One, who borrowed £1,000, and went to Rogers some time later with a business suggestion as to how he might pay it back, was told: 'Please yourself. I'd forgotten about it.'

He gives a quiet denial, however, to the idea that people are dropped who ask for increased fees. He said: 'Everybody gets the rate for the job. Anybody who doesn't want to work for me for the money I can afford to pay, can obviously drop out. I'm not happy about this when it happens, but it's usually done with goodwill on both sides. My old friend Eric Rogers, who has written and conducted the music for Carry Ons since 1963, decided that he couldn't afford to hire the sort of orchestra he wanted on the money I could pay for *Carry On England*. So he turned me down. But we're still good friends—and he'll be back for the next one.'

As a tactical move in his bid for more money, Kenneth Williams turned down the role of Leonard Marjoribanks, first officer on a holiday liner, offered to him in *Carry On Cruising*.

Rogers had got the idea for *Cruising* from a suggestion made to him by actor Eric Barker (who had appeared in *Carry On Sergeant* and *Carry On Constable*) to make a film based on a holiday coach tour. Rogers simply changed the mode of transport from a coach to a cruise liner.

'It's a pity you're turning this one down', Williams was told. 'You're throwing away a very good trip. It's all being shot on a P & O liner which is going out to the Mediterranean empty to pick up passengers and bring them back to Britain. On the trip out the cast will have all the amenities to themselves—and it's a luxury ship. Still, if your mind's made up . . .'

'Er . . . er . . . just a minute,' said Williams, his mind filling with pictures of casual strolls around the decks before breakfast, relaxing nights in the luxurious first class lounge and sunny Mediterranean resorts, 'perhaps I will think it over.'

He thought it over, decided to shelve his bid for more money, and accepted the role.

I'm looking forward to this trip', he said.

'What trip?' came the reply.

'This trip on a P & O luxury liner to the Mediterranean.'

'Oh, that trip', came the reply. 'Yes. Would have been very good.'

'Would have been?' said Williams.

'Oh, sorry, didn't anybody tell you? It's been cancelled. We're doing all the exterior filming now on a ship docked at Weymouth.'

Williams heaved a sigh. Ah well, he thought, it could be a lot worse. It was still better than being on a mock deck at Pinewood Studios; better than gazing into tanks of water with mirrors in them to reflect the ripples and the lights, making believe you were gazing over a ship's rail; better than that infernal wind machine blowing your hair 'to buggery', pretending to be a sea breeze.

At Weymouth there would be pink gins in the ward room with the ship's officers, and real sea breezes and all the luxuries would be the same—more or less. With a bit of imagination it would be just like being at sea. Yes, this would be all right. He had made the right decision in joining the film.

The next thing he heard was that the trip to Weymouth was off.

When filming began he was at Pinewood Studios . . . gazing into tanks of water . . . walking a mock deck . . . and there was that infernal wind machine.

'Mind you, I got my rise', he says. 'Though I haven't had another in the fourteen years since.'

Williams declined a role in the next film, *Carry On Cabby*, but was back for the one after that, *Carry On Jack*.

'Another sea film', he says. 'But where did I end up? Sharing a rowing boat on Frensham village pond with a cow and Charles Hawtrey. And Hawtrey was playing a cesspool cleaner. Oh, it's a glamorous life in the films!'

The top pay for an actor in a Carry On, apart from occasional stars like Phil Silvers and Elke Sommer, is £5,000 for five or six weeks' work. It is unlikely that Silvers or Sommer would appear for less than £25,000 or £30,000, unless they had some sort of profit-sharing deal.

Of the regular team, only Sid James and Kenneth Williams have achieved a constant £5,000 per film. It is likely that an average for the others is not much above £3,000 per film.

But, as Barbara Windsor says: 'Noboby's going to get rich playing in Carry Ons. We know that! Anybody doing them strictly for the money is in trouble! The reason we do them is, it's a great team.

'When you tell somebody: "I'm doing a Carry On film", you think to yourself: "I'm going to meet my old mates and it's going to be marvellous." Every one's a professional. Nobody throws a tantrum. I haven't seen all of the people for so long now, and I just want to go up and hug them.'

As Bernard Bresslaw says: 'The feeling I get when I'm going to a new Carry On is like going back to school after the holidays—eager to meet everybody, tell my news, hear their news. How's your rheumatism? How're the kids? It's a get-together. It's a feeling I've never had on any other films I've worked on.'

As Hattie Jacques says: 'The atmosphere on a Carry On is unique in my experience. You know that for as long as you're there, you're going to have a good old giggle. You may not necessarily be doing the sort of part you particularly like doing, but it's fun, providing you know your job. Working on a Carry On brings out the unselfish side in everybody. There are no stars, you're all equal, and if it's your turn to do a bit of "feeding" while the other person is getting all the laugh lines, you don't mind.' She smiles. 'You can't get more unique than that!'

As Kenneth Connor says: 'A pleasant atmosphere on the set, yes it's very nice, and there's something to be said for doing a Carry On for a small fee rather than something else for a gigantic fee and being taxed out of the country of your birth by dint of being successful! But it's not all laughs making a Carry On. We are normal people with the full set of emotions, and sometimes we like to be serious. There are some clever people on a Carry On and we have very good, deep discussions. It has been known, when we've been called onto the set, to say: "Whadya mean, time to get moving? We're in the middle of a vital debate here—sorting out the whole question of comprehensive education. Give us a couple of minutes and we'll have it settled. Can't you wait?"

'But the real joy of a Carry On comes later—when a lady with a string bag in awful weather stops you and says: "Thanks for all the fun you've given me." When that happens all criticism by others, all one's own niggly little feelings, just fly away. That woman will never know how much encouragement she has given. And that's the hallmark of the Carry Ons. That's what it's all about, as they say.'

There are other bonuses.

Rogers always has an end-of-film party for the cast. He also takes some of them, after every film, for a slap-up meal at one of London's leading restaurants, usually the Mirabelle.

He is held in awe by some actors, even feared and, occasionally, hated; and though he can be ruthless in order to stick to the budget of a film, Rogers is spontaneously generous, performing acts which he always denies if they are mentioned later, and can become tetchy about if the recipient is over-effusive with his thanks.

The home of Joan Sims had been burgled, and her mother was not well. Joan way crying on the set of *Carry On . . . Don't Lose Your Head*. A £10 note was pushed into her hand and a voice said: 'Buy yourself some perfume. Cheer yourself up.' It was Rogers.

Kenneth Williams said to Rogers one day, while making a Carry On: 'Did you see that last scene of mine? It was brilliant. Admit it—it was brilliant!'

Rogers said: 'It's the general consensus that you stink, and I've got the cure for it. Come with me.'

Williams followed him into the caravan where he works while a film is being shot. 'There you are', said Rogers. 'That'll fix you!' And he gave Williams a bottle of exclusive men's cologne.

While making a Carry On film, during the time she was married to John le Mesurier, Hattie Jacques learned that John had been taken ill in Malta. Says

Hattie: 'Immediately Peter Rogers, and of course Gerald Thomas, could not have been more helpful or concerned. "Leave at once and don't come back until he's well again", I was told, and they checked air schedules and booked a plane for me and did all that side of things. I was very grateful.' She laughs suddenly. 'But if you complain to Peter about money he thinks it's the funniest joke he's heard!'

Once, while the cast were having a meal on location, Rogers arrived in his Rolls-Royce. As he stepped out, Kenneth Williams said in a loud voice to nobody in particular: 'I wish we were back at the studio. At least we could get a drink there.'

Shortly afterwards six bottles of Chablis arrived for the cast. Rogers had been to a local off-licence and bought them.

Whatever apprehensions the actors may have about Rogers, they have none about Gerald Thomas, the Carry Ons' director.

'Gerry is the buffer between Peter Rogers and the cast', said one.

Thomas calls himself 'the ringmaster and the father confessor of the Carry Ons'. He says: 'I put the cast through their paces in front of the cameras and when they're not in front of the cameras they bring their problems to me, even between films. Of course I'm pleased to do everything I can for them.'

The Carry On team is unanimous in its praise for Thomas. Three samples:

Hattie Jacques: 'Gerry is a darling, benevolent headmaster. He knows his job and expects you to know yours. You can't turn up not having learnt your lines. But, apart from any other reasons, you just wouldn't do that anyway, for his sake. You wouldn't want to let him down.'

Bernard Bresslaw: 'You get the feeling from Gerry that he knows you can do it—even if you're not very sure yourself! He does a lot without rehearsing it first, because he now knows the capabilities of each person. He goes for spontaneity. Very often it is not until the end of a day's or a week's shooting that you realise just how helpful he has been.'

Kenneth Williams: 'Gerry creates a relaxed atmosphere while, at the same time, being able to push you when it's necessary. He's very good at guiding you, so that you don't miss opportunities. He'll say: "Don't worry so much about this next scene, but look at the one after that. It lends itself to good comedy. It could be a big sequence for you." And you take that advice gladly, because you know it is going to help the film and help you. It is going to be right.'

There are probably more jokes played on a Carry On set than anywhere else in show business, most with Thomas' approval. But he never allows them to get out of hand. The tight shooting schedule imposes a stern discipline and helps to shape his style. He goes for speed and simplicity.

Any cameraman who wants to spend time experimenting with different lenses is told very quickly: 'The lens and the camera aren't funny. The thing that matters is what's going on in front of the camera. So the lens you've got is just fine.'

Any cameraman who wants to move the camera to try for an unusual shot, is asked: 'If you move the camera over there, will it make this scene any funnier?' The answer is usually: 'No, but . . .' And the answer to that is: 'So let's leave the camera where it is, and get on.'

You're right—director Gerald Thomas is involved in a scene featuring two beauties. Two aspiring beauty queens, that is, played by Barbara Windsor and Margaret Nolan in *Carry on Girls*. As part of the film, Barbara and Margaret had a fight, during which Margaret's bra was ripped off. But no . . . this is *not* that bra. Filming is rarely so simple. As part of the scene, Sid James and Joan Sims had to react to the bra-ripping. So to shoot that bit, director Thomas had his cameraman wear the bra he is holding, at the side of the set. Thomas then ripped it off for Sid and Joan to react to. Says Thomas chivalrously (some would call him a spoil-sport): 'I didn't want to keep asking that poor girl to have her bra ripped off just to get the reactions I wanted from Sid and Joan. It wouldn't have been fair.' So that is why he is left holding two empty cups. Could he really be saying: 'Two tease please?' Part of the fight between Barbara and Margaret is on page 149.

As Carry On films are usually made in the spring and autumn (because the stars are often in pantomime or seaside shows in winter and summer) luck is needed to coincide outdoor filming with what, almost always, is a scarcity of sunny days. Thomas has a reputation for bringing off this feat with uncanny precision and regularity. His one momentous failure was *Carry On Cowboy* when it rained heavily for all of the first scheduled day of shooting on Chobham Common, Surrey. But that day is remarkable in a more outstanding way. For Thomas was never able to catch up on his schedule, and the film came in one day over its promised and allotted span, the only Carry On to go over schedule in twenty-eight films and nineteen years.

Yet Thomas names it as the Carry On he most enjoyed making. 'It was exciting to do', he says. 'A very meaty sort of film, with lots of action.'

One aspect of the film that he particularly remembers is that Jim Dale—the Errol Flynn of the Carry Ons—did all his own stunts, including falling off the top of a moving stagecoach.

Dale sees nothing remarkable in the deed. 'I was taught to tumble at a dancing school by an ex-commando,' he says. 'I'm trained in ballet, I've done a lot of variety. I'm used to that sort of physical action. It's like anything else—if you can do it, it isn't really dangerous. But mistakes of all sorts can happen, unforeseen problems can occur, so you have to consider the balance between the authenticity of doing a stunt yourself and what the film will lose, in terms of cost and a delayed schedule, if you seriously hurt yourself.

'I consider this aspect more now than I did when we made *Carry On Cowboy*. But I still maintain that if a stunt man had made that eight-foot dive from the top of a stagecoach, it would not have come out as well, from a visual point of view, as by doing it myself. The reason is that in a fall of that sort the audience is watching your face. A stunt man would have had to hide his face in some way, which would have lessened the effect of the scene.'

Dale now works mainly in Hollywood and, recently completed a Walt Disney adventure film. In his last Carry On, *Carry On Again Doctor*, made in 1969, he again spurned a stunt man, but this time injured his left elbow. The task was to hurtle down a flight of thirty stairs on a hospital trolley. So far as everyone could tell, Dale did it brilliantly. 'What they couldn't see,' he says, 'was that my left elbow was banging on a metal bar every time the trolley hit a step. After thirty of those it just came up like a balloon. I had to go to hospital, have it opened up and drained. Gerry was forced to alter the shooting schedule. In fact, this is an example of the sort of thing I was saying about unforeseen snags.'

The Carry On which director Gerald Thomas thinks works most successfully is *Carry On Up The Khyber*, followed by *Carry On Doctor* and *Carry On Nurse*.

Carry On Up The Khyber is also, after *Cowboy*, the one which he most enjoyed making. For a week the unit went on location to Snowdonia in North Wales.

They hired sixty local farmworkers and villagers to play fierce Khyber tribesmen, charging down a mountain pass, led by Bernard Bresslaw. 'I felt like Cecil B. de Mille', says Thomas. 'It's the only time I've had sixty extras in my life.' But he reckons they spent the whole time mocking him. Only one of them admitted to speaking English and he acted as interpreter for the rest who claimed to speak only Welsh.

When the interpreter was relaying one of Thomas' instructions, like: 'Come forward to this rock, then turn to Mr Wills', they would look at each other and

Carry On . . . Follow That Camel! He thought he was over the hump of his journey—and suddenly he was! Still, it's a stunning way to get off! This is former pop star Jim Dale adding a flip side to the role of Bo West as he drops in at a French Foreign Legion barracks to enlist. No, not as a flying officer! In a later bid to improve on this comical caper, one of Jim's boots became entangled in the trappings and the camel started chewing his foot. Fellow-actor Peter Butterworth had to beat off the beast with a brolly. Jim, of course, is only making it look as though, from this toss, it's: Heads, he loses. He is really winning hands down— at making audiences fall about.

shake their heads as if they did not understand, and the interpreter would explain to Thomas that there was Wills-the-bread and Wills-the-shepherd and Wills-the-post and Wills-the-pub . . . and which Wills did he mean?

As dedicated Welsh Nationalists were said to be in the district, a permanent guard had to be kept on the rifles being used. 'It certainly added an element of reality to the battle conditions we were supposed to be under', says Peter Butterworth.

When the Carry On contingent moved out, Gregory Peck moved in, making a film set in China.

Son of a sales director for a leading oil company, Gerald Thomas was born in Hull, Yorkshire. He looked destined to become a doctor, but the war interrupted his studies and he served as an officer, in the Royal Sussex Regiment, in France, Belgium, Holland, Germany and the Middle East.

When the war was over, rather than try to catch up on his studies, he followed his other interest, films, and got a job in the cutting rooms at Denham Studios for Two Cities Films.

He eventually became assistant editor on leading films such as *The October Man* and *Hamlet*, being appointed an editor for the first time on *Madness of the Heart*.

Two major breaks came in 1955 when he went to Hollywood to edit the Disney extravaganza *The Sword and the Rose*, and in the same year was editor and second unit director on the British film *Above Us The Waves*, directed by his brother, Ralph Thomas, at Pinewood Studios.

It was while working on this film that Rogers and Thomas, who already knew each other, had a coffee together in the canteen at Pinewood. Thomas told Rogers that he had been offered an associate producer contract by Rank, but that what he really wanted to do was direct.

'All right', said Rogers. 'Let's team up. You as director, me as producer.'

At this time, Thomas was one of the top half-dozen editors in the industry. Rogers was known as a writer and as an assistant producer on films made by his wife, Betty Box, though he had produced one or two pictures of his own, like *The Gay Dog*, which featured Wilfred Pickles and a greyhound.

Because his wife was better known, some people would annoy Rogers (purposely or innocently) by calling him Mr Box. To combat this he made up a joke, saying that he was hiding his light under a Box.

After his meeting in the canteen with Thomas, Rogers said to his wife that night: 'Gerald will never get a chance to direct while he is editing for his brother. I think he ought to be given that chance.' Betty agreed.

The rest of the film world did not.

'We did nothing for a year', says Thomas. 'Nobody wanted us.' But, gradually, they began to make pictures, like *Circus Friends*, featuring a thirteen year old future star, called Carol White, whom Thomas picked from an acting school. Then, in 1957, they made an impact with a film version of the Arthur Haley thriller *Time-lock*, starring Robert Beatty, about a bank official who accidentally locks his son in a vault, timed to open sixty-three hours later.

Though he has now directed more than forty films, including all the Carry Ons,

Timelock is still Thomas' biggest critical success.

Since the sixth Carry On film, *Carry On Cruising*, Rogers and Thomas have shared the profits on a fifty-fifty basis. Thomas first received a percentage of the profits after the second film, *Carry On Nurse*. They also take a fee for each film, probably in the region of £15–£20,000.

At the time of *Carry On Teacher*, the third film in the series, there was talk of turning six of the stars, Leslie Phillips, Kenneth Williams, Joan Sims, Kenneth Connor, Hattie Jacques and Charles Hawtrey, into the official Carry On team and giving them a share of the profits. 'But it was only ever talked about', says Leslie Phillips. 'It never progressed. We never had the chance to accept or otherwise.'

For about ten years now, the Carry Ons have cost £200,000 and upwards to make. *Carry On Henry*, the twenty-first, made in 1970, cost about £223,000. The latest, *Carry On England*, about a mixed anti-aircraft battery during World War II, could not be made for less than £250,000, with fees, budget and five-week schedule ruthlessly pared, and it is likely that no actor in this film was on the maximum of £5,000, or even £4,000. Eighteen years earlier another Army film, called *Carry On Sergeant*, much of it shot in the same field used for scenes in *Carry On England*, cost less than a third of *England's* budget to make, on a six-week schedule.

According to Nat Cohen, who backed the first twelve Carry Ons, profits were 400 per cent upwards and the first few covered their costs in days. The price of making a Carry On rose steeply after the first two or three, the sixth, *Carry On Cruising*, costing around £140,000, almost double the cost of the first one.

While there have been many later successes, *Carry On Doctor*, *Carry On Up The Khyber*, *Carry On Camping*, *Carry On Again Doctor*, *Carry On Up The Jungle* and *Carry On Loving*, for example, fewer cinemas means that it takes increasingly longer to make a major profit. *Carry On At Your Convenience*, made in 1971, was still struggling to show a healthy profit last year.

Married, with three daughters, Thomas says: 'I would not direct a film that I did not feel was going to be a financial success. But nobody can hit the jackpot every time. *Convenience* was one occasion when we misjudged peoples' feelings about an issue—in this case trades unions.'

Temperamentally he and Rogers are opposites. Rogers, 64 (for the astrologically-minded, a Piscean though born on 20 February, on the cusp of Aquarius) likes to be alone with his dogs, or to listen to music, and he tends to keep away from cocktail parties and aloof from actors, though he mixes readily with film technicians. In company he has a quick wit, however, and the Carry On humour is certainly his style. A brief example:

Scene: The lounge of London's Dorchester Hotel. Rogers orders champagne and the cork makes a louder than usual noise as the waiter extracts it.

Rogers (mocking): You love making a bang with those things, don't you?

Waiter: It won't come out softly.

Rogers: Oh dear. Mine does.

He has needed this sort of glibness since he launched the Carry On series, for there has never been a shortage of film executives ready to deride with comments like: 'Still making that crap, Peter?'

'If you call money crap, yes', is one of his replies.

But he would rather not have to bother, though he enjoys being the centre of attention in a small group of colleagues at a familiar bar, which has led some to doubt his declared shyness and embarrassment at personal publicity. A joke told about him takes the form of an inscription to be put on his tombstone: 'Here lies Peter Edward Rogers. He backed into the limelight'.

Thomas, eight years younger than Rogers (and a Sagittarian, born on 10 December) is gregarious, an optimist, relaxed in any company, likes travel, parties and show business functions, but is also a dedicated family man. While Rogers has porcelain figures of dogs on his desk, Thomas has pictures of his family.

Occasionally Thomas' voice, heavily disguised, can be heard in a Carry On film, producing the sounds of monsters and other non-human creatures. His latest vocal stardom is in *Carry On Behind*, made in 1975, in which he plays the voice of a mynah bird, uttering lines like: 'Show us your knickers!' and 'Get stuffed!'.

Despite being a lover of jokes, he seldom allows actors to add spontaneous funny lines to a scene. Carry Ons are made strictly according to a script, though, with actors like the Carry On crowd, suggestions abound.

One that did get in: Charles Hawtrey was about to be guillotined in the French Revolution comedy, *Carry On . . . Don't Lose Your Head*. Sid James suggested: 'Wouldn't it be funny if somebody came up and said: "I've got a message for you." And Charles said: "Drop it in the basket."'

Note that Sid's suggestion, as a sample of the team spirit, gave the funny line to another actor or, as it happened, an actress and not himself.

Another that was included: Khyber tribesmen are blowing up the British Governor's residency with artillery. Bernard Bresslaw, playing one of the tribesmen's leaders, suggested: 'Wouldn't it by funny if we see part of the residency blown up, then I say: "That will teach them to ban turbans on the buses."'

One that is said to be in, which was not meant to be in, and which I have not seen: it is alleged that in a scene in *Carry On . . . Don't Lose Your Head*, Joan Sims mouths the words: 'Piss off!'.

Apart from the brand of humour which it peddles the success of the Carry On series is based on a hatred of waste. So is Peter Rogers' status as Britain's most consistently successful film producer. For the hatred of waste is his.

Rogers hates waste on a budget—which eventually helps profits.

He hates wasting a script—which is how he came to turn the unwanted 'The Bull Boys' into the eagerly wanted *Carry On Sergeant* and, from a play he could not sell as a film, got the idea for *Carry On Nurse*.

While it has made him rich, this one-man war on waste has also provided for those regularly employed on Carry On films, their most lasting experience of security in the uncertain world of show business.

Typically Rogers underplays his success, but there is truth in his remark: 'If you've got some scripts you can't move, turn 'em into comedies. That's what I did—and look what happened!'

This underplaying of his achievement—a game in which others eagerly participate—is rooted in the paradox of his personality. For this purveyor of knockabout tomfoolery is a man of retiring sensitivity, deep emotions, unsuspected by many who know him, and with a sentimental streak as broad as the Carry On humour. If the face he presents to the world is often cold and the attitude sometimes abrupt, they are the shields behind which he hides his human vulnerability. As he puts it: 'You have to protect yourself.' The man who can laugh, and make up the most painful of puns, can go damp-eyed at the music of Schubert or Tchaikovsky; the man whom I have heard described as 'mean in business', embroiders cushions as a hobby.

The man who is the most successful comedy producer in Britain, and possibly the world, has been known, during a busy spell, to help out in the cloakroom of the Dorchester Hotel and to serve as a waiter in the restaurant at Pinewood Studios. 'They were a bit pushed and I was there', he says as explanation. 'Besides, I learn things from doing different jobs.'

Even a simple question like: 'When were you born?' can evoke a complicated and paradoxical answer like: 'I was born a long time before I was born.'

For a moment one examines the statement, looking for a Carry On twist. But there is none.

Rogers goes on: 'I know I have been here before, here on earth . . . probably as a writer, or even a musician.'

Can he be sure?

'I'm positive. In the same way that I know when a Carry On is going to take off. It is purely instinct, but I believe in instinct. I have a barometer in my navel. It never puts me wrong.'

Perhaps, then, his rapport with popular taste could mean that he was once born in working class surroundings? 'Possibly,' he says, 'but certainly I was never doing what I'm doing now, because I didn't know about film work. It was something I had to learn. In any case, films probably weren't around whenever I was here before. Whatever I was, it had something to do with being an observer of people. If I am any one thing, I am an observer of people.'

He ignores my repeated offer of the word 'reincarnation', saying instead: 'I think there is such a thing as thought transference from the grave.

'If you step off a kerb and a bus is coming, then you step back just in time without having seen the bus, who told you it was there? That's the sort of instinct I'm talking about. You must believe it when it brings you luck, as I believed it with the Carry On films. You must push that luck around a bit. You can't ignore it. It's there for your benefit.'

With films and music, animals are Rogers' overwhelming concern. Old and sick horses, dogs, Highland cattle and 'sex mad pigeons' have been given a home in a paddock behind his house in Buckinghamshire, a former convent and once the home of actor Dirk Bogarde.

He is devoted to his present dogs, Silver, a long-haired Alsatian, Cloudy, a Border collie and Cindy, who he describes as 'a black nothing' because he does not like the word 'mongrel' or phrases like 'Heinz dog'.

'People who invite me out but don't want my dogs, rarely get me', he says. 'I don't argue with people about it. I don't argue with people about anything. If I don't get my own way, I don't play.

'I love my dogs. I couldn't live without them. I want them with me as often as possible.

'It breaks your heart when you lose them. But they come back, you know. Every dog I've owned, which has died, has come back to me. Love goes on and on. Everybody who has loved anybody gets them back in time.'

There is an oak tree at his home with the name of every dog he has owned carved on it. The list is 30ft high.

One of his gambits when hiring people to work for him has been to invite them to his house for tea. While they are there they meet his dogs who sniff around them. If all is satisfactory, Rogers has then said: 'I like you. I just wanted to see if my dogs liked you—and they do. So I look forward to our working together.'

In the early days of his association with Rogers, Gerald Thomas used to take biscuits in his pocket whenever he visited Rogers at his home. 'Peter has always liked big dogs,' says Thomas, 'and whenever he left me alone in a room with the dogs he had then, I used to get apprehensive, so I would slip them these biscuits to keep their minds occupied! My concern was always whether I would have enough biscuits to last out until he came back, and whether I should save some in case he went out again.'

Unlike many wealthy film folk, Rogers has never considered living abroad to escape crippling taxes.

'I just wouldn't do it', he says. 'You don't get the same bird song in a morning abroad that you do in England. That's worth a lot to me. And what would my workers think if I came in from some foreign country to do a film? What respect would I get? They're here and I'm here. I'm happy to stay in Britain and pay my taxes.'

Such devotion, plus the overseas sales of his films, surely deserves official recognition?

Says Rogers: 'I've been offered accolades and I've turned them down. I don't want to be Sir Peter or anything like that. It would make it impossible for me to meet my friends, to meet the people who work on my films.'

One of the targets for most Carry On films is pomposity. Here is a link between Rogers and the comedy he peddles. 'I cannot stand pompous, hypocritical people,' he says. 'Pomposity is probably the thing I loathe most in life. I waste no time in cutting it down to size—in real life and in my films.'

He also reserves a special dislike for people at parties—which he often cannot get out of attending—who make the wrong assumption because he is the producer of the Carry On series, and say, almost as if calling the court jester: 'Peter, come and make me laugh.'

'The point is, I'm not funny', he says. 'So I tell them the most atrocious filthy jokes, getting four-letter words in whenever I can—and I know that they will never ever ask me again.'

There are those who say that Rogers' shyness is what gives him the common touch. Certainly the Carry On films might be seen as a shy man's defiant, rebellious thumb-to-the-nose at the hypocrisies and pomposities of daily life. Two fingers at all that he hates and fears.

The Carry On series that eventually the world wanted began with a script that nobody wanted. Even the Carry On title was secondhand, stolen from another film. As a recipe for world conquest the other ingredients, at first glance, were hardly more inspiring, bearing in mind that the subject was a military one and a comic one aimed at a largely working-class audience.

The recipe read:

take a very long, much rejected light-comedy script about the trials and tribulations of National Service;

take a title already used by another film;

take a shy producer from a middle-class, public school background, who had served in none of the fighting services;

take a director who had never before directed comedy;

take a writer who had never before written a film comedy.

There you have it. As a way to make people laugh it was an immediate success— you are probably laughing yourself already. So did several executives in the film industry. For, as a means of getting paying customers into a cinema, the result produced by these ingredients was considered by some to be . . . well . . . just laughable. Beyond a joke.

But it worked—better than any other laughter recipe or combination of comedy talent turned out by this country, and it is unlikely that any other film series will reach the same number of productions as the Carry Ons.

The producer was Peter Rogers. The director was Gerald Thomas. The writer was Norman Hudis. The much-rebuffed script from which they produced the first Carry On film was called *The Bull Boys* by R. F. Delderfield. The film that had the original Carry On title was . . . no, I'll come to that in a moment.

Rogers, Thomas and Hudis started re-thinking *The Bull Boys* into a broader comedy in 1957. They filmed it over six weeks in March and April of 1958 on a small budget of £74,000, and released it the same year with the title *Carry On Sergeant*. The extent of its success not only confounded those who had been mocking and sceptical about it, but surprised even Rogers and company. The original concept had been to turn out a one-off, inexpensive Army romp. But it quickly became the third most popular film in Britain for that year and the foundation of the record-breaking series. It also contains Hudis' favourite scene out of the six Carry Ons that he wrote. This is the first inspection by Captain Potts (played by Eric Barker) of the new intake of National Servicemen, which included Bob Monkhouse, Kenneth Williams, Charles Hawtrey and Kenneth Connor.

The Bull Boys originally belonged to Rogers' brother-in-law, the producer Sidney Box, who could arouse no interest in the script among backers and distributors. One of the script's faults was its length which, at 180 pages in first-draft form, was about twice what is needed for a ninety-minute film. Although there was comedy in it there was also too much preaching about the stupidities of Army 'bull'.

Rogers took the script over from Box and called in his writer, Norman Hudis, for a meeting with himself and Gerald Thomas. This was to be Hudis' major break as a scriptwriter. It was also Thomas' lucky day, for he had been Rogers' third choice as director, and the other two had turned it down. Rogers had first asked Muriel Box to direct the film. She was his wife's sister-in-law, married to Sidney Box. She refused because she would not direct anything to do with uniforms. Val Guest, Rogers' second choice, wanted more money than Rogers could afford.

So Rogers, Thomas and Hudis met, and what happened at that meeting—though according to Hudis it was not planned as such—was the conception of the Carry On comedy. Let Hudis tell it:

'I was originally called in to polish the script. In the course of discussion, however, the whole thrust changed and the notion of a group of incompetents getting

Carry On Sergeant Vested interest! Army Medical Officer Captain Clark (Hattie Jacques) is about to cure a pain in the neck—the hard way. She has lined up a bevy of medical specialists. Obviously, the lady has a vested interest. And there it is—the chap in the vest! He is recruit Horace Strong (Kenneth Connor) a hypochondriac and the biggest pain in the neck that ever made this wench wince. For Horace reports sick every day with a new complaint. But now he is about to catch a cold of a different sort, as each specialist gives him the once over and declares him A1. Little man you've got a busy (and disillusioning) day. Cough!

laughs all the way with their idiocy, then redeeming themselves at the end in senti-mental circumstances, was vaguely suggested by me and developed between the three of us. In short, the early Carry On 'formula'—a word I cordially detest—came into being.

'Delderfield's most developed aspect, as I recall, was the National Serviceman called up during his wedding breakfast, and we retained this and played with it quite effectively. (Bob Monkhouse was cast in this role.) The rest, owing something to his original, developed into the film we now know as the first Carry On.'

Rogers says that he did not ask Delderfield to revise his own script because he did not want Delderfield's kind of comedy. Hudis, in any case, was under contract to him at the time and he had decided that a change of style was needed if anything was to be done with the script. 'Hudis was very much on my wavelength', says Rogers. 'I used to have the shortest script conferences with him that I have ever known. I had only to hint at a comic idea and he knew immediately what I was getting at, and it was done.'

Another writer, John Antrobus, who had been sent to see Rogers by his agent, was asked to write a script for *Carry On Sergeant* and ideas from this were incor-porated in the final screenplay.

When news got around the film industry that Rogers was putting a cheaply priced comedy, culled from the unsaleable Delderfield script, into production, there were cries of derision. He was told, by people who claimed to have only his interests at heart, not to do it. 'Some of them thought I was mad,' says Rogers, 'but I'm stubborn and once I start something, I go through with it. Besides which, I thought we had a funny film.'

The contempt that some felt for the project pervaded not only the occupants of executive suites, but technicians and other workers at Pinewood Studios—even one or two who were employed on the film. Alan Hume, camera operator for *Carry On Sergeant*, and director of photography for later Carry Ons, recalls an example: 'This chap had quite an important job on the floor, but he was very sarcastic about the film. He deliberately showed boredom and contempt not only in words but in actions. He used to read a book on the set instead of keeping his mind on his job. He was caught out on one or two occasions. He's in television now.'

Even people connected with the film's financial backing began to have doubts when they saw the daily 'rushes' (un-edited film shot the previous day). Says Rogers: 'They used to tell me—"But Peter, it isn't funny!" I told them that was because they were seeing isolated shots and bits of scenes in no particular order. I said: "When the film is edited, in sequence and complete, it'll be funny." But they still had qualms, so I stopped them seeing rushes. I stopped everybody seeing rushes except those immediately concerned with production. There was a time when very few people actually believed in the film.'

But, out on location, the lads were doing their stuff. At Queen's Barracks, Guildford, in Surrey, where the parade ground sequences were shot, recruits Bob Monkhouse, Kenneth Williams, Charles Hawtrey, Kenneth Connor, Terence Long-den, Gerald Campion, Norman Rossington and the rest, under the watchful eyes of Bill Owen, playing a corporal, and the beady ones of William Hartnell, playing a sergeant, were a credit to the British Army to which they did not belong.

A visiting brigadier, not knowing they were actors, was so impressed after seeing them march across the parade ground as he drove past in his staff car, that he asked for their sergeant-in-charge to be brought to him to receive congratulations. 'That's the sort of marching that is a credit to the British Army', the brigadier told his subordinates. 'If every platoon here was as good as that one, we'd have something to be proud of.' He was then quietly told the facts about this peerless platoon, and Sergeant William Hartnell never did get to receive his congratulations.

The story of *Carry On Sergeant* is that of an ill-assorted, disinterested, in some cases incompetent, bunch of National Service recruits who, after blundering through most of the film, go all out in the final scenes to give their sergeant, who is on the eve of retirement, the only star squad of his career.

The original plan for filming the squad in its testing passing out parade was to shoot only close-ups of the actors and to use a real, crack Army squad as a stand-in for the more distant, yet more revealing, marching sequences. The actors' squad was so well drilled, however, that no stand-in squad was needed. The camera stayed on them the whole time.

Bob Monkhouse explains: 'A lot of the credit for that can go to William Hartnell who played our drill sergeant. Bill was a waspish, hard, tough man. When he said: "Tenshun!", we jumped to it because we knew that if we did it wrong and the director called for another "take", Bill would come across and snarl: "You bastards! Now we've got to do it again. Can't you blokes do anything right?" He and I didn't hit it off. I don't think he liked comedians. But he was the right man for that role. He terrified most of us—on and off the set!' (William Hartnell later became the first Dr Who in the long-running serial on BBC Television.)

For cameraman Alan Hume, *Carry On Sergeant* was a treat. It was a chance to see in action, for the first time, Kenneth Connor whom he found hilarious on radio. But the arrival of Connor on set provided Hume with a problem he had overlooked. He was such a fan that his laughter was in danger of ruining every scene in which Connor appeared. Hume's face-contorting struggles to stifle his guffaws became a familiar spectacle. Eventually the inevitable happened. There came a day when he just could not stifle them.

The scene was a fire-arms lecture during which Connor, playing a recruit who suffered from an abnormal variety of allergies and health fears, complained, with face contortions to rival Hume's, of the smell from the gun oil. The scene was shot and re-shot, but every time Connor said: 'It's the smell of the oil', a strangled whoop would come from behind the camera, quickly accelerating into uncontrollable giggles.

In the end, director Gerald Thomas had to send him off the set, get a stand-in to operate the camera, and shoot the scene without him. Hume has been sent off the set of several Carry Ons because of his uncontrollable laughter. He is not alone. Several others, whose spontaneous chortles have spoiled a succession of Carry On shots, have been shown the door.

A major selling factor of the series, recognised from the start by the makers, has been the Carry On title. The words 'Carry On', which are registered with the Film

Production Association of Great Britain and can be used by no other film-maker, were given to the founding comedy by Nat Cohen and Stuart Levy. They were partners in Anglo Amalgamated, the company which financially backed and distributed *Carry On Sergeant*, and went on to do the same for the next eleven films in the series.

How did they think of it? They didn't. 'Carry On' was not an original title. An earlier film, made by a different team for a different company, had been called *Carry On Admiral* (directed by Val Guest, whom Rogers had asked—but could not afford—to direct *Sergeant*). As the phrase 'carry on' was a normal Army expression, they decided to copy it. Who initiated the idea? Rogers is adamant that it was the late Stuart Levy, the partner with whom he dealt most directly. Cohen says the idea to 'pinch it' was his, but if anybody else wants to claim the credit, he is not worried.

Such are the ways of show business that *Carry On Admiral*, starring David

Carry On Sergeant **Just call me sergeant, lad— you don't have to kneel! Recruit Golightly (Charles Hawtrey) is no soldier of fortune. As you see, he is well down on his luck. Which is a pity, because he falls over himself—especially when** marching—to please Sergeant Grimshawe (William Hartnell), the stickler with the stick. If we were Golightly we would stay on our knees. It's an ideal position from which to pray!

Tomlinson and Peggy Cummins, which had been released in 1957, the year before *Sergeant*, was re-released in 1959, almost certainly to cash in on the success of the film (and the coming series) that had stolen its name. From the moment of its launch, the public took to *Carry On Sergeant* as though it belonged to them. It was not something to be viewed with wonder, made by unreachable gods on the other side of the Atlantic. It was not peddling luxury or magic or stars and made no pretence at superiority. They saw *Carry On Sergeant* and those that quickly followed as being part of themselves, a mate who showed them how to laugh at the problems and the people who pestered them and bossed them. The humour was the sort of humour they used themselves in pubs and clubs. Critics may call it corny, and lots of it was, but it was legitimate and true working-class humour. From its launch *Carry On Sergeant* was an old, winking, nudging, good-hearted, sentimental buddy, putting them and their kind of comedy up there on the screen where, only the previous week, the gods from Hollywood had been in residence.

Because it was their kind of comedy the public was quick to participate. The success of *Carry On Sergeant*, followed six months later by the even greater success of *Carry On Nurse*, brought an avalanche of suggested topics from cinema-goers for future episodes—everything from 'Carry On Coin Collecting' to 'Carry On Sewage Farming'.

When writer Norman Hudis received a suggestion for 'Carry On Stock Exchange', he realised one of the secrets of the Carry On success. 'The reason I would have voted against this idea', he says, 'is that one would have to spend five or ten minutes at the beginning telling *straight* how the Exchange works *before* one could poke fun at it. I realised that familiarity breeds laughter.'

Nearly twenty years after reaching that conclusion, Hudis sticks with it. He says: 'Much of the humour in a Carry On was anticipated by the audience, not because the jokes and routines were old, but because the general subject matter was so very familiar. Everyone had been in, or knew someone who had been in, the Army. The same applied to hospitals. Everyone had been to school. Everyone had some preconceptions about the police force. Thus—*Carry On Sergeant, Nurse, Teacher* and *Constable*. I was fortunate with these films in that I was dealing with topics of familiarity and so could get straight into the business of laughs—and if some of those were expected and chestnutty, that was all part of the fun.

'When we got to *Carry On Regardless* (about an agency that will help people in any way they want) I felt we were stretching away from the familiar, and it is my least favourite of those that I wrote. *Carry On Cruising* was also beginning to get outside the immediate warm, intimate range of peoples' everyday experience.'

While *Carry On Sergeant* was in the cinemas and *Carry On Nurse* was in production at Pinewood, Rogers announced, in November 1958, only eight months after *Sergeant* had begun filming, the titles of four more comedies in the series—*Carry On Teacher, Carry On Constable, Carry On Regardless* and *What A Carry On*.

Writer John Antrobus had been hired to do the script for *Constable*, two months previously, in September 1958. Later, another writer, Brock Williams, took over, and Hudis was not brought in until September 1959, two months before *Constable* went into production, to write the final script.

There was some discussion about hiring a Scottish comedian for *Constable*—the name of Chic Murray was mentioned—to boost sales north of the Border, but this was abandoned.

Of the four new Carry Ons announced by Rogers in 1958, three were made during the next two years, but nothing has since been heard of *What A Carry On* and even Rogers cannot remember what subject he had in mind for it. (An Army slapstick comedy called *What A Carry On* starring Jimmy Jewel and Ben Warris had been made, in fact, ten years previously.)

Shooting on *Carry On Regardless*, scheduled for November 1960, was postponed for two months because of the sudden illness of Hattie Jacques who had a leading role in the film. This led to a major rewrite, giving Hattie a much smaller part and creating a new lead role which was given to Liz Fraser.

In the same film, Sid James knocked himself out when he slipped while running down a flight of steps. He had the presence of mind, however, to say his lines before collapsing.

After the success of the early Carry Ons, colleagues who had been pessimistic or downright rude about the potential of *Carry On Sergeant* while it was being made, now told Rogers: 'With these successes you can get the backing to move on to epics.'

But Rogers was not interested in multi-million dollar epics. 'I believed the best future was in the Carry On films,' he says, 'and they all thought I was mad. But some of those who later went for epics soon slipped away.' He preferred the more controllable, familiar ingredients of a Carry On. He got big by staying small . . . and by staying British.

He turned down a suggestion that an adviser be sent over from America to show him how to adapt his films for the United States market.

The comedy, while remaining peculiarly British, has found many a foreign funny bone. Says Rogers: 'The success or otherwise of the Carry Ons is due to my own stubbornness and selfishness. It is a British series. It panders to the humour of no foreign country. Distributors and other people in the film industry are influenced by what is successful at any given time, by the box office success of others. They are always wanting to alter plans and pictures to fit in with what is currently popular. But I have never done that with the Carry Ons and I have never allowed others to do it. The Carry Ons have their own style. Change that and it would no longer be what it says it is—a Carry On.'

This does not mean that Rogers and director Gerald Thomas do not keep an eye on changes in permissibility, public taste, the over-exposure (in terms of number of appearances as well as bare flesh) of a star, and other factors that may affect the popularity of the series. *Carry On Dick* was Sid James' last film in the series for two reasons. Partly to avoid professional over-exposure (he was also starring on television in the comedy series *Bless This House*) but mainly because of the danger of distastefulness in a man of sixty chasing younger girls on the screen. As Jack Douglas says: 'There comes a time in every man's life when he can no longer lech without being labelled a dirty, old so-and-so.' Such is the perverseness of human nature, however, that film executives who told Rogers: 'Why don't you get rid of Sid James'? He's becoming a bore', changed their whine, after Sid died, to: 'The Carry Ons just aren't the same without good old Sid.'

A question mark was also put over Barbara Windsor as she approached the age of forty. How long could she go on playing provocative dolly birds of half that age?

Permissiveness and sexual innuendos have increased in the series as public taste has changed to accept them, but the accent of a Carry On has always been on suggestiveness rather than explicitness, with the latest, *Carry On England*, made in 1976, showing the most dramatic change of style, being more bold, frank and contemporary in its attitude to sex rather than cosy, blundering and cheeky. A permissive attitude in a Carry On film, however, like permissiveness in public thinking, is probably the Carry Ons' deadliest enemy. One of the attractions of the series was the way it exploited the vulgarity and the sexual thoughts in peoples' minds at a time when those thoughts could not be openly revealed and discussed in normal everyday life. There was a vicarious pleasure and release to be got from the *double entendres* of a Carry On, from the bare thighs and the partly bare, bobbing boobs. But nowadays when sex, adultery and all such things are no longer subjects of hush-hush embarrassment, some of the appeal of a Carry On must be lost for people over the age of about sixteen. It seems to me that if the Carry On series is to thrive it must become less permissive while other films become more so. It must go all out for its large following of younger fans, aged between seven and fourteen, who will also, in many cases, drag mum and dad along—and dad will not be displeased by the bonus of bottoms and boobs and frillies. It must not be panicked into competition with a series like the 'Confessions of . . .' sex comedies. (Producer Rogers and director Thomas had not seen one of these until 1976 when they went to an afternoon showing of *Confessions of a Driving Instructor* at a cinema in Slough, Buckinghamshire. Their previous, and only other, cinema outing together was in 1958, when, as dog lovers, they saw Disney's *Lady and The Tramp* at Putney, near London.) To get from the Censor, as did *Carry On England*, the first AA certificate of the series (meaning that no child of fourteen or below could see the film, even if accompanied by an adult) was one way to cut audiences dangerously low. Rogers and Thomas quickly appreciated this, however, and re-cut the film, after its release, leading to its re-grading as an A certificate. A strong possibility for future Carry Ons, however, is to make them more permissive, thus entering the already overcrowded more explicit sex market. I think it is a mistake, but do not be surprised if the next film in the series is the first Carry On with an x certificate.

The first eight Carry Ons were given U certificates. *Carry On Spying*, in which Barbara Windsor made her début in the series, started the run of A certificates. The first quick flash of bare breasts (Barbara Windsor's) came in the seventeenth Carry On, *Carry On Camping*. Made in 1968, this became Britain's biggest box office draw the following year. Second was another Carry On—*Carry On Up The Kyhber*. *Carry On Abroad*, in 1972, gave audiences their first proper look at Barbara's chest, and the following film, *Carry On Girls*, almost became the first to get an AA certificate.

Says Rogers: 'You only have trouble with the Censor if you dig your heels in. We appreciate he has a job to do and we try to settle everything amicably. We go along and talk to him, bargain with him.' Early in the series, to illustrate the type of comedy he was attempting, and to make the point that it was readily available on any seaside promenade, Rogers bought 150 saucy postcards from a publisher and sent them to the Censor. 'I only wanted him to look at them', says Rogers. 'I thought he would send them back after a few days. But he kept the lot!'

The Censor's cut most mentioned, and most regretted, by Carry On stars came in *Carry On Nurse* and involved actor Bill Owen (now best known by television audiences for his role in the BBC comedy series *Last Of The Summer Wine*).

In *Nurse* he played a patient called Percy Hickson, a Cockney building worker with a fractured right leg in plaster and raised at an angle by cords and round weights on overhead apparatus. During a disturbance in the ward the round weights fall off and roll all over the floor. A staff nurse, pointing at the weights, tells a subordinate: 'Nurse, pick up Mr Hickson's balls!'

When the scene was shot, everybody on the set was hysterical with laughter. It looked like being the roof-raising line of the film. But the Censor cut it. In the version shown to cinema audiences, the scene ends with the weights rolling around the staff nurse's feet.

In *Carry On Teacher*, Leslie Phillips plays a child psychiatrist, visiting a school, who falls in love with the gym mistress, called Sarah Allcock and played by Joan Sims. Bewitched by the very sight of his loved one, Phillips had to keep looking at Joan Sims and saying: 'Allcock, Allcock.' After reading the script, the Censor decreed that he would allow Phillips to keep muttering 'Allcock' providing he did not emphasise the first or the second syllable. Says Phillips: 'We had an absolutely hysterical day trying to do as the Censor had said. The whole set was full of people going around muttering "Allcock" just to prove they could do it. It's very difficult to say "Allcock" on one level because of those "k" sounds, but when you do succeed it sounds even more provocative than if you emphasise. Try it.'

In *Carry On Regardless*, Eleanor Summerfield had her entire appearance in the film removed by the Censor. She plays a woman who talks in her sleep and wants somebody to stay by her bed all night to report to her in the morning on what she says. Charles Hawtrey lands the job in error and, naturally, mistakes the reason for being in the lady's bedroom. The complete scene can be read on page 105-6.

Any series as mocking as the Carry Ons is bound, from time to time, to ruffle one or two of those who are mocked. The most notorious film in this respect was *Carry On Cleo*. At one time it looked as though the Lady of the Nile would be hauled up twice for a legal wigging. As it happened, she only appeared in court on one of the counts, and as this occurred in the week before the general release of the film it probably paid for itself in free publicity. On this occasion *Cleo* was defended by Mr Quintin Hogg QC (Lord Hailsham).

According to Peter Rogers, he got the idea to make *Carry On Cleo* after hearing of the amount of time Twentieth Century-Fox were taking to produce their version, called *Cleopatra* and starring Elizabeth Taylor. This was made at Pinewood Studios where the Carry Ons are also produced. 'Blimey,' said Rogers, 'I could make a "Carry On Cleo" in the time it's taking them to set up the scenery.'

As part of the joke he imitated as much as he could of Twentieth Century's epic version, including their advertising. One poster put out by Twentieth Century-Fox, showed Elizabeth Taylor lying on a divan, with Rex Harrison as Caesar and Richard Burton as Mark Antony, in the background. Rogers and his backers, Anglo-Amalgamated, reproduced this poster for *Carry On Cleo*, with Amanda Barrie on the divan and Kenneth Williams and Sid James in the background. What they did not know at the time, however, was that the Elizabeth Taylor poster was based on a Cleopatra painting by Howard Terpning and that by reproducing a version of it they were infringing Twentieth Century's copyright in the work.

So on 15 January 1965, *Cleo* in the shape of Anglo Amalgamated Film Distributors Limited, was taken to court by Twentieth Century-Fox. According to Rogers, they cast their defence in the way they would cast a film. 'We got Lord Hailsham to defend us as part of the fun', he says. 'He is an extrovert character with a good sense of humour and seemed absolutely right for the part. I was delighted when he accepted.' Sir Andrew Clark QC, appeared for Twentieth Century-Fox, and the action took place in the High Court before Mr Justice Plowman.

The result was that the *Cleo* posters had to be changed. 'But it was all very entertaining', says Rogers. 'There was no viciousness or anything like that. I think everybody took it in a spirit of good nature.'

Marks & Spencer was involved in the second complaint against *Carry On Cleo*. This was because of a scene which contained a slave market called Markus et Spencius.

It was not the play on their firm's name which bothered the heads of Marks & Spencer, however, but the fact that their trade mark colours of green and white had been used in the set.

'They learned about the colours because a critic, after the press showing of the film, rang and told them', says Rogers.

'We had not realised the importance of these colours to Marks & Spencer. I must admit, when I saw the film, they didn't mean anything to me. They were just colours. Afterwards I presumed that the people who had done the set had used them for a bit of authenticity.

'In any case, we were very nearly sued, and I am convinced that if an outside lawyer had been hired by Marks & Spencer, instead of the matter being dealt with by their own staff lawyer, we would have been. As it was, they asked me to write a letter, for insertion in the *Daily Express*, apologising for the use of the colours and explaining the matter.

'I don't know why they picked the *Daily Express* for this. It was in no way involved. But, in the end, after I had written the letter and sent it to Marks & Spencer for their approval, they dropped the whole thing and the letter was never sent to the *Express*.'

A problem for Rogers and director Gerald Thomas, from time to time, has been Charles Hawtrey. Though one of the longest-serving members of the Carry On team, appearing with Kenneth Williams, Kenneth Connor and Hattie Jacques in the founding *Carry On Sergeant*, Hawtrey has always been something of a loner and extremely wary of strangers.

'There is so much cardboard in show business that one must take a long time before accepting people', he says. It is a statement he bases on forty-two years as a performer, making his first appearance on stage in 1925 and in films in 1930. When he knows you and trusts you he is full of funny stories about the people he has met and worked with—people like Groucho Marx and Will Hay.

A dedicated actor, he has also directed, produced and scripted plays. Though he has had no music lessons, he has an acute ear. Whistle a tune and he will play it on the piano. He also plays the horses. Like Kenneth Williams, though more privately, he rates professionalism among the front-ranking qualities that he looks for in others. His own supreme professionalism is one of the facets which has kept him a member of the Carry On team for so long. As Jack Douglas puts it: 'Only an experienced professional can stand the pace of a Carry On. You've got to be able to turn on the acting ability, the mood, the reaction, immediately it is wanted, for as long as it is wanted . . . and get it right first time.'

Hawtrey's professionalism is what has caused Rogers and director Thomas and members of the Carry On team to close their minds to the fact that, on some afternoons, it is evident that Hawtrey has been sipping something in the lunch hour rather stronger than the bottles of lemonade which he often brings in a carrier bag to the studio. Just as everybody has pretended not to understand the coded messages that Sid James would ask his stand-in to telephone to a certain number on the occasions when he had positively, definitely and indubitably given up betting on the horses, after warnings from his wife Valerie and from producer Rogers, who sometimes loaned money to Sid to settle his gambling debts.

In 1962 Rogers dropped Hawtrey from *Carry On Cruising* and gave his part— as the chef on a holiday liner—to Lance Percival because, says Rogers, Hawtrey insisted on having a silver star on his dressing-room door and was pushing for bigger billing. Says Thomas: 'It was a difficult situation. But with the best will in the world we just could not bill him above Sid James, for example.'

Says Rogers: 'He reached a point where he did not fit into the team, and team work is vital if these films are to be made in the allotted time. He was not pulling with us, but standing alone. He used to say I was drunk with power, but power is something I have very little use for.'

Hawtrey was back for the next film, *Carry On Cabby*, made in 1963. He also came to an arrangement that he would never be less than third in the billing, and though he almost missed a part in *Carry On Screaming* in 1966 (see page 121), he had a role in each of the seventeen Carry Ons made during the next nine years.

Then, at the end of 1972, says Gerald Thomas, came another serious collision about billing, this time for a television show called *Carry On Christmas*, being made by Thames TV.

According to Thomas, Hawtrey wanted top billing and would not take second place to Hattie Jacques. Thomas says he made sustained efforts to get Hawtrey to change his mind, as he wanted him in the show. Hawtrey refused. The day came, says Thomas, when he had to finally decide if Hawtrey would be in the show. He rang his home and got no reply. Knowing Hawtrey's liking for dining out in the restaurants of large departmental stores, such as Dickins & Jones and Bourne & Hollingsworth, Thomas began a systematic search by telephone.

'I found him', says Thomas, 'having lunch at Bourne & Hollingsworth and, again, over the telephone, tried to talk him into changing his mind. In the end, I said: "Well, this is it. You have to make up your mind finally right now, before you hang up. Will you accept second billing or won't you?"

'There was a pause at the other end of the line, then he said: "No", and hung up. I was very, very sad about it.'

Hawtrey has been in none of the four Carry On films made since that telephone conversation and I, for one, have missed his entrance with, what became his catch-phrase: 'Oh, hello', and that owl-like stare behind glasses which had no lenses. A routine was also adopted of giving his entrances an element of surprise by casting him in roles which contrasted with his appearance. The Red Indian chief Big Heap in *Carry on Cowboy* is an example.

Neither Rogers nor Thomas can adequately explain Hawtrey's attitude. Says Thomas: 'Charles is a bit of a lonely man, I think, so, more than any other member of the team, he used to volunteer to go to various cinemas all over the country to

Carry On Cruising **This'll cook his goose! First Officer Marjoribanks (Kenneth Williams) and ship's doctor Arthur Binn (Kenneth Connor) plot a two-stage cure for the continual seasickness of chef** Wilfred Haines (Lance Percival). First a tranquil-lising tablet—then a great hypodermic needle up the backside!

help promote one of the films. Of course he would be wined and dined and made a big fuss of and all I can think is that possibly this gave him a false sense of his own importance.'

The last time Hawtrey appeared in a Carry On film was as the hard-drinking mother's boy Eustace Tuttle in *Carry On Abroad*, though Rogers says: 'Nobody is dropped for ever from the Carry Ons. They can all come back.' So do not be surprised if Hawtrey turns up in future Carry Ons. After introducing a bevy of new talent in the last two films, *Carry On Behind* and *Carry On England*, an experiment which did not have the sort of immediate box office impact hoped for, 'It is probably back to square one with all the old names for the next Carry On', says Gerald Thomas.

Because of her appearances in the Carry On series, resulting in a lot of fan letters from the younger teenagers, Barbara Windsor calls herself: 'The fourteen year olds' pin-up.' But in 1973 the Press got a hint of a story that she was more than just a pin-up to Sid James; both denied it with mocking laughter. Sid's attitude was: 'It's the most stupid thing I've heard. Barbara and I have known each other for years. We're old workmates. If something was going to happen it would have happened years ago, wouldn't it? I mean, I'm only flesh and blood. Anything can happen to anybody. But ask yourself: Why should it suddenly happen now, after all this time?'

Indeed, by the autumn of 1973, Sid and Barbara had appeared in seven Carry On films together, four of them (*Camping*, *Henry*, *Abroad* and *Girls*) on close screen terms without Sid's attitude toward her being anything more than friendly and professional. And while he would act leery and girl-chasing on-screen, such conduct off-screen was distasteful to him.

His only other love, next to his wife and family, was gambling. Occasionally, of the £5,000 which he received for making a Carry On film, only £3,500 was paid into his bank in the normal manner. The remaining £1,500, about which he claimed his wife knew nothing, was then paid to him separately. This was Sid's gambling money. He called it his 'back pocket money'. The money for his other love.

Sid's disinterest in socialising while he was working, his need to turn off and be a private person whenever he could, and the wary eye which he kept on his health after his heart attack in the spring of 1967, meant that he rarely joined other members of the cast for a lunchtime drink, or a meal in the studio restaurant, while working on a Carry On at Pinewood. He lived not far away and preferred to go home for lunch. Possibly the money he saved by doing this was another reason. It does not matter. It is Sid's life pattern that matters, because in this lies the reason why his attitude to Barbara remained merely friendly-professional until the end of 1973, and why it slowly became something else after that.

The change was brought about by Peter Rogers' launching, that winter, of the first Carry On stage show, called *Carry On London*, at the Victoria Palace where the Crazy Gang had once reigned for so long.

In a stage show the life pattern of the stars is vastly different from that while making a film. Let Barbara Windsor tell it:

'You don't get to know anybody much in films. I had a lot of scenes with Sid in

Carry On Abroad and *Carry On Girls*, but I didn't know him, and he didn't know me. We did our scenes and went home.

'But when you're rehearsing a stage show, you're brought into closer contact. You're rehearsing in some dirty old hall, doing the same bit of dialogue or business together over and over again. You're making each other coffee. In the breaks there's nowhere to go, so you talk to each other.

'Besides this, Sid saw me doing things like singing and dancing that he didn't know I could do. All he'd seen me at until now was wiggling my bottom and my boobs around a Carry On set! Now he started to admire me professionally. I used to see him standing at the side of the stage watching me with amazement and admiration all over his face.

'It shows what our relationship was like when we started this show: After I'd sung something for the first time, Sid said: "I didn't know you could sing." And I turned on him. I said: "It's typical of you not to know anything about your fellow artists, Mr James!"

'He also saw me putting blokes down who fancied their chances, and that got him admiring me as well. But I've had a lot of experience at putting blokes down. When you've had to go home alone from a show to the East End on a late night bus as often as I had to in my early days, you learn a few tricks . . . but quick! You'd better!

'Sid used to call me Tiger. He said one day: "The thing I like about you Tiger is that you're kind, but you don't knuckle under." I said: "I'm kind to everybody lower than me in the show because I know what it's like down there. I spent a very long time in the chorus."

'I realised he was getting fond of me when he started being over-protective, defending me against people. "What's all this with Sid?" they used to say.

'Once I was late turning up for the night's show, and Sid was waiting for me by the stage door, worried out of his mind.

'He used to send me a dozen red roses every week and write nice little notes. But I never played on it. I love my husband.

'Was Sid in love with me? Yes, I think he was or, at least, I think he believed he was. I thought he was perhaps going through the male menopause. We became very close and fond of each other, but I wasn't in love with Sid.'

Early in 1974, as well as appearing in the stage show, *Carry On London*, Sid and Barbara began filming at Pinewood in what was to be Sid's last Carry On, *Carry On Dick*, in which he played Dick Turpin. Barbara was a housemaid who dressed as a highwayman and accompanied Turpin on his robberies.

Says Barbara: 'For about six weeks I was spending more time with Sid than with my husband, and we became very close at this time. We were together on the film set during the day and together in the show at night.

'I felt we were becoming too close and that it was affecting my work. Before this film it didn't bother me to do all that wiggling in front of Sid, but I had a scene in *Carry On Dick* where I had to seduce him—and I just couldn't do it. I couldn't shake everything about in front of him. The change in our relationship had put a wall between us when it came to doing things like that in a scene.

'Sid said: "What's the matter with you? You're acting like I've got leprosy. Come on, let's get on with the scene." But I couldn't. I just couldn't. I broke down and wept and Gerry (director Gerald Thomas) had to talk to me, help me.

'Though Sid's death was sudden to most people, it wasn't to me. I knew he wasn't well, and he was overworking. His death hit me pretty badly, though. It happened just before they started filming on *Carry On England*. I was glad I wasn't in that one. I don't think I could have handled it—not just then.'

Sid James died in the last week of April 1976.

For all the Carry On stars there is the professional danger of being type-cast and the frustrating prospect of not being picked for other kinds of films by other directors, even though few roles give world fame faster than stardom in the Carry Ons.

Whoever they touch is marked for life. Actors who have not starred in one for years continue to be mobbed by cheering foreigners from Hamburg to Honduras, their performances in other, more recent, roles brushed aside by the heavily

Carry On Cruising **With this lot behind me I'm sunk! Captain Crowther (Sid James) of the holiday cruise ship *Happy Wanderer* feels seasick—but not in the usual way. He feels sick at the thought of going to sea with an inexperienced and blundering** First Officer (played by Kenneth Williams) and ship's doctor (Kenneth Connor). How right he is! Soon the ship could be re-named 'The Slap-Happy Wanderer'!

accented chant 'Carry On, Carry On', though, judging by a recent example, the famous Carry On label does not always stay on the package. For its 1977 opening in Germany, *Carry On Abroad* was re-titled *A Mad Holiday*.

Leslie Phillips, who starred in his third and last Carry On in 1959, is one of those still recognised, not only abroad but in Britain, as a Carry On star.

'The Carry Ons have had this effect right from the very beginning', he says. 'I remember going to a film festival in South America not long after being in *Carry On Nurse*. I had also, shortly before that, been to Hollywood to appear in the musical *Les Girls*, which was a big, glossy job with people in it like Gene Kelly, Kay Kendall and Mitzi Gaynor.

'When I was asked about the films I'd made I began listing them, including *Les Girls* of course. But somebody interrupted me. "What about *Carry On Nurse?*" they said. "The greatest film of all!"'

Phillips has also been heavily castigated by a film critic for his performance in a

Carry On Doctor **This'll cut him down to size! The chap on the table is Doctor Tinkle—for whom, you might say, the bell tolls. The three musketeers of surgery are patients Ken Biddle (Bernard Bresslaw), Charlie Roper (Sid James) and Francis Bigger (Frankie Howerd.) They are indulging in this bit of sharp practice to scare a confession from Tinkle that he and Matron unfairly gave the professional chop to young Doctor Kilmore (Jim Dale). What dare Tinkle say? 'Yes, I put the knife in' . . . 'Cut it out, fellas' . . . 'You've got the edge on me.' Difficult. For all he knows, once the theatre gets in their blood, anything could incite them to incision.**

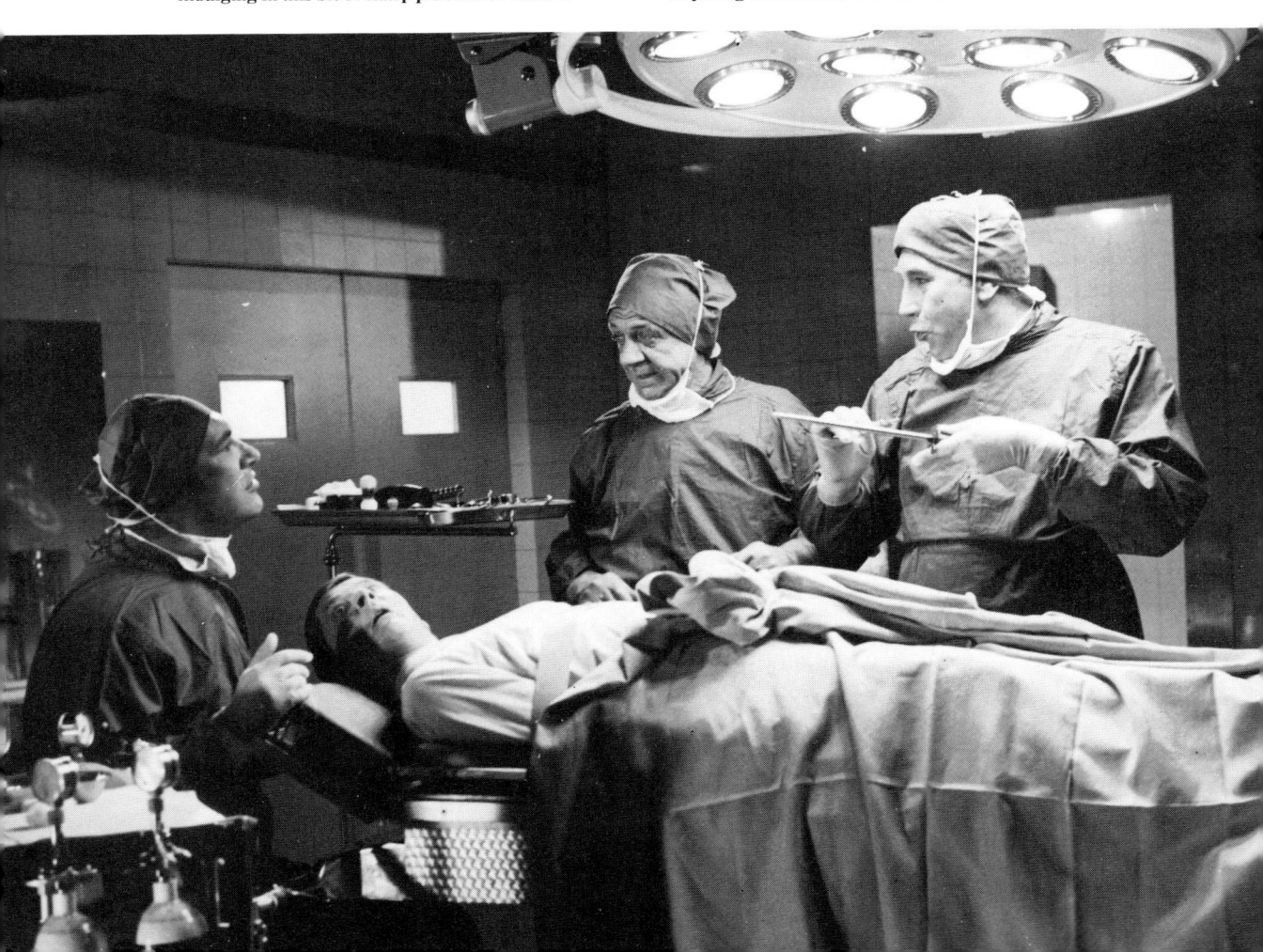

Carry On in which he did not even appear! Says Phillips: 'That was *Carry On Regardless*, and I was given an absolutely appalling notice in a newspaper in Bristol. I immediately wrote to the editor and got an apology. But that's the sort of thing that happens. Once your name is linked with the Carry Ons, everybody thinks you're in all of them. This critic chap obviously hadn't seen the film and didn't bother to check.

'Of course, the fact that these films are now appearing on television also makes sure that you are for ever a Carry On man.'

Kenneth Williams is another of those with the mark of Carry On upon him. In eastern Crete, after trekking to see a remote fifteenth-century monastery, he arrived to be greeted by a monk with the words: 'Ah, Carry On!'

Frankie Howerd, who has been in only two of the films, *Carry On Doctor* and *Carry On Up The Jungle*, has been hailed as a Carry On star in places as far apart as Mombasa and Singapore, and when he visited a town in Borneo, what was on at the local cinema—a Carry On film.

Sid James, shortly before he died, visited Phnom-Penh in Cambodia on his way back from a tour of Australia. While there he met a rich businessman who invited him to dinner. Afterwards the man said: 'And now I will take you to the cinema.' Sid did not *really* want to go, but he politely agreed. When they got there he discovered that the man not only owned the cinema but that it showed nothing but Carry On films twenty-four hours a day.

'And it was packed', said Sid. 'As for me, I was greeted like the second coming. Since doing the Carry Ons there is nowhere in the world I can go for a rest. All round me, everywhere, in a million different lingos, people are saying "Carry On, Carry On". Whenever I arrive somewhere fresh I think: "Maybe here I won't be recognised?" You've gotta be kidding!'

From the major cities of the world to remote South Sea islands the words 'Carry On' are an international passport not only to the guffaw and the belly-laugh but to a sound they have made their very own, which I call 'the groaning grin'.

This strangulated cry, often given out by critics laughing against all the laws of sanity, reason and judgement, is brought on by the gall of the puns, the flagrant cheek of the *double entendres* and the bludgeoning, persistent, endless audacity of the slapstick.

The series is a loud, broad, incorrigible phenomenon which puts its mark on words as well as on people. Any attempt at historical setting down looks like hysterical sending up when applied to, or influenced by, the Carry On films. After seeing one of them, momentous speeches by politicians, newspaper leader columns, even the innocent conversation of friends and loved ones become a Carry On script. Words like 'it' and 'posterity' and 'circumspect' adopt uncontrollable, mischievous double meanings. Somebody says: 'I must go now', and the phrase transforms itself in the mind into an urgent visit to the loo. One cannot even describe the Carry Ons as a bastion of British comedy without being aware of the mocking twinkle in the eye of that word 'bastion'.

In the film industry the Carry On series is a voluble, comic drunk who has blundered into a hushed lounge bar full of people trying to look worldly, important and wise. While most of them frown and give the drunk looks of distaste, they eagerly take the large drinks he buys them.

In the sacred galleries of cinematic art the Carry On series is a gaudy, winking, seaside picture postcard among the Rembrandts. And British to the 'Cor!'. As Jim Dale says: 'Where else in the world can you buy a postcard of an old man looking out to sea with, underneath, the words: "I haven't seen my little Willy for ages"?'

The whole of the film industry eagerly watched the early Carry Ons, if only to try and analyse their success and jump on the bandwaggon. But because there have been so many Carry Ons since, and because over the years it has become almost a reflex action of some critics and members of the industry to knock them (the 'in' thing to do) the later good ones have tended to be underestimated by many and bundled with the later not-so-good as mere tits and titters. Like Bernard Bresslaw, however, I believe that the best of these Carry Ons, like *Cleo* and *Up The Khyber*, are funnier, better constructed, more cleverly written than many glossier, more prestigious comedies such as one or two of the *Pink Panther* series.

Carry On dialogue, especially from 1963, is a work of anarchy. The dictionary is turned into a jack-in-the-box. Words you have used for years adopt the manners of a skunk, turning into derisive stink bombs.

Just as the Carry On scripts of Norman Hudis are distinguishable by their strands of pathos, so those of Talbot Rothwell, who took over from Hudis in 1963, are the ones most responsible for this knockabout, mocking, sometimes brilliant trickery with words, plus situations of genuine satire.

Rothwell has written twenty of the Carry On scripts out of the twenty-eight so far produced, beginning with number seven, *Carry On Cabby* and ending with number twenty-six *Carry On Dick*. Number nine, *Carry On Spying* he wrote in collaboration with Sid Colin.

Rothwell was already a successful scriptwriter, aged forty-six, when his agent suggested, in 1962, that he send some samples of his work to Peter Rogers. At that time he had written for the stage, radio and television, including scripts for the Crazy Gang, Terry-Thomas, Arthur Askey and Ted Ray. 'Though it is true to say I was comparatively unknown', says Rothwell.

Talbot Rothwell. He has written twenty consecutive Carry On films, from *Carry On Cabby* to *Carry On Dick*.

The script he wrote was called 'Poopdecker RN' and was a burlesque of the Captain Hornblower books. Rogers received the script in the post one morning at his home and read it in bed before going to the studio. 'If something doesn't absorb me in the first two pages then I don't bother with it', says Rogers. 'This interested me all the way through.'

The next thing Rothwell knew was that he had been invited to meet Rogers in the lounge of the Dorchester Hotel in London.

Says Rothwell: 'I remember he ordered tea for two then, without any more fuss, said that he liked my story and wanted me to do a screenplay of it immediately. He made a few suggestions about the sort of characters he would like—and left the rest to me. That is how I came to write for the Carry On series. The first script was eventually called *Carry On Jack*. I suppose it took me about three months to write. When I delivered it he gave me another!'

This second script was not a Carry On at the time, but was titled *Call Me A Cab*. It was a rush job and Rothwell turned it out in two weeks. Rogers and Thomas filmed it in the spring of 1963, before *Carry On Jack*, and, on the suggestion of their distributors, later retitled it *Carry On Cabby*.

Rothwell (full Christian names Talbot Nelson Conn) was born at Bromley, Kent, into a family with a stockbroking background, though his father was what he calls 'a high class electrical engineer'.

In a biography which he wrote as part of the publicity for the launch of *Carry On Jack*, Rothwell describes his birth like this: 'It was November 12th 1916 that I fought my way out of my first tight spot. Even at birth I was an out-of-the-ordinary child. The doctor took one look at me and said: "This child will get ahead." In fact the head arrived a couple of days later.'

And schooling: 'At school I took school certificate three times and matriculation four times—failing brilliantly in all subjects. But I excelled at games of all kinds—in the first fifteen with rugger, in the first eleven with cricket and in the first twenty with the caretaker's daughter.'

Leaving school he spent three months as a failed clerk at the Town Hall, Brighton, then joined the Palestine Police. Two years later he transferred to the Royal Air Force. When World War II began he was a pilot officer with Coastal Command in Scotland. Flying a Lockheed Hudson on a bombing raid over Norway in June 1940 he was shot down by three ME 109s. Though wounded he managed to bail out and was captured by German troops when he drifted down onto a beach.

Like Carry On star Peter Butterworth, a wartime pilot with the Fleet Air Arm, who was shot down off the Dutch coast trying to bomb a tanker, Rothwell ended up in the notorious prisoner of war camp Stalag Luft 3. Both were involved in the now-legendary escape operation which featured a wooden vaulting horse.

It was at Stalag Luft 3 that Rothwell began to write plays and scripts for the camp theatre ('one of the tortures that the prisoners had to go through', he says) on a typewriter sent out from Britain as part of a Red Cross parcel.

After joining Rogers, he turned out two Carry On films in most years (as well as screenplays for other Rogers' productions) until the end of 1973, when something very odd happened to him.

This is how he describes it: 'I was nearing the end of my work on *Carry On Dick*. It seemed a normal sort of morning when I awoke. I had my breakfast, then went to my desk to begin my day's work on the script.

'I sat down opposite my electric typewriter, but instead of working I found myself staring at the keys. I couldn't work. I had a sort of mental blockage. I just stared at those keys and thought: What is all this ASDFG? (*Note to non-typists:* That is the order of letters at the start of one row of a typewriter keyboard).

'I thought: "What do they mean? It's ridiculous."

'That's all I could think: How ridiculous the typewriter keyboard was. It wasn't that I couldn't think up dialogue. I could. It wasn't that I couldn't physically type. It was simply that every time I went to type, my brain said "no". My brain said it was ridiculous.

'In the end I had to get my daughter Jane to type it for me. It wasn't all that much of a problem because I had done a pretty fair copy of a draft. She just typed from that.'

A doctor later told Rothwell that he was simply suffering from eye strain and overwork, both of which would quickly disappear after a little rest. 'But it was worrying at the time', he says.

Rothwell's mammoth contribution to the Carry On series cannot be overstressed. Yet, ask him to name his favourite bits of word play, the puns which gave him the most relish, and he laughs.

'To tell you the truth,' he says, 'once I've written them, I forget them. But, yes, at the time I get pleasure out of one or two, though I'm usually so busy I don't get time to laugh!' A selection from Rothwell's worderama is in Part Three of the book along with quotations from the other films.

If Rothwell does not consciously remember gags, his subconscious certainly has its favourites. The miracle is, in his type of writing, that he has not repeated himself more often.

A joke about 'Do you believe in free love?' . . . 'Well I'm certainly not paying for it?' appears in the consecutive comedies *Carry On Matron* and *Carry On Abroad*.

A joke on the lines of: 'You wouldn't think that I was once a weak man, would you?' . . . 'Once a week is plenty for any man', turns up in *Carry On Doctor*, *Carry On Loving* and *Carry On Henry*, with a variation on 'once a knight' (night) appearing in *Carry On Dick*.

You can hear the one about 'chaste—but not caught', in *Carry On Henry* and *Carry On Dick*, and the city of Bristol jogs the mammary in *Carry On Cleo*, *Carry On Henry* and *Carry On Girls*.

The gag: 'May his radiance light up your life.' Reply: 'And up yours', in *Carry On Up The Khyber* is cantered out under slightly different colours in *Carry On Dick*.

'Don't forget your bag.' . . . 'She's not coming', or something similar adds to *Carry On Cleo* and *Carry On Dick*.

Bidets fascinate Rothwell. Apart from being an integral part of the plot of *Carry On At Your Convenience*, Bidet is the name of a character in *Carry On . . . Don't Lose Your Head* and *Carry On Henry*.

Burke is a good Carry On name, which is probably why it turns up twice, in *Carry On Cowboy* and *Carry On Doctor*.

Desiree is such an obvious Carry On name I am surprised it has only turned up twice—in *Carry On . . . Don't Lose Your Head* and *Carry On Dick*, both times played by Joan Sims. (She got stuck twice with Chloe, however, in *Carry On Doctor* and *Carry On At Your Convenience*!)

As in the Restoration comedies, Henry Fielding and funny books and plays down the ages, names are an important part of the Carry On ensemble. Names like: Lord Hampton of Wick, Sir Roger de Lodgerley, Sir Sidney Ruff-Diamond, an unmarried mother called Miss Willing, a surgeon called Sir Bernard Cutting, a block of flats where somebody has 'a bit on the side' called Rogerham Mansions, the prophet Mustapha Leke, Indian leader the Khasi of Kalabar, the Reverend Flasher and Bunghit Din. In a Carry On, Finishem Maternity Hospital simply had to have a Bunn Ward, just as a lavatory attendant had to be called Mr Dan Dann. Names have also ranged from the obviously vulgar Long Hampton Hospital to the think-about-it-for-a-minute Fircombe-on-Sea.

Next to bedrooms, showers and baths are a favourite Carry On fun spot—as Barbara Windsor can tell you! But a pretty girl is not always part of such splash-stick comedy. Leslie Phillips, Kenneth Williams, Charles Hawtrey and Kenneth Connor were featured in Norman Hudis' shower scene in *Carry On Constable*. Rothwell's *Jack, Cleo, Camping, Jungle, Matron* and *Abroad*, and Dave Freeman's *Behind* (*Carry On Behind*, that is) are some of the other places where water and waggery happily gurgle round the parts and down the plughole.

And have you noticed how badly made the women's clothing often is in a Carry On? A man has only to touch it—and it falls off!

Amazon beauties feature in two Carry Ons—*Carry On Spying* and *Carry On Up The Jungle*, and there is a fascinating variation by two different writers of the mistaken identity–marriage agency gag. This is about a chap expecting to meet a blind date from a marriage agency who becomes mistakenly involved with another girl. The gag revolves on the fact that there are so many different kinds of agencies. In Hudis' *Carry On Regardless*, Liz Fraser turns up from an agency to clean a gent's flat. But he thinks she is the blind date he is expecting from a marriage agency. Comments from her of the type: 'Shall I start on the settee?', bristle with different meanings for him. In Rothwell's *Carry On Loving*, Richard O'Callaghan meets Jacki Piper in a bar and thinks she is his marriage bureau partner. Jacki, playing a struggling actress, thinks he is the pin-up photographer from a modelling agency that she is waiting to meet. So she takes him back to her flat and starts to strip off . . .

While an increasingly more open-minded attitude to sex and kindred matters, like unmarried mothers, has given Rothwell a freer hand and more comedy scope than Hudis had, he has had to deal with the often difficult marriage of violence and comedy. In several, *Jack, Cleo, Cowboy, Don't Lose Your Head, Follow That Camel, Up The Khyber* among them, violence was necessary if the situation was not to become totally false, unbelievable and even unfunny. The realism of the violence was necessary to help the comedy. But a fine balance had to be struck, because one of the functions of the comedy was to tone down the violence, to provide a defusing element of unreality.

In cinematic terms, *Carry On Cowboy* is the most realistically violent film of the series, though well within the bounds not only of what children will accept, but expect. A point worth making is that the baddies in a Carry On are not always played by actors in supporting roles, but by beloved members of the Carry On team, often without the usual comedy excuses of plotting disaster in ignorance because of wrong information, and causing death (to a baddy, of course) by mistake or comic clumsiness. In the case of Sid James, for example, death or dastardly deeds were calculated in *Cleo* and *Cowboy*, and it was goodies who were the intended victims.

Such is the advantage of the Carry On repertory system (in which anybody plays almost anything) and the non-star mentality of most of its members where the series is concerned. I know some comedy actors who would have refused the parts that Sid took in *Cleo* and *Cowboy* on the grounds that it would not be good for their lovable image with the public to be nasty or underhand on the screen. They would have calculated that any romantic associations that Mark Antony (the part

Carry On Constable Anything you say will be taken down, as the policeman said to the girl in the underwear department. And these odd customers *are* policemen, right down to their legal briefs. They are PC Benson (Kenneth Williams) and Special Constable Gorse (Charles Hawtrey) all dressed up to catch shoplifters. But as disguised policemen they are not much cop. They end up being mistaken for shoplifters themselves, thanks to this assistant, played by—wait for it— Mary Law!

Sid played in *Cleo*) may have, are lost the moment he becomes a broad character. In the same way, the persuasiveness of his motive in plotting to murder Caesar (because he is blinded by his love for Cleopatra) is also lost, and Mark Antony becomes just a sneaky assassin.

Some stars will not appear in drag. But one of the subjects for laughter and leg-pulling among Carry On actors is who will be lumbered with the false boobs and knickers in the next film—for there is usually a drag role in every Carry On, and lots of wisecracks and wolf-whistles when the girlie-garbed victim for a particular film appears.

It is time to reveal the unknown star of the Carry On series. She is not an actress nor a member of any branch of show business; she has never appeared on the screen, nor has her name ever been on a cinema poster. But her contribution is the most famous among the total of twenty-eight Carry On films so far made.

First her contribution.

In terms of publicity and audience reaction the most successful Carry On scene comes at the end of the second film, *Carry On Nurse*, when a daffodil appears to be used to take the temperature of Wilfrid Hyde White—via his backside.

Wilfrid Hyde White plays a character called 'the Colonel', who has his own private ward. He has also an itchy finger for the button which summons a nurse in case of emergency. The incident with the daffodil is done as a lark by two nurses, played by Joan Sims and Susan Stephen, to pay the Colonel back for all the unnecessary running about he has caused them to do by pressing the emergency button for trivial reasons.

They enter his room saying that they have to carry out a final test. When the daffodil is in position and they are preparing to photograph it, they see Matron, played by Hattie Jacques, approaching and they scarper. The film ends with:

Matron: Colonel, whatever's going on?

Colonel: (lying on stomach) Come, come Matron, surely you've seen a temperature taken like this before?

Matron: Oh yes Colonel, many times. But never with a daffodil (and she plucks it out).

Wilfrid Hyde White was not there when the scene was being shot at Pinewood, but as Hattie Jacques moved, as if pulling out the daffodil, somebody watching made a noise with his mouth like a popping champagne cork. The stern face of Matron immediately creased into laughter, joined by everybody else. The take was ruined. So was the next . . . and the next . . . and the next. Hattie could now not do the scene without laughing. In the end the shot had to be abandoned until the next day.

Because Wilfrid Hyde White could not remember making such a sequence, his agent threatened legal action on the grounds that the actor had been hoodwinked into participating while thinking he was doing some other scene, or that trick photography had been used, or that somebody else's rear had been superimposed on his body. In effect, that his bottom was being exploited without his knowledge or permission. It was all very much like a Carry On scene.

The fact is, however, that nobody's bare end appears. The idea in 1958, when

Carry On Nurse was made, of showing on-screen a backside with a daffodil stuck up it was unthinkable. The whole effect is achieved by a quick succession of images and the final picture of this medico-horticultural phenomenon appears only in the minds of the audience. It is in the best Carry On tradition and one of the reasons for the success of the series: vulgar suggestiveness rather than vulgar explicitness.

Audiences loved it, even eventually and surprisingly, in America where prejudice and opinion, based on exaggerated arguments about a different sense of humour, unintelligible accents and technically inferior productions, had long declared that no British comedy film could be a hit on that side of the Atlantic.

After being rejected by major American film distributors, *Carry On Nurse* was taken up by David Emanuel who ran an independent company called Governor Films. Under his guidance *Carry On Nurse* led with its behind—and smashed through the American laughter barrier. In a country which cannot resist a gimmick, Emanuel provided one. He projected the posterior temperature scene by having a plastic daffodil presented to each member of the audience as they left the cinema.

After an exploratory introduction in California *Nurse* found the funny bone and the chuckle muscles of Uncle Sam in the most unlikely places as Emanuel trundled the cans of Carry On film from cinema to cinema in the boot of his car.

It was not long before a host of golden, plastic daffodils sprouted across America, from Los Angeles to New York.

The film, made in black and white for a modest £71,000, with a wardrobe bill of less than £480, broke box office records in Britain and America, beating all comers from lavish Hollywood and elsewhere to become the biggest money-making film in Britain for 1959, recovering its cost and going into profit in a matter of days. It has now made about £1 million.

In America it ran for more than a year at the Crest cinema in Westwood, Los Angeles and became a cult on university campuses. The only place where the bloom of *Nurse* faded was in New York where it was given a gala opening with director Gerald Thomas and star Shirley Eaton in attendance and a bumper crop of plastic daffodils. But the comedy was too basic for the city's more sophisticated audiences. There was no doubt, however, that *Carry On Nurse* and its daffodil had got to the bottom of what made the rest of America laugh.

One trans-Atlantic telephone call to Carry On producer Peter Rogers told him: 'Your film is playing out here in places where they don't even wear shoes.' In London restaurants he would be advised by visiting Americans who knew he was in films but did not yet connect his name with the series: 'You've just gotta see *Carry On Nurse*. It's a riot!'

The film's scriptwriter, Norman Hudis, on his first visit to Hollywood, in 1964, was in a waiting room. When his name was called to go in for a meeting, a stranger, who was also waiting, rushed up to him speechless with emotion and practically kissing his hands. When the man could speak he told Hudis that in a desperate attempt to stay in the film business, which had recently treated him unkindly, he had invested his last few hundred dollars in the company which had distributed *Carry On Nurse* in America. And now he was rich. *Carry On Nurse* had saved him.

Despite the stubborn Britishness of the humour, the only scene that appeared to puzzle Americans was when Joan Sims, as the blundering Nurse Dawson, had a L-plate stuck to her backside. They do not have L-plates in America.

The success of *Carry On Nurse* blazed a golden trail for the next film in the series, *Carry On Teacher*, which was also a trans-Atlantic hit, and pioneered the way for other British comedies.

Says Rogers: 'I was more pleased that the film was doing well where they didn't wear shoes than disappointed that it was dying in New York. The Carry Ons are not made for a West End-type audience. I was against the gala launch in New York and wild horses wouldn't have got me over there. *Carry On Nurse* was not suited to that kind of treatment. I have always been more interested in the opinion of a char than in that of her boss where my films are concerned.'

Subsequent Carry Ons in America failed to repeat the bonanza of the early ones after bigger distributors (who had originally said there was no market for Carry Ons in the United States) now moved in on the gold mine and squeezed out the independent David Emanuel. Eventually a situation was reached where major American distributors bought the rights of Carry On films simply to hoard them and so prevent smaller competitors from possibly repeating the *Carry On Nurse* breakthrough.

Nine years after *Nurse* was written, a different scriptwriter paid homage to the daffodil joke in *Carry On Doctor*, the fifteenth film of the series: Frankie Howerd is a patient in a private ward. A nurse, played by delectable Valerie Van Ost, enters carrying a vase of daffodils. She places the vase on a locker beside Howerd's bed, then takes out one of the daffodils. Howerd reacts. 'Oh no you don't!', he says. 'I saw that film!'

'I thought you'd like to smell it', she says, sniffing the daffodil. 'Mm, lovely.'

'Yes, well, that's different', says Howerd. 'You have to be careful here, you know. They stuff you full of everything.'

So who invented this legendary scene—a scene which film chief Nat Cohen, whose Anglo-Amalgamated company backed *Nurse*, has no doubt was the dynamo of the American success? The obvious answer—scriptwriter Norman Hudis—is wrong. This golden gag was set on its bawdy world travels by an Irish housewife called Ethel Good.

Mrs Ethel Good. Mother-in-law of Carry On scriptwriter Norman Hudis. She invented the most famous gag in the Carry On series—the daffodil up the backside in *Carry On Nurse*.

She is the unknown star of the Carry On series and not until now, nearly twenty years later, has the fact been revealed. Who is Ethel Good? She is scriptwriter Hudis' mother-in-law.

Confessing that the gag was not his and offering 'belated, but deserved credit', to his mother-in-law, Hudis explained: 'My dear mum-in-law was never a nurse. But, born in Ireland and a very lively lady indeed, she is greatly experienced at polishing off a jar or two with friends and neighbours and swapping stories both true and otherwise, but always deeply amusing. She tells 'em well too, with a good sense of the dramatic.'

It was during such a session at Hudis' home, then in Rickmansworth, Hertfordshire, while he was writing *Carry On Nurse* in 1958, that Mrs Good came out with the daffodil yarn.

Now living in County Mayo, Eire, Mrs Good told me: 'The daffodil was one of those stories which one visualises on the spur of the moment, especially after a few jars. As far as I'm aware it originated from myself.'

Says Hudis: 'Ever a snapper-up of well considered non-trifles, the story was on paper before the air around us had a chance to change back from the bright blue she had created with the yarn.'

But that is not the end of the story. When Hudis wrote *Carry On Nurse*, he put the daffodil joke about three-quarters of the way through the film, and that is where it stayed during script conferences with producer Rogers, during filming with director Thomas, during editing, and during the music stage. With the film completed, shown to the distributors and ready for the public, the daffodil scene still remained where Hudis had placed it and where they all felt it served well.

When Rogers and Thomas saw the finished film, however, they had a small doubt which grew into a big decision. A Carry On usually builds to a finale of what they hope will be the loudest laugh, the most riotous slapstick, or, in a Hudis script which more than those that followed, mixed pathos and 'heart' with the guffaws, a major emotional climax.

Rogers and Thomas had known all along that they had a good, romantic, happy-every-after ending to the *Nurse* film. This was the resolution of a love affair between Staff Nurse Dorothy Denton (played by Shirley Eaton) and local-reporter-cum-appendicitis-patient Ted York (Terence Longden).

What Rogers and Thomas now knew, however, was that the daffodil scene would make a better ending.

They also knew that at this stage it was impractical, even foolhardy, to re-edit parts of the film to make the change. But they did it, putting the daffodil sequence last, because one reason takes precedence over all others in a Carry On—what will get the biggest laugh where?

As for the original ending. Next time you see *Carry On Nurse* on television, notice how the music starts to build to a louder than usual crescendo at the close of that Shirley Eaton–Terence Longden scene, though crescendo and scene have been shortened to fit better in their new position in the film.

'It was a change we thought worth doing at the time', says Rogers. 'And I think we were probably right.' He smiles at the understatement.

A Carry On usually begins with Rogers thinking of a theme and title. Ideas mostly come to him on one of three occasions—while taking a bath, while gardening, or while sitting, relaxed, on the steps of a large, 150 year old gipsy caravan parked in the grounds of his home in Buckinghamshire. 'Of the three I suppose the most fruitful place has been the bath', he says. 'I think it's the hot water round the parts that, in some mysterious way, gets my brain working. You could say that I come to a genitals agreement'

Rogers' first twinge about the possibilities in a hospital theme, however, was generated by a play called *Ring For Catty* written by actor Patrick Cargill and Jack Beale. This was not a broad comedy, though it had stiff-upper-lip humour worked into the theme of death in a sanatorium for tuberculosis patients. Rogers' wife, Betty Box, best known as producer of the 'Doctor' series and the 'Percy' comedies, had seen the play performed at Richmond in Surrey and thought it might have film possibilities. Rogers found a copy lying about the house and read it. Professionally, apart from the accident of founding the Carry On series, he has never done himself a more rewarding favour. For while there is nothing of *Ring For Catty* in *Carry On Nurse* (though he gave Cargill and Beale a screen credit for the idea, a small payment and a small percentage of the profits), he began to see the comic potential in a hospital setting.

There have been more Carry On films about hospitals (always with Hattie Jacques as the matron, though other members of the team have varying roles) than about anything else—and all of them have been hits. As somebody jealously punned: 'The way Rogers turns illness to gold makes me sick.' Or: 'Sick benefit is the money Peter Rogers makes out of his hospital comedies.' Apart from the initial bumper injection, there have been booster doses called *Carry On Doctor*, *Carry On Again Doctor* and *Carry On Matron*, with a fifth merry medical mixture, *Carry On Again Nurse*, ready for dispensing. Rogers has also produced a hospital comedy called *Twice Round The Daffodils* (those lucky daffodils again) which is more solidly derived from *Ring For Catty* and is really just an injection of Carry On with a less blunt needle. The gags are not as punful to the senses.

Under contract to Rogers and given *Carry On Nurse* to write, Hudis made some preliminary notes which left him totally dissatisfied. 'They were soppy and sentimental,' he says, 'idealising the nursing profession and lacking that robust humour which had flowed so easily when I wrote the previous *Carry On Sergeant*.'

A publicist for J. Arthur Rank films before turning to scriptwriting, Hudis had written more than twenty low-budget second-feature screenplays when he got his break with the Carry On series. Until that time his biggest hit was *The Tommy Steele Story*. At one stage, *Nurse* did not look like being fit to tie the guitar strings of that film. The fact that Hudis' wife, Marguerita, was a nurse and could help in the writing of the new Carry On by supplying authentic funny stories was a boon, but it was not enough. In the writing of *Carry On Sergeant* Hudis had been able to draw on the experience of the six years he had served in the Royal Air Force, for even though *Sergeant* was about the Army, the basics of rookies, routine and training were similar enough. He had the feel of service life.

Luck, however, was a feature of the foundation of the Carry Ons. By chance the

Norman Hudis. He wrote the first six Carry Ons.

series made its début at a time when music hall had died in Britain and its broad, unpretentious, irreverent parading of the embarrassments, belittlements, resentments, indignities, lusts, vulgarity, arrogance and helplessness that beset or dwell within us all, made it the natural heir. Enlarged to laughable proportions, it showed people as they saw themselves—in a never-ending struggle to get their share, or even to keep the bit they had, in the face of life's unremitting opposition and malevolent mockery. Not that any of those involved in the making of the Carry Ons, and probably few of those who queued to see them, had any thoughts about these things in connection with the films.

But the luck which attended the beginning of the Carry Ons adopted a grey, if not black, hue in the solving of scriptwriter Hudis' lack of knowledge of hospitals. As he pondered the awfulness of his first ideas for *Carry On Nurse*, Huddis felt a twinge of pain low in his guts which had nothing to do with the notes he had written. He had developed acute appendicitis and was rushed to the Peace Memorial Hospital, Watford, for an emergency operation. Says Hudis: 'This was free research as well as being entirely fresh to me. In the few days I was there I realised something of what British nursing was about, I got a line on it which gave me the right direction and mood. First, it was aggressively unsentimental and yet, because of the archaic discipline and the pitiful pay, those involved had to have heart and drive and fulfilment as their motives and reward. Second, it was rich in natural, earthy humour, especially in a mens' ward.'

Back home again, Hudis now based the film on his own situation—a trained observer admitted to hospital with appendicitis for ten days. This is the part played in the film by Terence Longden, as a local reporter told by his editor to make notes for a series about hospital life. In Hudis' words, the writing of the first draft of the script was now 'shudderingly quick', taking about a week. Apart from his own newly acquired knowledge and sense of atmosphere there was his wife's contribution as a professional nurse. 'I used anything she was able to tell me,' says Hudis, 'frequently calling downstairs from my office for another "funny" from her.

at one stage, among the financial backers of *Carry On England*, made in 1976.

Rogers was so good-looking as a boy, say friends, that everybody thought he should have been a girl. His mother warned him that his looks would create enemies. 'It would be wrong to name names,' says Rogers, 'but she was right.'

With his brothers, at the age of seven, he went to King's School, Rochester, for what, for him, were the eleven most miserable years of his life. His only friend there was a coloured boy, the son of an African prince. 'What I hated about school', says Rogers, 'was a feeling of being caged, that awful frustration of sitting at my desk knowing that I could not move until I was told, of looking through the window at the trees and the grass and the sky and not being able to go out to them when I wanted to.'

The boy who grew up to spawn such hits as *Carry On Up The Khyber* and *Carry On Jungle Boy*, spent all of his spare time writing highly dramatic plays full of Christlike figures. By the time he was twelve he knew that he wanted to be a writer rather than go into his father's business. But it was another six years before he dared to tell his father, though his mother knew.

The revelation that a member of his family wanted to do something so bizarre as write for a living, baffled his father and worried him. Could you make a living by writing? Was it possible? Writing was a world the father knew nothing about, and like most men he was frightened of the unknown. But once Claude Rogers was convinced that it was not a whim on his son's part, he did not insist that the boy drop such foolish ideas and cleave to the solid, substantial world of property. He let him have a go, first as a reporter for the *Kentish Express* at Ashford, nearly thirty miles away and later, when that failed, made his son a generous offer, though Rogers claims that his father was also doing himself a favour: he paid him the same amount of money to stay at home and write that he would have paid him if he had gone into the business.

'I think he felt,' says Rogers, 'that I would have made such a mess of things in the business, it was worth paying me this money to keep me out of it. I do know that this suggestion was made to my father by a man who worked with him—and he was probably right!'

Not that Rogers' chosen careers went well.

He was hired as a reporter by the *Kentish Express* after writing a review of a local play and sending it to the editor. His first job was to cover an agricultural show at the seaside resort of Margate on the Kent coast.

What happened after the show is almost like a Charles Hawtrey sequence in a Carry On film. Arriving back at Margate station, Rogers pointed at a train and asked a porter: 'Is this going to Ashford?'

'That's right', said the porter.

But he did not tell the shy young man *when* it was going to Ashford. The trip was a thirty-minute one. But Rogers sat in a carriage for three hours, from 6 pm to 9 pm, before the train moved.

When he walked into the office he was greeted by anger and pandemonium—an ugly duo. Even the police had been called to try and trace him. All sorts of solutions had been concocted to explain his mysterious disappearance on a simple agricultural show story. Now that he was back, and in one piece, it was obvious to everybody where he had been. He had been enjoying himself, hadn't he? It was obvious. Living it up on the fairground, revelling in all the frivolous pursuits of the seaside . . . in office hours . . . and almost certainly with a girl! It was a mistake to send young reporters to places like seaside resorts.

Nobody believed Rogers' story—the bit that he told. But the full truth was that he had been too shy to approach the porter again to make further inquiries. So he had sat there . . . hour . . . after hour . . . after hour. Meanwhile, trains to Ashford had been leaving other platforms on regular thirty-minute trips.

A reporter as painfully shy and sensitive as this obviously could not last. He was hopeless at interviews. He would not collect the names of mourners at funerals, refusing to intrude on their grief and, most damning of all, his lodgings were at a public house—the Kent Arms. This was the blackest stroke against him because the news editor of the *Kentish Express* was a stern teetotaller. It looked as if Rogers just could not win.

'Why do you stay at a public house?' the news editor kept asking him, his tone heavy with the inference that not only did he consider Rogers useless, but an alcoholic, and that, just as he had thought, drink was at the root of his problem, just as it was at the root of every problem.

The facts were the simplest. Rogers stayed at the Kent Arms because it was owned by a friend of his father, and he was looked after better there than he would have been anywhere else.

The end came when Rogers was sent to interview a farmer whose wife had just died. The farmer met him at the door with a shotgun. He would not let Rogers in. He would not answer questions. Furthermore, he wanted Rogers off his land— fast. Rogers did not argue. He agreed with the man. He hated this sort of inter- view, this sort of intrusion into the most personal, emotional aspects of peoples' lives. When he arrived back at the office without a story he was fired.

He went home to Rochester happy, with a deep feeling of relief and release. Though only thirty miles from home, he had longed to return, and had done so on every day off and at every available opportunity. It was the antidote to those fearful requests to crawl round the pews of strange churches, asking people their names and what relation they were to the deceased.

Now his father made the gesture of paying Rogers to stay at home and try his hand as a playwright. 'What you've got to remember,' says Rogers, 'is that in those days parents placed their children in professions and apprenticeships. It was looked on as part of their responsibility. It wasn't like today when children are left to their own devices and drift onto the dole.'

He wrote many plays and sent them off eagerly to agents and theatres. They all came back as the doubters had said they would. He received some encouragement, however, and astutely showed only the encouraging letters to his father.

When he was twenty-one he silenced the doubters briefly by having two plays performed in London. One was a drama about unconsummated marriage ('of which, naturally, I knew precisely nothing', says Rogers) called *Human Straws*. It was put on at the Players Theatre and W. A. Darlington, renowned critic of *The*

Daily Telegraph, wrote that Rogers would be better employed pushing a punt up river, rather than writing plays of this standard. After a run of seven days the curtain came down for ever on *Human Straws*.

The other play was the public's first sample of comedy from the man who was later to set the world laughing. It was called *Mr Mercury* and was the story of an Australian's inheritance of the possessions and position of a snobbish family in England. Like a Carry On film it was full of puns and gags and made a point of puncturing the selfimportant and licking the toffee-nosed into shape. 'I have always liked writing about snobs', says Rogers. 'I hate 'em.' The critic of the London *Evening Standard* wrote: 'We have a new comedy writer in our midst.' Few wanted to know. The play, which was staged at the Arts Theatre, closed after ten days. Says Rogers, with a quick smile which signals his habit of making a quip to hide a more complicated truth: 'As the comedy ran longest I decided that was what I ought to concentrate on!'

But the Carry Ons were nearly a quarter of a century away and, apart from one offer, what followed his London début was six years of failure and depression. The offer was from the Warner Brothers film company inviting him to go to Hollywood as a dialogue writer. Most struggling playwrights in their early twenties would have whooped with delight and caught the next boat. Rogers turned it down. From what he knew of brash, bustling, high-living Hollywood, it was not for him. Besides which, he had been homesick living less than thirty miles away from Rochester, so what would he be like living 5,500 miles away? Today, a successful movie millionaire, he has still not been to Hollywood. He has never been to the United States, and has no desire to go. 'I don't talk the language over there,' he says, 'and neither do my dogs.'

One of the few places he will go is Cyprus; the South of France is another. But he is never eager, and needs persuading. This reluctance is illustrated by the following incident. His wife, producer Betty Box, talked him into going on holiday to Cyprus for Christmas 1975. On the day before he was due to go he was sitting in warm luxury in the back of his Rolls-Royce, being driven by his chauffeur along London's Bond Street. It was cold and raining and all around the car were shoppers, wet, pushing and irritable. Rogers looked at them and said to himself: 'Oh, you lucky, lucky people. You don't have to go to Cyprus tomorrow.'

Rolls-Royces and Cyprus and the agony of being talked into holidays abroad were a long way off for Rogers in the 1930s.

He continued writing plays, encouraged by the brief staging of *Human Straws* and *Mr Mercury*. But he never sold another one. Indeed, there was one dark, deflating day when seven of his plays were returned in the same post and an agent wrote asking him never, never, never to submit anything again . . . please!

In the succeeding, richer years Rogers has met and done business with the agent who sent him that letter. 'I don't think he remembers anything about it', says Rogers. 'Why should he? It was a long time ago. I certainly would not dream of mentioning it.' He pauses, then adds: 'I've bought the rights of other people's work from him.' He gives a brief chuckle: 'And I've rewritten them!'

By the time he was twenty-seven, with no further success to show for his efforts, most of Rogers' relatives and their friends were convinced that he was wasting his time, and that his hopes of becoming a successful, professional writer were doomed to perpetual failure. 'The chorus of "We told you so" grew', says Rogers. 'Those years were a complete trough of depression. But I was determined to go on. What else could I do, anyway?'

Fate decided otherwise, and the time of the first daffodil was nigh.

In the spring of 1941, came even more trouble. His health failed. He became dangerously ill with meningitis, a disease of the brain and spine. Even today, meningitis is rated as 'very serious' by doctors. Forty years ago it was an odds-on killer.

The onset of the illness was gradual, and for a time he was treated at home. But his condition worsened and he was admitted to hospital at Sittingbourne. On the same day he received his call-up papers for the Army. Rogers defuses his closeness to death with the crack: 'You can't have better timing than that—to go into hospital on the day you're called up!' But he knows that, at the time, despite expert treatment, his chances of dying in hospital at Sittingbourne were higher than if he had gone to war.

He admits that as he lay in hospital, drifting into periods of unconsciousness, he thought his life was over.

Then one day when Mrs Morgan, his mother's daily help, came to visit him, she brought a daffodil in a pot. After she had gone, it stood on the table beside his bed—tall, firm, bright. Every day it was there, unchanging, challenging the unnatural surroundings of the hospital, not needing a garden in which to thrive, but living and growing in a little pot away from the sky and the breezes and the sun and all the things that, ideally, it wanted and needed to survive. But it *was* surviving, defiantly surviving, and not only surviving but blooming.

Gradually a resolution formed in Rogers' mind: If that daffodil can grow here, where everything is wrong for it, then I too can hang on to life, I can get over this illness. Every morning when he woke he looked first for the daffodil to see if it was still blooming, and the fact that it always was strengthened his own defiance.

Meanwhile, all around him in the ward, patients with a similar illness to his own were dying.

But the daffodil lived on and, gaining strength from it, so did Rogers. 'I believe quite firmly that it was the daffodil and the resolve it put in my mind that got me through that illness', says Rogers. 'I thought: if it can live, so can I.'

In the end, he was the only patient in the ward who did not die. In the end, only he and the daffodil were left.

Look who's playing a toilet role! Producer Peter Rogers and director Gerald Thomas sat in on some off-screen lavatory humour while *Carry On At Your Convenience*, twenty-second film of the series, was in the pipeline. Some would call it sheer loo-nacy. But, then, some said that the first Carry On was a pipe dream, and one or two meant these sort of pipes! But Rogers and Thomas refused to be bogged down by such sentiments. They closseted themselves, linked their talents, pulled together and produced a great wind of change in British comedy. Now they are recognised as film men of the first water, and many are willing to pay more than a penny to be privy to the secret that has set the whole world laughing like a drain.

Rogers grins. 'Little did I believe at the time that one day I would stick it up somebody's backside', he says.

After recovering from meningitis, Rogers found that he was unable to concentrate on three-act stage plays, so he turned to writing shorter plays for radio with which he had quicker success. Some of the plays he had broadcast were: *The Man Who Bounced*, *Mr South Starts A War* and *Cards On The Table*. He later did a documentary feature series called *War Report*.

In 1942 he was hired by J. Arthur Rank to work on religious films. The boy who had filled his plays with Christlike figures now earned his living '. . . gagging up Jesus Christ, giving it all a lighter touch.' (In later years he bought the company, called GHW, where he had been, in effect, Christ's publicity agent.)

A spell with the film division of the Ministry of Information followed before he returned to Rank where, most notably, he created the original story and co-scripted *Holiday Camp*.

When Rank drastically reduced its production programmes, Rogers was one of those out of work, and he went back to journalism, as a feature writer with *Picture Post*. As with the *Kentish Express* it was not a successful venture and he was fired (by Ted Castle, journalist husband of Barbara Castle). 'We just didn't seem to hit it off', is Rogers' comment on this cul-de-sac of his life. He then joined the journalist's trade magazine, *World's Press News*, but, within a few months, was back in films as scenario editor of Gainsborough Pictures, working as an associate producer as well as a writer and being involved with a dozen films, including *Here Come The Huggetts* and *Dear Murderer*.

At this time he met and married (in 1949) Betty E. Box, his boss's sister, his boss being the studio head Sidney Box.

When Gainsborough closed down, he and Betty, having already worked together as writer and producer (one of their early films was prophetically called *Marry Me*) set up an independent production company, making a number of successful films, with Rank backing, like *Appointment With Venus* and *Clouded Yellow*.

However, in this partnership, Rogers was the prince consort to his wife's queen. Though he went on to produce several films of his own, Rogers was forty-three when he set out to make the unpretentious one-off comedy, eventually to be called *Carry On Sergeant*, which led to the series. This not only shot him permanently into his own illuminated galaxy, but rocketed his backing company, Anglo Amalgamated and its partners, Nat Cohen and Stuart Levy, into a land of wealth, power and influence. They made twelve Carry Ons together, but when Levy, who became a close friend to Rogers, died, Rogers took his series to Rank.

In 1978, after making sixteen Carry Ons with Rank, Rogers plans to put future films in the series into production with another company. He is also set in 1978 to launch a film called *That's Carry On*, a compendium of some of the funniest scenes from the series, in co-operation with Rank and EMI. He is leaving Rank after that, he says, because he does not feel they push the Carry Ons strongly enough.

The Carry Ons went into television in 1972 with an annual show called *Carry On*

Christmas. In 1974 and 1975 there was a television series called *Carry On Laughing*, made by ATV, but with which Rogers was not entirely happy. 'It was not what we set out to do', he says. 'There were too many producers and other people involved and though I had the power of veto I felt it could only make matters worse to use it. But I have no future plans for a TV series of this sort.'

The Carry Ons became a stage show in 1973, called *Carry On London*, at the Victoria Palace. In the summer of 1976 another stage show was put on at the Royal Opera House, Scarborough, in Yorkshire, called *Carry On Laughing*.

Anything else for the future? 'I'd like to bring the Carry On films to a total of thirty. I wouldn't mind buying a pier, and I'm trying to write a book about gardening', says Rogers. 'But I can tell you what future Carry Ons will not be about. They will not be about the Royal Air Force and it will not be about the fire service. There's a lot of comedy in those subjects, but I consider them too dangerous. Actors, and others, can get hurt. If I made a Royal Air Force picture there'd be no flying in it!' I suspect that the next Carry On will be closer to a bed than to an air field. Rogers already has a script called *Carry On Again Nurse*, and Australian writer Lance Peters has turned in what could be the Carry Ons first X-Certificate *Carry On Emanuelle* for possible production by Hendale.

Kenneth Williams is an oboe.
Sid James is a trombone.
Hattie Jacques is a euphonium.
Charles Hawtrey is a piccolo.
Joan Sims is a cello.
Barbara Windsor is an alto-sex . . . sorry, I'll start again . . . an alto-saxophone.

That is how you have mostly *heard* some of the stars of the Carry On series in twenty-one films from *Carry On Cabby* to *Carry On Behind*.

They are the instruments that Eric Rogers, who has composed the music and directed the orchestra for those films, often uses to depict the personalities of the characters as they appear on the screen.

But he would object to my use of the word *heard*. For Eric Rogers (no relation to producer Peter Rogers) is adamant that the only music you should hear in a film is the title tune. After that, if you are aware of the music, then it is bad film music, according to Rogers. You should absorb it without noticing the intrusion of a single note.

Eric Rogers is the man who translated all the music of the hit show *Oliver* from the thoughts and the la-la-la-ing of Lionel Bart to the page. 'The originality of the ideas was Bart's, says Eric. 'But, because he could not write music, I was the means of communication.' He grins: 'So it is truthful to say that I *wrote* every note of *Oliver*.'

After the show was a stage hit, Eric became associate music supervisor to Johnny Green on the film version and, with Green, won an Oscar.

From 1954, for three years, he was music director at the London Palladium and composed the signature tune for the television series *Sunday Night At The London Palladium*.

Eric Rogers. He has written the music for twenty-one consecutive Carry Ons, from *Carry On Cabby* **to** *Carry On Behind*. **Though he turned down** *Carry On England*, **he will be back for future films in the series.**

He takes two weeks to write the score for a Carry On film. 'But that's concentrated work', he says. 'I don't go out during that time.'

Before he begins his two-weeks musical exile, he and producer Peter Rogers have long chats. 'Peter knows a lot about music,' says Eric, 'and makes some very good suggestions.'

They have their private jokes in most of the films. In *Carry On Up The Khyber*, for example, for a scene in which Sid James is writing a comic letter, they had a version of the letter music from Tchaikovsky's opera *Eugene Onegin*. 'Nobody else will notice, but *we'll* know,' Peter Rogers had said.

For *Carry On At Your Convenience*, Eric did a jazz version of 'Three Old Ladies Locked In A Lavatory'.

The music for *Carry On Behind* was based on a Scott Joplin style, using the initials of producer Peter Rogers' wife, Betty Evelyn Box.

Carry On Henry was enlivened by a jazz version of 'Greensleeves'. Says Eric: 'I also did a lot of research for *Henry*. The music in it is the genuine style for the period.'

But Eric Rogers takes special pride in the principal theme for *Carry On Up The Khyber*, about a Scottish regiment's need to prove that its troops wore nothing under their kilts.

'The basic tune for that just had to be "Cock 'o' the North,"' he says.

Eric is given full charge of the music budget for each film, taking from it his fee as composer and conductor, and hiring players for the orchestra.

'The reason I did not do the music for *Carry On England* (made in 1976) was because, on the budget that Peter was able to give me for that film, I could only have hired twenty musicians instead of the forty that I prefer', says Eric. 'So I declined. But I'm back next time.'

Even before Eric Rogers became the Carry Ons' music man, Charles Hawtrey was a flute noise, Hattie Jacques had that euphonium-tuba sound and Kenneth Williams was a reed warbler, but expressed with a clarinet rather than an oboe.

For that is how Bruce Montgomery, who was commissioned to do the music for the first six Carry Ons, also saw them . . . or rather, heard them. Sid James, however, he did not depict in brass, as does Eric Rogers, but as a bassoon tune.

Montgomery, also well known as a crime novelist under the pen name Edmund Crispin, whose tenth book came out in 1977, was hired for the first Carry On, *Carry On Sergeant*, after doing the music for an earlier Peter Rogers–Gerald Thomas film, *Circus Friends*. Before that, he had worked for Betty Box.

'There was a lot of marching music in *Circus Friends*, so I suppose they thought I would be all right for an Army film', says Montgomery. 'I used the band of the Coldstream Guards all the way through *Carry On Sergeant* and they were very good.'

Why did he leave the series?

'Peter Rogers was rather annoyed because I let him down on *Carry On Cruising*', he says. 'I had the flu and I was also getting a bit stale so far as the Carry On music was concerned. Douglas Gamley had to be brought in to finish it.

'Eric Rogers makes a better job of it all than I did. He has the flair. I think I was rather too intense. I tried to make it all too musically significant.

'Eric, in fact, helped me out with the title music for *Carry On Constable* and *Carry On Regardless*, because they wanted them jazzed, and that was not quite my style.'

Question: 'Are the Carry On films out of touch with reality?'

Answer, by Kenneth Connor: 'A chap earns £20,000 a year and people say: "The bastard".

Another chap wins £75,000 on the football pools and people say: "Good on ya, mate!"

Now there's comedy.

Anybody who works and earns money is a bastard.

Anybody who wins it by putting crosses on a bit of paper is a good bloke.

And people have the cheek to say that the Carry Ons are out of touch with reality.

Look around. Read the newspapers. The whole world's out of touch with reality. It's all far barmier than the Carry Ons.'

'What is my comedy secret? Please don't ask me. I see talented people trying very hard to be funny and some of 'em, poor devils, falling flat on their faces. I play it straight—and everybody laughs.' (Sid James).

Part Two

The Fun (and a few tears)

You can treat actors like rubbish and pay them well and they'll slog away cheerfully.
You can treat them marvellously and pay them peanuts and they'll still slog away.
But to treat them like rubbish *and* pay them peanuts is really expecting too much.

(Kenneth Williams, on working for the Carry On films—of which he has made twenty-four!)

The ordeal that worries most actors and actresses appearing in a Carry On film for the first time is that most of the stars are likely to be Carry On veterans—veterans who know the routine, know the pitch of the comedy, know the producer, the director, the camera crew. But, most of all, veterans who know each other, with the bonuses of personal chemistry, acting rapport and knowledge of foibles, likes, dislikes, and varying ability in varying situations that this brings.

Some of those who are now well known members of the Carry On team felt this way when they first appeared. A new arrival can turn up at Pinewood Studios, at 8 am, for the opening day's work, fearful of the clannishness, isolation and other terrors, like the mockery of Kenneth Williams, or that slogging work schedule which wraps up a Carry On film in five or six weeks.

Though invariably exaggerated in an actor's mind, the fears have a factual basis. The pace can be killing to somebody who cannot learn lines quickly; who expects to create a characterisation as the film begins and goes along, rather than arriving with one already defined. Many scenes are shot without a rehearsal. As for Kenneth Williams—he *can* be acidly witty. He loves to shock. He loves a verbal battle. He loves people who can counter his comments with some just as sharp. Fail to do that and you could be in trouble. He can trounce those who do not come up to his own standards in any given aspect of their craft or personality. The boastful or egotistical he makes ready fodder. One aspect of his personality is that of a demonic schoolboy. For mischievous reasons (never bitterly serious or Machiavellian ones) he likes to add a touch of spice to life and give it a little stir.

Jim Dale tells a story of how, on *Carry On . . . Follow That Camel*, Williams went to him and said: 'Just a friendly piece of advice. Peter Butterworth hates your guts. I'd watch him if I were you. He's out to steal every scene you have together.' As Dale and Butterworth practically did a double act in the film, playing a young man of high breeding and his manservant doing penance in the French Foreign Legion, Dale was concerned about what Williams had said. He thanked him for the tip, and for most of the film was wary of Butterworth, watching him closely, analysing his every move. It was not until near the end of the shooting schedule that Dale learned Williams had gone to Butterworth at the start of filming and said: 'Just a friendly piece of advice. Jim Dale hates your guts. I'd watch him if I were you. He's out to steal every scene you have together.' This done, Williams had merrily sat back to enjoy their antics.

Shortly after Dale found out about the prank, the butt of his rifle crashed onto one of Williams' feet while they were doing a scene together. Williams screamed loudly. 'You've broken it! You've broken my foot!' he yelled.

'Of course it was nothing like as bad as he claimed,' says Dale, 'and I reckon he thought I'd done it deliberately for the joke he'd played on me. But I hadn't. One simply accepts that these sort of pranks are one side of Kenny's personality. Really, he's a helluva nice fella.'

It was largely because of Williams, says Dale, that he got into the Carry On series. He was playing the member of an orchestra in the Peter Rogers' film *Raising The Wind*. Williams played the conductor. At one point he had to blow a raspberry at Williams on his brass instrument, and was asked to stand up.

'Where's your music?' said Williams.

Before he said his lines, Dale thought—what can I do to be noticed? He decided to do an impersonation of Williams.

'I haven't got it', he said in a burlesque of Williams' voice. Then: 'I was sitting on it all the time.'

Williams' eyes dilated. Then outrage filled his face. He turned to director Gerald Thomas and spoke vehemently with emotional gesticulations.

'Blimey,' thought Dale, 'I've had it now. I'm out.'

But what Williams said to Thomas was not: 'Get rid of him. He's taking the mickey out of me', but: 'Use him, use him! He's marvellous!'

There are those who say that Williams' attacks are really a form of defence. A man attacking before he is attacked. There seems little doubt that they are a way of finding out the personalities of strangers, a quick test of whether he is going to like them or not, based very much on their response.

There is no doubt at all that he likes an audience. Any women's club or other group of people being shown round the studios, and Williams' face adopts a little smile as he goes across to them. 'Aye, aye, we'll watch this', say other members of the cast. 'This could be good.' The entertainment is provided by watching the expressions of the visiting ladies under their big hats. The first response they show is usually one of shock—a response Williams loves. But soon the group is beaming cosily. If they were dogs or cats or horses they would be eating out of his hand.

Though he has been known to visit a sick member of the film crew without mentioning the fact to anyone, Williams has also been known to refuse to open a door for a tea-trolley girl on the grounds that, 'I don't ask her to say my words.'

A complicated man, with many sides, including a learned one, his knowledge of a multitude of subjects constantly surprises his colleagues.

In the main, the most barbed words of Kenneth Williams are only directed at newcomers if he feels they do not come up to his ideas of professionalism, but he can also still outrage seasoned members of the Carry On team, like Joan Sims. They had a cold war which went on for several days after Williams made what Joan considered to be a 'disgusting' suggestion about what she could do with asparagus tips. But, as we shall see, Joan Sims is quite capable of taking care of herself and played one of the most successful getting-your-own-back gags on Williams in the history of the series.

His own most notorious mocking spree involved the American comedy actor Phil Silvers (television's Sergeant Bilko) who starred with Williams in *Carry On . . . Follow That Camel*. This is how it began.

Williams, like all the Carry On team, arrives on set each day knowing his lines, but he can be more uncompromising than most in his professional attitude towards others. He makes no allowances to newcomers to the series. He knows his lines and expects everybody else in the film to know their lines. Speed and efficiency, in any case, are vital aspects of the work if a film is to be 'in the can' within five or six weeks. His opinion of Phil Silvers was, therefore, immediately coloured when Silvers became the only actor in a Carry On film to use cue cards—his lines written on them in large letters and held off-camera for him to read while acting.

Williams was shocked, angry and alarmed.

'You haven't done the scenes as Gerald wanted', continued Joan. 'They haven't time to re-shoot. So they're putting somebody else's voice over them . . .'

Before she had finished speaking, Williams was stalking across to director Gerald Thomas.

'I think it's utterly disgraceful what you're doing to me', he screamed at Thomas. 'My voice is one of my most individual and important characteristics. To put somebody else's all over my scenes is . . . well . . . well . . .', Williams was speechless.

Gerald Thomas grinned. 'Don't be a fool', he said. 'I suggest the answer lies in what is going on behind you.'

Williams turned. Joan Sims was convulsed. An all-heaving, screeching portrait of hysterical laughter. Kenneth Williams had been had.

Despite his professionalism where the words and acting are concerned, Williams is not as technically knowledgeable about filming as, say, Charles Hawtrey—but, then, few actors on a Carry On set are.

When called for a scene, Williams does not always know where his cue light is (each star has a light on set to which he must go when a scene comes up) and his lively, ribald mischievousness makes him the one most likely to 'muck about' and send up a scene.

In a sequence with an actress he will suddenly end a speech to her with the impromptu words: 'You filthy old whore', and director Gerald Thomas will call 'Cut'.

When speaking feed lines off-camera to help the reactions of an actor or actress doing a scene on-camera, Williams invariably pulls funny faces to throw them, make them laugh.

But it is not the sort of larking about that Sid James, for one, would tolerate. 'Cut that out', he would tell Williams when he came off the set. 'I'm trying to do a scene.'

To Sid, acting, even in a Carry On, was not something that you tried to enjoy. It was something that you did, and went home.

He hated appearing 'in drag'. While playing Sir Rodney (the Black Fingernail) Ffing, a take-off of the Scarlet Pimpernel, in *Carry On . . . Don't Lose Your Head*, about the French Revolution, Sid had to dress as a giggling girl, being interviewed by Williams as Citizen Camembert, chief of the secret police.

When Sid appeared in wig and dress, Williams purred: 'Ooh, I couldn't half fancy you!' And other actors and the camera crew joined in with wolf whistles and invitations.

'Shut up, the lot of you!' snapped Sid, embarrassed. 'Let's get this scene shot and out of the way', and he stomped onto the set, skirts arustling.

Jack Douglas joined the Carry On team in 1971, and was launched in champagne. His agent was keen to get him in the series, but the first part available, that of an expectant father in *Carry On Matron*, was so small that Peter Rogers did not think it suitable.

Douglas' agent persisted and, in the end, it was agreed that he would play the part not for money, but for three bottles of champagne.

Shortly afterwards a black Rolls-Royce pulled up outside Douglas' home and the chauffeur carried in his fee—with a bonus. There were not three bottles of champagne, but twelve.

Since then Douglas has appeared in five more Carry On films, nineteen Carry On programmes for television and two Carry On stage shows—at the Victoria Palace, London, and in Scarborough.

But, though an experienced performer, adept at ad libs, Douglas had apprehensions when he turned up for his first appearance on the lot at Pinewood Studios.

'I needn't have worried', he says. 'The entire team were marvellous. Everything they said was designed to help and always has been, telling me how they thought a scene could best be played.

'In a later film, *Carry On Girls*, Sid James pulled me to one side and said: "Let me give you a tip. Stick close to me in this next scene, otherwise it's a one-shot, with just my mug in it. They won't see you."

'I know lots of actors who wouldn't have said that', says Douglas. 'They would have kept their mouths shut and hogged the camera and the scene to themselves.'

Jim Dale appeared in several films with Sid James, but they worked particularly closely in *Carry On Cowboy*, *Carry On . . . Don't Lose Your Head* and *Carry On Again Doctor*.

'On the day Sid died in 1976,' says Dale, 'somebody from the television programme *Nationwide* rang me up and asked if I would go on the programme and talk about him. I refused. They rang up other people from the Carry On films, and they refused too. The programme had a hard job finding anybody who would go on television and talk about Sid James that night.

'The reason was not that he wasn't liked. It was the reverse. It was too soon to ask us. I simply could not have gone on TV that night and talked about Sid in the past tense. I didn't want to believe it.

'Sid was respected and he was liked. He was a gentle man . . . and I mean that as two words. There was nobody, in my experience, he would not treat as an equal. I never heard him be vicious about anybody.'

A group of Very Important People were visiting the Carry On set one day. They had been treated to a luxurious lunch and had possibly drunk a little too much. One of the most important men in the group took a fancy to one of the gorgeous girls who was in the film. He went across to her and began saying things which, perhaps, without the benefit of the lunch he would not have said. One or two people, apart from the girl, were becoming embarrassed. But the man *was* very important . . .

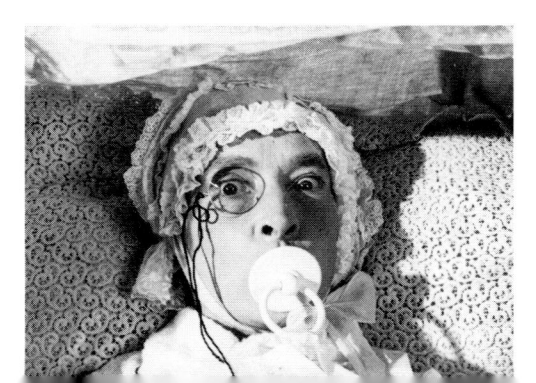

Carry On . . . Follow That Camel Hi there, sucker! It's a boy, and the image of his . . . father's Commandant! When Bo West (Jim Dale) leaves the French Foreign Legion and marries Lady Jane Ponsonby (Angela Douglas), who has pursued him to his barracks in North Africa, their first child looks like this . . . Commandant Burger (Kenneth Williams), Bo's former commanding officer. So that's what the CO meant by a dummy run!

Then somebody said to the important man: 'Here, that's enough of that. Just cut it out.' The somebody was Sid James, demonstrating one of his most resolute traits—he would never stand by and see a woman treated badly.

'He was generous and helpful to most people,' says Hattie Jacques, 'but especially to women.'

'He had feelings of protection, chivalry almost, about women which some may find old-fashioned these days, I suppose,' says Joan Sims. 'But I know I appreciated them, and I think most women still do.'

'Women were crazy about Sid', says Jack Douglas. 'He used to pooh-pooh it all, but Sid was a sex symbol.'

But, as an actor involved in comedy, Sid James was haunted by a constant fear. It was a dread embodied in people like Kenneth Williams, Kenneth Connor and Jack Douglas. It was a dread based on the one aspect of comedy in which Sid was a beginner—the ad lib, the spontaneous, off-the-cuff remark made in the middle of a carefully rehearsed script.

It was because of his inability to cope with an ad lib that Sid made efforts to keep Douglas out of the stage show *Carry On London* at the Victoria Palace.

Sid wanted actors around him who would stick to the script. One unrehearsed gag, thrown in off the top of the head by another actor, and Sid was lost. His expression would become one of utter bewilderment.

In a stage show, whatever the conditions, whether the theatre was a quarter full or packed to the doors, Sid gave the same performance. It never got better and it never got worse. Even an Irish bomb scare at the Victoria Palace, which affected some members of the cast, made not the slightest difference to Sid's performance.

After a few weeks he called Douglas into his dressing room at the Victoria Palace, and over a drink, confessed: 'I didn't want you in this show, Jack. I tried to get you out for the one reason that you ad lib. I don't. I'm an actor.

'I'm telling you this now because I want to thank you. During all the time we've been doing this show you've never once ad libbed while I was on the stage. I'm grateful.'

'Of course I haven't ad libbed when you were on the stage,' said Douglas, 'for the very reason that you mention. You would be at a disadvantage, and I don't think this business is about that sort of thing.'

A few weeks later, carried away by the response of the audience, Douglas found himself, on reflex, playing up to them and ad libbing. The realisation came when he saw Sid's glassy stare and he quickly returned to the script.

Kenneth Connor, a superb raconteur, has also forgotten himself while on stage with Sid and, encouraged by the audience, has gone off at a comedy tangent—until he has seen Sid's blank face.

Like Peter Rogers, Sid loathed being reminded of any act of sentiment or kindness for which he was responsible. He hated any outward sign of emotion, although he helped several people secretly. Without telling him, Sid put Kenneth Williams up for a part in a film (a non-Carry On film). Williams only found out much later through a third person.

One of the favourite stories about Kenneth Williams among the Carry On team occurred in *Carry On Up The Khyber*, set on India's North-West Frontier in 1895.

Williams played a rajah, the Khasi of Kalabar, who is passionately pursued by the governor's wife, Lady Joan Ruff-Diamond, played by Joan Sims.

Declaring her feelings, Lady Joan panted in one scene: 'Ever since I first saw you I haven't been able to get you out of my mind. I lay awake at night thinking of your strong arms around me, your . . . (pant, pant) . . . hot lips on mine and our . . . (pant, pant) . . . our bodies entwined in Oriental passion . . .'

At which point, by way of reply, Williams broke wind.

'It's disgusting', said Joan Sims. 'How can you play a love scene with people farting all over the place?'

'Oh shut up!' said Williams. 'Valentino used to sound off all the time in love scenes.'

'Maybe so,' said director Gerald Thomas, 'but they were silent films, Kenneth. This one of yours is much worse than that. It's on the sound track!'

Because of Williams' habit of 'mucking about', everybody was highly suspicious during a coach trip to a film location when he tried to persuade the driver to stop at a public house on the way. Their suspicion was increased by the fact that they were all made up and costumed for their parts in the film.

Sid James, in any case, was against the idea, because he was involved in a game of pontoon, playing for money—and he was winning. But Williams persisted in his pleas.

'It's a trick to make us miss the location', somebody said.

'Don't be daft', said Williams. 'I'm making a generous gesture. Pull in at a pub—and I'll buy you all drinks. What can possibly be conning about that? You've all heard me. You're all witnesses.'

So the coach pulled in at a public house. Williams led the way inside and announced to a startled barmaid: 'Here to patronise your humble hostelry I bring a distinguished gathering.'

Williams then took everybody's order, passed them the drinks and asked, grandly, how much was the bill?

'Seven pounds', came the reply.

Williams put his hand in his inside pocket—and realised that, because he was in costume, he had no money with him.

In consternation he had to turn to Sid (who was typically and conscientiously having nothing more than a small sherry because he was working) and ask to borrow the money.

'You conniving swine', said Sid. 'I knew it was a con. I didn't even want to come in here in the first place!' But he forked out some of his pontoon winnings and paid for the lot.

And nobody ever believed that Kenneth Williams had not been playing one of his little games, even though he swears: 'This was on the level. I really did want to buy everybody a drink, for no other reason than that I like them all.'

When Barbara Windsor arrived at Pinewood Studios in the spring of 1964 to appear in her first Carry On film, *Carry On Spying*, she was terrified.

Bernard Cribbins was starring in the film along with Kenneth Williams, Charles Hawtrey, Eric Barker, Dilys Laye and Jim Dale. All had appeared in previous Carry On films. Williams and Hawtrey had been in all eight.

Barbara knew Bernard Cribbins and told him of her terror. 'All these people know each other', she said. 'What are they like?'

'Don't worry. They're all right', said Cribbins, then paused and added: 'Kenny Williams might wind you up.'

From that moment Barbara was keen to find a weakness in Williams, a vulnerable aspect of his personality and ability. But she did not have time. Their first clash came very quickly.

Williams was playing British secret agent Desmond Simkins. Barbara was trainee agent Daphne Honeybutt. In a scene in which Williams wears a false moustache and beard, Barbara, in her nervousness, got her lines wrong.

Putting on his most superior accent, Williams cried out: 'Darling, do please *try* to get it right!'

Carry On Doctor **Laughing fit to bust! Barbara Windsor in side-splitting pose as Nurse Sandra May. While she is lying sunnyside up on a roof at the nurses' home, Dr Kilmore (Jim Dale) tries to rescue her, because he thinks she is going to commit suicide. She may be covered in sun tan oil, but she's not that browned off . . . is she?**

Barbara's nervous tension snapped. Pointing a trembling finger at Williams' falsely-whiskered face she yelled: 'Don't you shout at me with somebody's minge hair round your face! 'Cause I won't bloody stand for it!'

A short silence followed, during which Barbara, and everybody else, waited for Williams' acid or explosive retort. Instead, he clapped his hands and with a broad grin said: 'Ooooh, isn't she marvellous!'

At the end of the day's shooting he went up to Barbara and said: 'I like you.' They have been friends ever since. Indeed, how deep can friendship get? Williams even went with Barbara and her husband on their honeymoon to Madeira.

Barbara had married businessman Ronald Knight on the day that the film went into production. She was not needed on the set that day, but was told to be on standby and not to leave home in case the shooting schedule changed.

'How can you get married and not leave your home?' enquired husband-to-be Ronald.

'I don't know', said Barbara, and worried about it until the last moment, when she took the telephone receiver off the hook, dashed away to the registrar's office, returned home as Mrs Ronnie Knight, and rang Pinewood Studios to say that people had been ringing her all morning and had they tried to get her while her telephone was engaged. They said they hadn't, but how conscientious of her it was to ring up and enquire.

When Barbara told Kenneth Williams she was going on honeymoon when the film was over, he said: 'I need a holiday. I'll come with you.'

'You've gotta be joking', said Barbara. 'This is my honeymoon.'

'I know, I heard you the first time', said Williams. 'How long have you known this bloke?'

'Two years', said Barbara.

'Well, you're not gonna tell me you haven't had it off in all that time,' said Williams. 'I shall work on the basis that you've already had the honeymoon. Which means that everything's settled—right?'

When Barbara and her husband arrived at the airport to catch the 'plane to Madeira, Williams was waiting for them. With him was his mother and his sister.

'Have you come to see him off, then?' said Barbara.

'See me off? Good gracious no', said Williams. 'They're coming.'

Barbara spent most of her honeymoon with Williams' sister, while he and her husband went off on jaunts together.

Contrary to the all-boobs-and-bottom image that she gives in the Carry On films, Barbara is basically shy and sensitive and does not like baring more than is absolutely necessary of her 38–22–35 torso.

Nor is she a diligent reader of the non-dialogue parts of a script—the sections that describe the setting and action. It came as a surprise to her, therefore, in *Carry On Camping*, that in one scene she had to lose her bra.

Her first reaction, when the day arrived to make this scene, was to screech and declare that she would not do it. Her second reaction was to demand a closed set with only the director, the necessary actors and the minimum camera crew present.

This request was found to be ludicrous on the grounds that the scene was not being made in a studio, but in a field. 'Then close the field!' demanded Barbara.

Accordingly, everybody not necessary to the scene was shooed as far away as possible. The scene showed Barbara and other girls from the Chayste Place Finishing School for Young Ladies being given some keep fit exercises by their headmaster (played by Kenneth Williams) while on a camping holiday.

Though set at the height of a sunny summer, the film was being made during a wet autumn, so the girls wore bikinis and wellington boots because, as they did their exercises, they were sinking in thick mud. Before the scene started, and throughout the making of the film, the autumn leaves, the grass and the mud were sprayed a succulent, summer green.

During an arm stretching exercise Dr Soaper (Williams) calls to the girls: 'Now really make those old chests come out. And fling. And in. And fling. And in. And fling . . .'

At this point Barbara's bra was supposed to snap, fly off and hit Williams in the face. It was easy to make it snap. What they could not do was make it fly. It just kept dropping down.

Then somebody had the idea of hooking a fishing line to the front of the bra and swinging it up in the air and across to Williams' waiting face, like bringing in a wriggling 7lb catch.

In an attempt to spare Barbara any further embarrassment, the oldest prop man they could find was given the task of reeling in the bra. 'I suppose they thought he wouldn't get as much out of it as a young bloke', laughed Barbara. 'But it worked. I did find it less embarrassing than having some leering youngster ripping my bra off!'

What did not work, at first, was the fishing line idea. When the old man pulled the line the bra remained stubbornly in place, and he pulled with such force that Barbara fell into the mud and was dragged through it head first.

After she was given a sponge down everybody tried again, and this time the bra snapped, flew through the air on the end of the line and wrapped itself round Williams' face. As she felt it go, Barbara slapped her hands over her breasts, congratulating herself that nobody had seen naked the most famous boobs in the Carry On series.

But all in vain. A second later Hattie Jacques, playing the school matron, came up, grabbed one of Barbara's arms and dragged her off, in the process exposing, for all to see, the bouncing double feature of her vital statistics.

In a later film, *Carry On Henry*, Barbara went to a lot of trouble to make sure that only the most necessary people were present for her bare boobs scene. Then, when it was all over, she discovered there was a technician above her, in the flies, whom everybody had forgotten and who had most certainly got a boggling bird's eye view.

A friend, working in an adjoining studio on Ken Russell's controversial film *The Devils* said: 'What? You had a closed set for half a bum and half a tit! You want to see what's going on next door for everybody to see.'

It was while working on *Carry On Henry* that Barbara got a telephone call saying that Ken Russell would like to see her in his office at Pinewood Studios

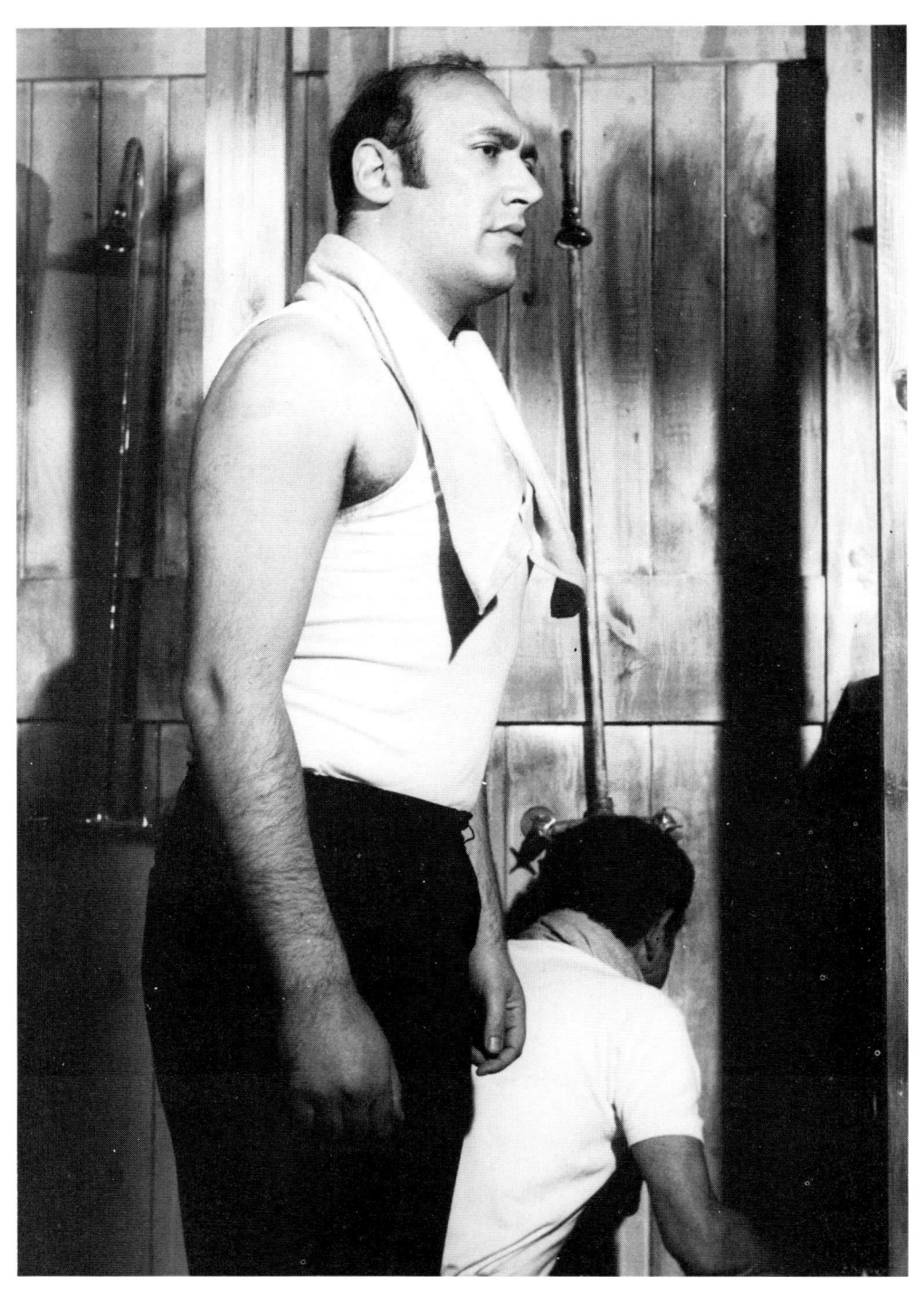

Carry On Camping **What low down trick is this? Sid Boggle (Sidney James), true to his surname, peeks through a knothole into the girls' shower-room, while on a camping holiday. Meanwhile, his mate, Bernie Lugg (Bernard Bresslaw), stands silently disapproving. Not a peep out of him! Though he does keep a lookout while Sid takes a look in. Sid's attitude is: the camp is called Paradise, and it's about time I had a glimpse of it!**

after the day's shooting. Barbara looked around, could not see Kenneth Williams, but deciding, anyway, that it was obviously a Williams' joke, said: 'Yes, sure, I'll be there', and instantly brushed it from her mind.

Next day, Ken Russell went up to her at Pinewood and said: 'I waited for you last night, but you didn't come to see me. I want you for a part in my next film, *The Boyfriend*.' Barbara was speechless at the thought that she had almost missed the opportunity.

Despite a repetitious need for Barbara to bare something or other in a Carry On film, she has never got used to the idea—even if everybody else has.

In the 1974 Carry On film, *Carry On Dick*, she was all set to clear the studio for her baring bit when she saw, to her annoyance, that nobody had turned up to watch, except the people who were in the scene with her.

'What's going on?' she said. 'Doesn't anybody want to look?'

'We've seen those boring things before', somebody said.

'Well at least come in and pretend to look interested', said Barbara. 'At least give me the satisfaction of having people thrown out!'

Though she moans on the set at the spartan conditions under which she has to work ('there's no pampering and "will you wait in your dressing room" and that kind of thing. Your part of a ruddy great conveyor belt') Barbara enjoys the Carry Ons.

'The first thing you think about when you sign to do one of these films is—I'm going to see all my mates', she says. 'It's a great get-together. Nobody throws tantrums and, providing you know your lines and are on set ten minutes before your scene, you have nothing to worry about.

'I think it's disgusting that the Carry Ons haven't had some sort of official acknowledgement, when you consider all the money they're bringing into this country.'

Barbara's most famous moaning session occurred on *Carry On Camping* after days of floundering in green-painted mud.

'I can't go on', she told director Gerald Thomas. 'Look at my feet, they're disappearing in the bloody stuff!'

'If you were being employed for your feet you wouldn't be in the film', cracked Thomas. Barbara grinned and went on to do a scene.

But as the scene ended and Thomas shouted 'Cut', Barbara turned to Kenneth Williams and said: 'We're treated like a load of sheep. I'm not kidding, you couldn't pay me to do another Carry On film. Look at me—mud all over the place, bitten by midges, and does anybody care? Not on your life! They've all buzzed off for lunch and just left me here. I tell you, we're treated just like a load of rubbish.'

Next day, after watching the rushes (un-edited scenes) of the previous day's filming, Peter Rogers said to Barbara: 'Would you stay behind for a minute.' He then ran a little scene between Barbara and Williams over which had been dubbed Barbara's harsh words about the mud and the midges and the spartan Carry On life.

Unbeknown to Barbara, while she had been giving vent to these outspoken views, Williams' throat microphone had not been turned off, so it had all been recorded.

When Barbara turned up a few months later for another film, *Carry On Again Doctor*, Rogers said to her: 'I thought you weren't going to be treated like rubbish again?'

Director Thomas gagged: 'Here to be treated rotten again?'

Though frightened of horses, Barbara rode one in *Carry On Dick*, and though she cannot drive she rode a motor-bike along Brighton promenade in *Carry On Girls*. 'The point is I don't like letting Gerry down and I also don't like other people knowing that I can't do something', says Barbara. 'I would rather hurt myself than admit that something is beyond me. When I rode the motor-bike I said to Gerry: "I don't want to rehearse it. Just go for a take." I knew that if I started trying to rehearse it I would have time to think and get even more petrified. So I just got on the bike and that was it.'

If only it had been that simple for Bernard Bresslaw when his turn came to ride a motor-cycle in *Carry On At Your Convenience*.

When asked by Peter Rogers if he could ride a motor-bike, Bernard said 'yes' on the basis that he could ride a bicycle, and a motor-bike was just a bicycle with an engine—or so he tried to convince himself.

But his niggling misgivings turned to admitted defeat when he went into the studio on the morning before the afternoon he had to ride it, and saw the huge, glistening monster covered, to his eyes, with a baffling assortment of gears, dials and knobs. 'Ride it, I can't even get on it,' he confessed to himself.

But that confession was the easiest one. The hardest was the one he felt he now had to make to Peter Rogers. He put it off all morning. At lunchtime, however, he went into the bar, bought Rogers a large drink and blurted out: 'Er . . . about this motor-bike . . . I can't ride it . . . I thought I could . . . but . . . I can't ride it . . .'

According to Bresslaw, Rogers' change of expression rivalled anything seen in his films. To call it incredulous is like calling World War II a difference of opinion.

'For a second I thought he was going to belt me,' said Bernard with a laugh. 'Then he began thinking what could be done.

'The production manager's son was an expert motor-cyclist. So I was rushed off to him to get a few quick lessons during the lunch break. It helped, but it wasn't a long enough time. When shooting began again I could ride the bike, but only in a straight line. I couldn't turn corners.'

That was no good to director Gerald Thomas, so Thomas' first assistant, who was about the same burly build as Bernard, rode the motor-cycle in long-shots.

There was one scene, however, which Bernard had to do himself. But no problem was envisaged because, while the scene involved the motor-cycle, Bernard did not actually have to ride it. He just had to sit on and, as the camera turned, jolt backwards with his body pretending to have drawn up and applied the brakes, get off the machine, prop it up on its stand, knock on a front door, and deliver a pair of trousers.

The street set was at Pinewood and the trousers belonged to a character being played by Kenneth Cope who had lost them in hectic and hilarious circumstances.

Nothing could be easier, thought Bernard.

'Take one', said the clapper boy. Bernard jolted his body, got off the motor-bike, but could not get it to pull up onto its stand.

'Take two', said the clapper boy. Bernard jolted his body, got off the motor-bike, pulled it up onto its stand, collected the trousers from over the tank, turned to walk to the front door . . . and the motor-bike began to fall over. He ran back and caught it.

'Take three', said the clapper boy. Bernard jolted his body, got off the motor-cycle, pulled it onto its stand, collected the trousers and . . . as he walked towards the front door the trousers caught on a protruding part of the machine and pulled it over.

'Take four', said the clapper-boy. Bernard jolted his body, got off the motor-cycle, pulled it onto its stand, walked to the front door, knocked and . . . realised he had left the trousers on the motor-cycle.

Take five . . . six . . . seven . . . eight . . . nine . . . ten . . . came and went in uproarious, side-splitting succession as Bernard tried to deliver the trousers and each time something different went wrong, not always his fault. One take, at least, was ruined because the cameraman was laughing so much the camera was shaking.

As he became more anxious to do the scene right, however, Bernard became more tense . . . and other things began to go wrong. Take eleven . . . twelve . . . thirteen . . . fourteen . . . fifteen only added to his embarrassment.

By now everybody on the set was helpless with laughter, everybody except Bernard. 'I can't understand it', he kept saying. 'It's such a simple scene.'

'Take sixteen', said the clapper-boy, grinning. By now nobody expected it to go right, and they were stuffing handkerchiefs in their mouths to stifle the guffaws. They were not disappointed. Bernard jolted his body as if coming to a halt . . . and slowly the machine began to fall over with him helpless to stop it.

Sixteen takes for one scene, without, even then, getting it right, is a rarity on a Carry On film (almost something to tell your grandchildren about) where, with speed and efficiency at a premium, to capture a scene in one take is commonplace.

'I think we'll abandon the rest of this Carry On,' announced director Gerald Thomas with a grin, 'and make a film exclusively out of these takes!' He then revised the scenes, shooting it in three short takes instead of one long sequence. But the real laugh is that, after all this, most of the scene ended up on the cutting room floor and is not in the film.

Thomas, when the production schedule allows, is not averse to playing jokes on the cast, like waiting until Jim Dale and Peter Butterworth were buried up to their necks in sand for a scene in *Carry On . . Follow That Camel*, before calling a tea break, and leading everybody else off the set, leaving the two actors (but only temporarily) helpless, exasperated and gasping.

Sometimes such jokes are unintended. Bernard Bresslaw is convinced that Thomas played one such gag on him in *Carry On Cowboy*, Bresslaw's first Carry On, but Thomas says it was purely coincidental.

Bresslaw is scared of heights. For a man who is 6ft 7in tall, it sounds like a joke. In *Carry On Cowboy*, he was playing a Red Indian, Little Heap (son of Big

Heap, played by Charles Hawtrey). For one scene he had to climb 50ft up a tree, in woods behind Pinewood Studios, lean out from a branch and shoot at Sid James and Percy Herbert, playing a couple of baddie gunslingers.

Besides heights, Bresslaw is frightened of guns. So, to climb 50ft and fire a Winchester rifle was his idea of hell. But he told nobody of his phobias, though the expression on his face as he went up the tree on a rope ladder, told director Thomas a lot.

'There's a technique to climbing a rope ladder,' says Bresslaw, 'and I didn't know it. But I kept going, with the ladder twisting and bucking and turning under me. And I kept looking up. I knew that if I looked down, just once, I was lost, I would just stiffen and not be able to move.

'At the place up the tree where I was supposed to go, they'd built a little platform. The most terrifying bit was getting from the rope ladder to this platform, and when I'd managed it I just flopped out, face down, panting away and feeling absolutely exhausted, not with the physical effort of climbing but with terror. I suppose I lay there for about two minutes and all the time I was thinking of the next, most forbidding, thing I had to do—stand up, lean out with a rifle and, the thing I least wanted to do, *look down* and fire at Sid and Percy who were approaching me on horseback.

'"Well, it has to be done", I thought. So I gingerly got to me feet and was just feeling very proud of myself when Gerry shouted: "All break!"

'I thought, No! Now I've got to do it all again! Make a terrifying climb back down to the ground, get my tea and bun and make another terrifying climb back up here.

'I was convinced Gerry was playing a joke on me. But I didn't mind. I thought—if people play jokes on you it means that they accept you as one of themselves.'

In fact, Bernard did not have to make that frightening descent on the rope ladder to get his tea and bun. He was told to stay up on the platform and they sent his snack to him on a winch. When the time came to play the scene, he had got used to his eyrie, the adrenalin had started flowing and he was able to lean well out from the tree, pumping away at Sid and Percy with a Winchester.

Director Thomas says he was not playing one of his gags with Bresslaw. He just had not realised it was time for a break and felt a bit concerned about it all, especially when he saw, from Bernard's expression, the effect that heights had on him.

Bresslaw is frequently cast as a fierce chief of one sort or another. When playing the scimitar-wielding leader, Bungdit Din, in *Carry On Up The Khyber*, his make-up was so complicated that he had to be at the studios by 6.30 am in order to be ready for filming by 8 am.

In *Carry On . . . Follow That Camel* his convincing robes and make-up, as Sheikh Abdul Abulbul, had a car park attendant almost bowing and scraping.

Much of the film was made at Camber Sands and a car park had been set aside by the local council for the exclusive use of Carry On personnel. Bresslaw was made up as the sheikh at a local hotel where he had stayed overnight and drove to the film's location in the back of a long, black limousine provided for this purpose.

They're barking up the wrong tree if they think I'm climbing this! You don't expect a tall bloke like Bernard Bresslaw to be scared of heights. But he is. So when, as a Red Indian called Little Heap, he had to go up a wobbly rope ladder to the top of this tree, for a scene in *Carry On Cowboy*, he became the only paleface in the tribe! Here he is giving a trunk call for help. But Bresslaw believes in branching out, and faced up to this tree-mendous challenge. When he made it, he felt heap big brave. (We don't know which one!)

When the car arrived at the appropriate car park, however, the attendant stiffened, was over-deferential and went to a lot of trouble to make sure that Bernard really was part of the film.

'I felt I was being treated like royalty', said Bernard. 'The expression on the man's face really was something to see. Then I remembered that the newspapers were full of news and pictures about a royal visit from Saudi Arabia!'

Bresslaw knows nothing of the leg-pulling on this film involving Phil Silvers. One of the delights of making a Carry On film for Bresslaw, Sid James, Terry Scott and others, is that there is always a good poker school going between scenes. Phil Silvers became a regular member of the Carry On poker school and Bresslaw got to know him well, being particularly fascinated by Silvers' stories about Hollywood, New York, Las Vegas. A sample story was:

Silvers had a flat above the club in which Dean Martin and Jerry Lewis gave their final concert before splitting up as a double act. All their friends and admirers turned up. The place was full of stars and the entertainment went on until the early hours of the morning.

Unable to sleep because of the noise, Silvers put a dressing gown over his

The laughtermakers—and they even make each other laugh! Just because the cameras stop rolling does not mean the wisecracks also stop. Here, onscreen warmongers continue as offscreen laughtermongers during a break in *Carry On . . . Follow That Camel* at Camber Sands, Sussex. Kenneth Williams (who plays Commandant Burger of the French Foreign Legion) has obviously heard a gag full of Eastern promise from Bernard Bresslaw (who plays Sheik Abdul Abulbul), though Bernard no longer remembers what he said! Third member of the tittersome trio is Peter Butterworth (Simpson, a gentleman's gentleman turned legionnaire). The Laughing Cavalier . . . huh!

pyjamas, went down to the club, walked onto the stage and said to Martin, Lewis and the entire audience: 'Haven't you got any homes to go to?' The audience cheered and applauded and Silvers ended up as part of the act, swapping jokes with Martin and Lewis.

Bresslaw also admired the way in which Silvers, when faced by a British slang phrase he did not understand, never took the easy way out offered to him by changing it to something which he did understand. 'Tell me about it. Tell me what it means', he would say. 'Then let's go ahead and play it according to the script. It's just that I can't play something I don't understand.'

At the time he made *Carry On . . . Follow That Camel* in the spring of 1967 Silvers was unwell and had domestic problems. Because his eyes were bothering him he wore contact lenses and spectacles at the same time, but still occasionally had difficulty reading the cue boards. In addition any fears that a British actor had about joining the Carry On team with their 'in' jokes and lively camaraderie were more than doubled in his case. He was in a country that was not his own, among actors who were strangers (except for Peter Butterworth who worked with Silvers in the film *A Funny Thing Happened On The Way To The Forum*) and playing comedy which presented unfamiliarities of language, accent and style.

For many reasons, therefore, it is not surprising that Silvers went to his hotel room after a day's shooting and kept himself to himself rather than joining the team for a drink, though this attitude got him tagged as unsociable.

11 May, however, was Silvers' fifty-fifth birthday. Filming was then taking place at Camber Sands in Sussex and Silvers was staying at a different hotel from most of the team. A party, including Jim Dale and Peter Butterworth, decided to invite him to have a birthday drink and went round to see him. Because he had always refused to join them, they expected another refusal on this occasion. Silvers, however, did join them briefly, then went off complaining of a headache.

As a gag, Jim Dale and Peter Butterworth got a blank hotel bill and filled it in with a list of drinks, costing a horrendous amount of money. 'Many thanks for the drinks. Happy birthday,' Dale wrote at the bottom of the bill. They then asked for it to be presented to Silvers at breakfast next morning.

Says Dale: 'He never mentioned the incident, but we heard that he had gone white and hurried off to the hotel manager when he got the bill.'

So why was he in the film? Silvers was hired because Rank, the new distributors of the series, wanted an American in the cast to try and boost sales in the United States. Though not approached, comedy actor Woody Allen was also considered for the role. It was a move opposed by Peter Rogers who was against any sort of dilution of the series' British style of comedy. He also did not think the plan would appreciably help sales in America, and in this he was right.

There is little doubt that, apart from Kenneth Williams' guying of Silvers about cue cards, there were some who resented the importing of an American in the top billing role of the woman-mad, double-dealing Sergeant Nocker of the French Foreign Legion.

The admirers among the cast, like Bresslaw, that Silvers collected, he got because of his supreme gift for the witty ad lib and for his gags and stories about Hollywood. 'I could have listened to him all day', says Bresslaw. 'It didn't even worry me if he repeated a story.'

German beauty Elke Sommer, who starred in *Carry On Behind* as a Russian archaeologist, is the only guest star that the Carry On team has taken to en masse. And it happened in less than a week.

When she arrived on the set for the first day's shooting, Elke was frightened. She had worked in several British films, including three for Peter Rogers' wife, but she had never starred in a film with such an established team.

For four days she was out in the cold, treated politely, but in a businesslike way. Then Kenneth Williams, who was playing an English archaeologist, brought her into the fold. 'She was marvellous', he said. 'No edge, knew her business. I liked her.'

When you have to be funny, sometimes energetically funny, at eight o'clock in the morning, it is unwise to go on a binge the night before. But there have been occasions when stars have been 'overtired' on set.

Joan Sims had a scene in *Carry On Regardless* in which she had to attend a wine tasting, drink too much and end up causing shattering, slapstick chaos. It was a good scene, it worked well and Joan's impersonation of a drunken woman attempting to remain ladylike, poised and coherent was hilariously realistic. 'Like hell!' says Joan. 'I'll tell you what happened. This scene was the first being shot that morning. So I went on and started sampling drinks as it said in the script. Of course they weren't real drinks, just water, cold tea, that sort of thing. Then I tried one that really burnt my throat. I took a good swig—and it was neat gin. I thought—you bastards. You're at it again. Playing practical jokes. But I kept on with the scene, though the drink began to take a bit of effect. I mean—neat gin at eight-thirty in the morning! When the scene was finished I went across to Gerry (director Gerald Thomas) and the rest, who had started to laugh now. I said: "You really are a load of so-and-sos." Gerry said: "I thought it worked a treat. Your reaction when you drank that gin was exactly the one I wanted." And they say women are devious!'

But what happened to Charles Hawtrey in *Carry On Spying* was not the result of a jape. While being one of the longest-serving members of the Carry On team, Hawtrey is basically a loner. He can be hard to get to know and is suspicious of interviews. Though outwardly he can appear defenceless and vague, he is inwardly tough. However, he brings out the mothering instinct in women and Joan Sims and Hattie Jacques keep a caring eye on him, maintaining contact even when no

Carry On Regardless **Stop the room, I want to get on! The glassy-eyed gal at the wine-tasting (getting bottled in Britain) is Lily Duveen (sweet, heady, full-bodied), who works for a helping hands agency. But in real life, Joan Sims, playing Lily, also got a touch of that hic, hic hurray feeling—thanks to the film's director, Gerald Thomas, who turned the wine tasting into a ginkhana! For, as a joke and to add a spirit of authenticity, Thomas put undiluted gin in Joan's glass, instead of the usual, innocuous, non-alcoholic stuff. Verdict: neat acting. Vintage performance.**

Carry On is in production. Barbara Windsor has cleaned up for him when he has been ill during afternoon filming. As a rule, Hawtrey does not eat with most of the team in the Pinewood restaurant but goes off to the canteen. Despite being bone thin, he is a voracious tucker-away of food and drink and, apart from what he buys at the studios, arrives on set on most days with a carrier bag containing sandwiches, bottles of lemonade and Woodbines. One day, while trudging along the road from the bus stop to the studios, a chauffeur-driven Rolls-Royce pulled up beside him and a voice from the back of the Rolls said: 'Hello Charles. What are you doing lumbering that carrier bag along here? Don't they give you transport?' It was Laurence Olivier who was also filming at Pinewood, and as long as he was there he used to meet Hawtrey off the bus and drive him up the road to the studios.

As a film performer, Hawtrey is one of the most astute in the team, his comedy experience going back to Will Hay and filming in the 1930s. Jim Dale claims to have added to his own experience by watching Hawtrey, citing as an example a small part that Hawtrey had in *Carry On Screaming*, where he played a men's lavatory attendant. 'He entered carrying a pile of towels', says Dale. 'Most people would have held them against their chest, with their face visible. Hawtrey held them high, obliterating his face, then brought them down as he got up to the camera. The result was funny and eye-catching whereas for the majority of actors it would just have been an entrance.'

However, there have been occasions during afternoon filming when Hawtrey has not been at his best. The most notorious occasion occurred during *Carry On Spying*.

Kenneth Williams, playing a British secret agent, with Bernard Cribbins, Barbara Windsor and Charles Hawtrey as trainee agents, are trapped in the underground headquarters of the evil Dr Crow, leader of a subversive organisation called STENCH (Society for Total Extinction of Non-Conforming Humans). In their bid to escape, they end up on a conveyor belt in a devilish processing plant, struggling to avoid pounding machinery, crushing rollers, spinning cutters and steaming vats of acid.

At one point they are picked up by hooks and swung forward, looking like carcasses in an abattoir, to be dipped in the acid vats. It became apparent to director Gerald Thomas, Barbara Windsor and others, however, that this terrifying ordeal held no horrors for Hawtrey. He looked more of a dead weight than any of them. Hawtrey had passed out.

A first aid man was called, who looked down at the prostrate Hawtrey and said: 'Have you tried giving him brandy?' And everybody laughed.

In *Carry On Nurse*, Kenneth Connor played one of the patients—Bernie Bishop, a boxer with a broken wrist.

Awakening at his Middlesex home at 5.30 am Connor's day could go like this: get up, take off pyjamas, have a bath, put on outdoor clothes, drive to Pinewood Studios, undress, put on different pyjamas, put on make-up, and be back in bed, this time on the set, by 8 am.

If he did not have a scene to play, he would begin to doze, and at the same time a buzzing sound would be picked up by the sound mixer. Production would then stop while the third assistant walked down the ward, tapped Connor on the

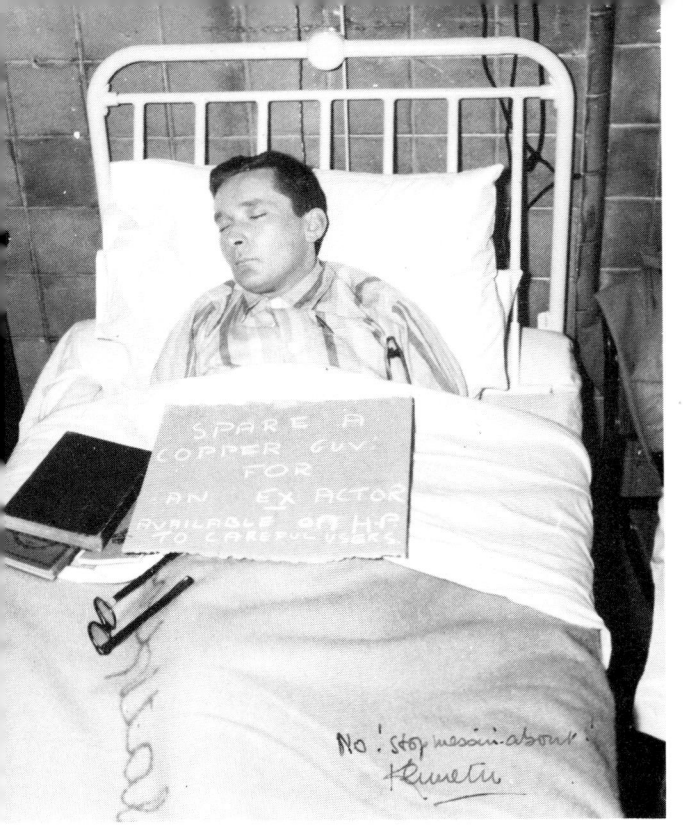

Caught napping! This nodding acquaintance is Kenneth Williams during the making of *Carry On Nurse*, when the early morning start, the heat of the studio lights and the fact that they were in bed, had many of the actor-patients snatching forty winks . . . and not only at the 'nurses'! Because Williams denied that he ever slept on set, director Gerald Thomas had photographs taken, of which this is a sample. The notice, part of the gag, reads: 'Spare a copper Guv for an *ex*-actor. Available on HP to careful users.' Williams has written on the bottom of the photograph: 'No! Stop messing about! Kenneth.'

shoulder and said 'Could you stop snoring please, Mr Connor, it's being picked up by sound?'

Come lunchtime it was out of bed, out of pyjamas, into outdoor clothes, lunch, back to the set, into pyjamas, into bed.

If he was not needed for any scenes the lunch inevitably began to take effect— and he dozed off, to awaken once more to the tap of the third assistant, this time saying: 'We've decided to put a mock-up wig on your bed Mr Connor as your snoring is still getting onto sound. So why don't you go to your dressing room and have a good kip?'

At the end of the day it was out of pyjamas, into outdoor clothes, drive home, have a meal, get back into pyjamas, go to bed—and spend the night frustratingly unable to sleep!

The warmth of the bedclothes and the arc lights had the same effect on Kenneth Williams. 'You fell asleep in that last long-shot', director Thomas would say to him.

'Nonsense, absolute nonsense!' Williams would protest. 'I'm a professional Thespian. I don't do that sort of thing!' It was all said with mock outrage but the next time he dozed off, Thomas had a couple of photographs taken. In one, for good measure, a banana was stuck in Williams' hand, and, in both, a notice was laid against his chest reading (SPARE A COPPER GUV FOR AN EX ACTOR AVAILABLE ON HP TO CAREFUL USERS).

The next time director Thomas accused him of dropping off to sleep and Williams indignantly denied it, Thomas, amid laughter, produced the photographic evidence. 'It's all fake, fake!' cried Williams.

Catching Williams napping in 1958 proved much easier than catching him full in the face with a large cream cake for the final, slapstick scene of *Carry On Loving* in 1970.

In this scene, all the allegedly happy couples, brought together by a marriage bureau run by Sid James and Hattie Jacques, attend a banquet to celebrate Sid's marriage to Hattie. One of Sid's earlier peccadillos catches up with him, however, and anger and pandemonium escalate until everybody is hurling food at each other. In one shot Jacki Piper aims a large cream cake at Joan Sims who ducks, and Williams gets the lot full in the face.

To put this on film in the easiest, or apparently easiest, way, director Thomas broke up the shot. For the final moment when the cake splatters over Williams' face, he planned for somebody, anybody, to throw a cake off-camera directly at Williams.

It looked the simplest of actions. All the thrower had to do was to stand beside the camera and hurl the cake a distance of 6ft at Williams. The only restriction was that whoever threw the cake should not let their hand be seen in the shot, as the cake, on screen, had to appear to come from Jacki Piper.

With a mock-malicious grin, director Thomas decided he was the one who was going to do the throwing. 'Unfair, unfair!' yelled Williams. 'Can't we have somebody who's cross-eyed?'

Thomas took the large, oozy, creamy-looking cake, grinned at Williams, aimed, threw—and missed! 'We *have* got somebody who's cross-eyed!' cried Williams triumphantly. Then he stopped crowing, for director Thomas had another large cream cake in his hand and a more determined look in his eye.

Thomas weighed the cake in his palm, took aim, threw—and missed again!

Williams' banter knew no bounds. 'Williams the conqueror, Williams the unhittable!' he cried. 'Action', called director Thomas, picking up a third cake and whizzing it with great force. But, unbelievably, yet again he missed!

'Of course we could be here all day', said Williams. 'You'll never do it. Nobody can do it.'

Director Thomas turned to actor Julian Holloway: 'You play cricket', he said. 'You have a go.'

'And here we are at the Oval,' said Williams in a mock-commentator's voice, 'and the bowler is taking his run and . . .'

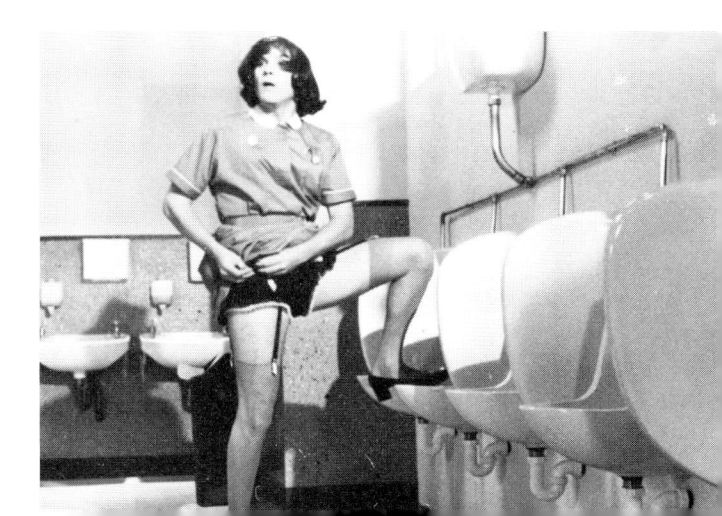

Carry On Matron Flash in the pan! A brief interlude in what is obviously an undercover job. Crook Cyril Carter (Kenneth Cope) is disguised as a nurse to discover the layette . . . er . . . layout of a maternity hospital as part of a plan, conceived by his father, to steal contraceptive pills. But when Cyril is caught short he goes into the 'gents' instead of the 'ladies', risking unfrocking, as it were, especially as he does not yet have the right knack with the knicks. Hence this picture which we call: Watching Brief, or Suspended Animation. Of course, somebody comes in, but they don't discover that Cyril is no lady!

'Action', called director Thomas, and Holloway picked up a cake, threw it—and missed!

Bernard Bresslaw was the next to have a go—and he missed too.

Soon almost the entire cast was lined up to hurl a cake at Kenny, and eventually somebody hit him, without getting their hand onto the film. There was such hilarity and so many people had a go that nobody is absolutely certain who threw the winner, but a general consensus lays the honour at the feet of Lauri Lupino Lane, a variety performer with a lot of experience in hurling custard pies.

'Now I know who hates me', gagged Williams.

When Bernard Bresslaw says that he often seems to fall for the parts in Carry On films which have long, flowing robes, he means it literally. Playing the desert leader, Sheikh Abdul Abulbul, in *Carry On . . . Follow That Camel* he had to lead his army in a charge on a French Foreign Legion fort. 'There's no dialogue in this scene, so we'll try it without a rehearsal', said director Thomas. 'Come at the cameras from behind those sand dunes, yelling and waving swords.'

Simple, thought Bresslaw. 'Action', called Thomas. Bresslaw charged, looking his fiercest, followed by a yelling horde of extras. Then it happened . . . his foot caught in his flowing robe and he was down, with all the extras trampling over him giving him a mouthful of sand. Nobody had shouted 'Cut', so over the dunes went the extras, charging down at the camera, leaving their leader more hurt in dignity than body. 'Cut', said Thomas, 'Where's the fierce Arab leader?'

'Here', came a plaintive voice from the other side of the sand dunes.

In *Carry On Abroad*, Bresslaw was playing Brother Bernard, the cassock-clad member of the religious order of St Cecilia. Trying to prevent curvy Sally Geeson, playing Lily, from tripping over a plank at a continental hotel, he accidentally rips off her skirt. As she screams and runs into the hotel he follows her, anxious to return her skirt.

Again, it was a straightforward scene. 'There's no dialogue, so we'll try it without a rehearsal', said director Thomas. 'Just run after her through the swing doors of the hotel.'

The doors were made of glass. Not the usual, imitation glass used in Carry On films, but real glass.

'Action', called Thomas. Sally Geeson fled into the hotel. Bresslaw followed, waving the skirt until . . . his foot caught in his cassock, and he did a somersault through the glass swing doors, shattering them from top to bottom.

For a moment an apprehensive hush settled on cast and crew. Then, as Thomas was about to call 'Cut' (an unfortunate word in the circumstances) and investigate, fearing like most that Bresslaw could be slashed to ribbons, the actor unrolled, surrounded by broken glass but unharmed, and said blushing: 'I'm awfully sorry about that, Gerry'. Everybody burst into laughter. 'You twit!' said Thomas. 'Why did you have to speak? I was going to use that!' Then, grinning broadly: 'I'll tell you what. You couldn't do it again, could you Bernard?'

In the next film, *Carry On Girls*, almost as if planned, Bresslaw, dressed as a woman, had to trip over his dress. 'Believe it or not,' he said, 'I was worried whether I'd be able to do it convincingly.' He did.

Travel agents in Slough, Buckinghamshire, were worried. A new agency had opened in the town and was offering a four-day, long-weekend holiday abroad for £16. What is more, the trip was to a new, exciting island. Four of the agents, two English, two Indian, formed a deputation and went along to the shop where they delivered a stern warning about price cutting, and how they should all stick together and not try to put each other out of business. The men in the shop, who were putting up holiday posters and displays, listened patiently. 'In any case,' added one of the deputation, 'where is this "Paradise Island of Elsbels", anyway, that you're advertising. In the Med?'

'No, in *Carry On Abroad*', came the reply.

The empty shop had been taken over and turned into a travel agency for sequences in the new film.

In *Carry On Matron* Kenneth Cope had to dress up as a nurse in order to get into a maternity hospital to steal their supply of contraceptive pills. 'It gave me a new insight on what it's like being a woman', he said. 'I found that the click-click of my heels aroused great interest in men. They would turn round to eye me up and down. I had on all the frilly undies, black knickers, black stockings, suspenders, the lot, and I used to flaunt myself something awful. Any strange man whose interest was aroused by my clicking heels (and I used to lay the clicking on a bit, too) I would flash my suspenders and my legs at him. At that stage some of them would get embarrassed, frightened even and start backing off. That's when I would flaunt myself even more.' Cope ended up chasing a coloured man, in order to offer himself. 'He was terrified', said Cope. 'It was a great lark.'

Carry On Constable **What a drag! The 'ladies' in this arresting pose are policemen in disguise—as part of a department store's counter measures to catch shoplifters. They are Special Constable Gorse (Charles Hawtrey) and PC Benson (Kenneth Williams). But as this is a between scenes shot, taken on location at a store in Ealing, London, they decided to display the leg rather than the arm of the law! 'My feet are killing me,' wrote Williams on the picture, which is loaned by director Gerald Thomas.**

Charles Hawtrey and Kenneth Williams, playing policemen, were disguised as women to watch for shoplifters in a large store for sequences in *Carry On Constable*. As part of the film they were mistaken for shoplifters themselves and chased by the assistant manager (played by Robin Ray) out of the store and down the street. When shot in West Ealing, London, the scene was so realistic that a local policeman on his beat, seeing the chase, joined in and was gaining on the runaway Hawtrey and Williams when he heard director Thomas, behind him, shout 'Cut'. Realising what had happened, the policeman stopped running, blushed, looked highly embarrassed—and then had a good laugh at himself.

During the making of the same film, a woman member of the public was walking along with a dog which suddenly started to foul the pavement. At the same time, the woman saw Leslie Phillips and other actors, in police uniform, coming towards her. Thinking they were local bobbies she turned and ran off, dragging the reluctant dog behind her, still fouling the pavement.

Again in *Carry On Constable*, during location work in West Ealing, London, Kenneth Williams, as a policeman, had a sequence in which he took a deaf old lady (played by Esma Cannon) across a busy road, blithely unaware that she did not want to go. Another old lady, this time a member of the public, watched the scene without realising it was part of a film. She then asked Williams, thinking he was a real bobby, if he would take her across the road. 'Of course, darling', said Williams, and filming temporarily stopped while he held up the traffic and escorted the old lady across.

Actors taking part in *Carry On Sergeant* had a lot of fun during location work at Queen's Barracks, Guildford, in Surrey. Those, like Eric Barker, who were playing officers, received salutes all day from troops and officers of a lower rank stationed there. Other actors, like Bob Monkhouse, Kenneth Connor, Bill Owen and Terence Longden, playing rookies or junior NCOs, were sometimes bawled at by officers and sergeants for walking about the barracks with their hands in their pockets or for being improperly dressed. Soon the barrack's officers and NCOs became wary of disciplining the slovenly in case they turned out to be the Carry On mob. It was a glorious time for Army 'scivers'.

They have painted autumn leaves and autumn mud green to look like summer grass in *Carry On Camping*. They have made snow, frozen on the boughs of trees, look like delicate spring blossom in *Carry On Behind*. They have made the stagecoach in *Carry On Cowboy*, in reality going through thick mud and puddles a foot deep on Chobham Common, Surrey, appear to be throwing up the dry dust of a Western trail, by having a man lying on the floor of the stagecoach puffing out clouds of fuller's earth with a pair of bellows. They have been unperturbed by hailstones and a fort covered in thick snow at Camber Sands, Sussex, while filming *Carry On . . . Follow That Camel*, a French Foreign Legion romp set in sweltering Africa. In the same film they have made gallons of Polyfilla look like gallons of gum Arabic, which they have poured into a trench around a fort and covered with sand, fixing a sticky end for attacking tribesmen, led by Bernard Bresslaw. But, when it came to a camel, they decided to have the real thing. A genuine, humped, spitting, biting camel. So they hired Sheena for three days, complete with her Irish keeper, whom they promptly disguised as an Arab. The actors may be pretending, the palm trees may be false, the location may be thousands of miles from where it is supposed to be, and the season may be wrong. But Sheena was the real thing. Of course, like all living creatures, she had her little quirks. Sheena's idiosyncracy was that she would not walk on sand. They had hired a camel that was frightened of sand. The explanation was that Sheena had never seen sand before. She was born at Dublin Zoo and now lived at Chessington Zoo in Surrey. She was used to concrete, not sand. So for most of the first day they had to put boards on the sand for the camel to walk on. After that she got used to it. Almost as if she had been designed for it.

In *Carry On Up The Jungle*, Bernard Bresslaw played a native tracker called Upsidasi, who was guide to an African expedition. Part of his role consisted of taking orders in English from the big white hunter (played by Sid James) and passing them on, in their own language, to native bearers. A conscientious actor, Bresslaw was not happy about making up a lot of gibberish for the film and pretending it was some African tribal language. Especially as the actors chosen to be bearers would, obviously, be genuine Africans. Especially when he had an elder brother, Stanley, who could speak a tribal dialect from Rhodesia called Ndebele.

So Bresslaw went to see his brother, showed him the various phrases he had to pass on from Sid James to the bearers, and got them translated into Ndebele. Painstakingly he learned the Ndebele words and how to speak them correctly. He felt that when he arrived at Pinewood Studios for the first day of shooting, all the African bearers would be impressed. He could hardly wait to use the first phrase. When the time came, he turned to them proudly and said it, expecting looks of amazement, perhaps a few words of praise. Instead they looked at him blankly. None of them understood what he was talking about, because none of them was from Africa. His painstaking work had been in vain. All the actors chosen to play bearers were from the West Indies.

Said Bernard: 'It wasn't completely in vain. Sid James, who came from South Africa, knew it was the genuine article. And I did find one other, years later, in Bournemouth! I went into a shop to buy a pair of shoes. As he served me, the assistant said: "Where did you learn to speak Ndebele?" That made it all seem worthwhile—well almost! And, of course, if the film is ever shown in Rhodesia I'll be a big star over there—the only chap talking the local lingo!'

Don't get the hump with me, young lady! What do you say to an aloof film star camel like Sheena, the one in the title, *Carry On . . . Follow That Camel*? 'I want you for my next picture, "The Hunchback of Notre Dame,"' might help. Whatever the answer, Charles Hawtrey obviously knows how to chew the cud without getting her back up. He's certainly within spitting distance of finding out! Indeed, Hawtrey (as Captain Le Pice of the French Foreign Legion) and Sheena make a great military team. While he provides the polish, she provides the spit. But usually in the eye! And don't think those glasses will save him. There are never any lenses in them.

In the final scenes of *Carry On Up The Khyber*, the British Governor in Northern India (Sid James) and his wife (Joan Sims) entertain guests (including Peter Butterworth as a missionary) and staff to a sumptuous dinner, while an Indian army outside (led by Kenneth Williams and Bernard Bresslaw) blows the building to pieces with artillery. Apart from the set crashing about them and all sorts of debris dropped on them and piled on them, the actors had to contend with the stench of rotting fruit and other food which, under the intense heat of the arc lamps, had begun to go off by the end of the scene. But though, under all this rubbish, the actors could not see director Gerald Thomas, they could hear his encouraging voice telling them how well they were doing, and to keep reacting . . . keep reacting. So they stayed there, acting away, ignoring the discomfort. The show must go on. They then began to notice how quiet it had gone. Peter Butterworth cautiously peered out from under the table. The studio was empty. The camera was not turning. Gerald Thomas and the crew had crept silently off to lunch.

After a scene in *Carry On Constable*, in which Leslie Phillips, Kenneth Williams, Charles Hawtrey and Kenneth Connor showered in freezing water, the cameraman complained that their bare backsides were 'flaring', meaning that they were too shiny to give a sharply focused picture. So the four were marched, naked, to a trestle table to have the matter corrected. One or two of them moaned at the indignity of it, but the make-up man who was called in shamed them all to silence. 'I've been in this job all my life,' he said, 'and this is how I end up. Making up asses.'

'I am the world's biggest physical coward', says Kenneth Williams. 'Any hint of violence, the simplest stunt, the faintest chance of danger, the remotest possibility of a scratch and I say: "Not me, matey! No way!"' So when director Gerald Thomas told Williams that for a scene in *Carry On Spying* he had to put his bare fist through a glass panel, the actor's response was a blank refusal. In the scene, Williams had to back towards a glass-panelled door, and feel for the handle. At that moment, actor Richard Wattis would push the door open from the other side.

At least, that was the idea. But assurances, the wiliest persuasion, even a bit of mickey-taking met with unyielding resolve. It made no difference when director Thomas pointed out that the panel was not made of real glass but a substance, designed for safety, known as 'sugar glass'. Finally Thomas said: 'Look, I wouldn't ask you to do anything dangerous. I wouldn't ask you to do anything I wouldn't do.' With that he crashed his own fist through the pane, stuck his hands casually in his pockets and said: 'There you are, nothing to it.'

Williams was persuaded. 'Very well,' he said, 'but I'm wearing a knuckle-duster and a flesh-coloured glove.' This was agreed. The scene was shot. Williams' hand smashed through the 'sugar glass'. Director Thomas then removed his hands from his pockets. The one he had used in the demonstration, which had convinced Williams there was no danger, was lacerated and covered with blood.

Barbara Windsor and Joan Sims sat in the restaurant at Pinewood waiting for Paul Newman. They had heard he was at the studio. 'I just know he's going to walk through that door, see me . . . and KEPOW! That will be it', said Joan. 'Love at first sight.'

'Yeah, me too', said Barbara. 'And not only that, I just know he's going to be the very next man who comes in here. I have this feeling . . . and my feelings are never wrong. Watch that door. I betcha. The very next man . . .'

They fixed their eyes on the entrance. A moment later a figure appeared. It was a man . . . and he was looking at them. Now he was waving at them. 'Hello darlings', he called. It was Charles Hawtrey.

'Let's get pissed', said Barbara.

'Yeah, let's', said Joan.

If you walk into the Pinewood canteen and see a group of Carry On stars talking to a sausage, the chances are they are doing an impersonation of their director, Gerald Thomas. Let Kenneth Williams explain: 'When you see a love scene in a Carry On film or a bloke getting in a lather over some girl's boobs, the chances are that, in reality on the film set, there is no girl there at all. Once Gerald has got all the shots he wants of the girl, he sends her home. Then he takes her place. So the reaction shots you see on the screen of a bloke getting going, are done opposite Gerald. He sits there and prompts you: "Come on," he says, "you're throbbing with it. She's getting them out! You can't believe your eyes!" And, of course, you respond to this like mad.'

So when you see a group of Carry On stars talking to a sausage and saying: 'I love you. You're beautiful, magnificent, sexy . . .' they're doing an impersonation of director Thomas getting reaction shots. Even Bernard Bresslaw, who has a gargantuan appetite, could not really feel that way about a sausage!

Travelling by coach from ATV's Elstree studios to a location, during the making of the television series *Carry On Laughing*, Joan Sims sat next to Bernard Bresslaw, who was reading *The Times*. As he turned a page, Joan saw a picture of South African cricketer Tony Greig. 'Cor, now that's what I call a good looking man', said Joan.

'It's funny you should say that,' said Bernard, 'but lots of people have mistaken me for Tony Greig.' Joan laughed, as Bernard looks nothing like Tony Greig. 'No, true', said Bernard. 'Look, can't you see the resemblance.' He turned his face this way and that, showing off his profile, putting on various expressions. Joan began to get one of her giggling fits.

'I'm sorry, Bernard', she managed to say. 'But I just don't see it.'

All day during breaks in filming, Bernard would go up to Joan and start posing in front of her, pointing at his face: 'Tony Greig', he would say. 'Surely you see it now. Everybody says I look like Tony Greig.' After a while he adopted a South African accent. 'Now do you see it?' he asked. Joan shook her head. She could not speak. The giggles were growing. 'Wait there', said Bernard. 'You're bound to see the resemblance now.' He walked away from her, then came back at a run and bowled an imaginary cricket ball at her. 'You must have seen the likeness, then', he said. 'I mean, that action. The way I move, the look on my face.' Joan exploded into laughter and shook her head. 'Honestly', said Bernard. 'Hundreds of people come up to me in the street and say: "Could I have your autograph Mr Greig." '

Next day the cast assembled in the rehearsal room at Elstree. 'It's a bit chilly outside', somebody said.

Carry On Dick It's the Fuzz! Technically you need three of anything in a row to make a hat-trick, but this is a good start! Bewigged, bothered and bewildered is Sir Roger Daley (Bernard Bresslaw), chief of the Bow Street Runners. Brimfull of beauty is his lady wife (Margaret Nolan). This is a rehearsal for a scene in which they have just been robbed by Dick Turpin but, luckily, have a splendid pair of titfers between them, with which her ladyship can hide her embarrassment and Sir Roger can hide his pride. Judging by her ladyship's grin, perhaps Big Dick, as he is known in the film, helped himself to more than her jewellery and clothing! Not that Sir Roger can do much about it, except to shake his fist. He can't even shake two fists . . . can he? (PS: I wonder if that's why it is called a titfer?)

Carry On Dick Hello cheeky! Bernard Bresslaw and Margaret Nolan (playing the robbed Sir Roger and Lady Daley) laughingly spot the photographer trying to get to the bottom of what, if anything, they are wearing under their hats. As if they haven't, apparently, laughed off enough already! Just one of many off-screen larks during the making of the Carry Ons. Note director Gerald Thomas—centre, in dark glasses. Well, he is the director!

'Well, it is October. Whadya expect?' somebody else said. At that moment the door opened and Bernard Bresslaw entered, dressed in a cricket outfit. Cap, pads, the lot. He marched straight up to Joan and said: 'Now can I convince you?' Everybody in the room exploded into laughter.

Says Bernard: 'Of course I don't look anything like Tony Greig. It was all a gag. But I didn't half feel a fool walking about in cricket gear in October. I put it on before I left home and drove to Elstree. I must say, I got some funny looks from other motorists, and from people when I got to the studios. My wife helped me to get the gear together. I know we went into the subject very thoroughly. There was one serious discussion about whether the trousers ought to be lengthened or whether they looked funnier a bit short. But it was all done for a laugh. Joan doubled up when she saw me.'

In *Carry On Up The Jungle*, Terry Scott played a Tarzan-like character, dressed only in a short loin-cloth like a pair of tatty underpants. During the shooting of one scene everybody on the set began to laugh. 'I thought "Hello, what's all this about?"' said Terry. 'It can't be the dialogue because Sid James gets all the jokes. Then I looked down. I'd indecently exposed myself.'

For a scene in *Carry On . . . Follow That Camel*, Peter Butterworth was buried up to his neck in sand. 'They dug a hole, put a barrel in, put me in the barrel, then filled in the hole with sand', he said. 'The scene was supposed to take place in the burning desert. But we were at Camber Sands and it was freezing cold. The sand

was wet and icy. I was covered in goose-pimples, but they used glycerine on my forehead and face to give the effect that I was sweating. They also kept giving me swigs of brandy to keep out the cold. It's quite an experience to be nice and merry while up to your neck in sand. At least it means you don't fall over!'

For the same film Phil Silvers wore a medallion, on a chain round his neck, which had the star of David on one side and St Christopher on the other. 'With a medal like this you can go practically anywhere and be greeted as a friend with just a little twist of the wrist', he gagged.

Jim Dale was redecorating a house, getting it really spick and span before moving the bulk of his furniture in. He had a bed there and a few pieces of furniture, and, while working on the house, he could not be bothered to cook, so he lived off snacks. On this particular day he had brought a large pork pie. Kenneth Williams called round to see him. Dale apologised for the state of the place and for not being able to offer Kenneth a meal. 'Oh that's all right', said Williams. 'I understand. Don't worry.'

The next time Dale went on a Carry On set he found that people were feeling sorry for him, asking if his luck had improved. 'What are you talking about?' he asked. He discovered that Williams had told everybody that things were not going too well for poor old Jim. He was living in this house which needed redecorating, had hardly any furniture and nothing to eat in this hard, cruel world but 'a mouldy pork pie'.

This story is about the day that Kenneth Williams suffered the most frightening injury of his life. He and Joan Sims were in a store scene for *Carry On Regardless*. Williams was demonstrating children's toys and Joan was in a negligee and swimsuit to demonstrate 'Cleopatra Bath Bubbles' which 'Make Every Woman Feel Like A Queen'. At one stage Williams was supposed to be rocketed off a see-saw (because Charles Hawtrey had landed heavily on the other end) and plunge into Joan's bubble bath. While standing on a twelve-foot high rostrum waiting to do this (by swinging down on a rope), Williams fell off backwards and injured the most private part of his body. 'Oh my parts, my parts!' he screamed (only using another word for 'parts'). As somebody who, in producer Peter Rogers' words, 'wants a blood transfusion every time he cuts a finger', Williams staggered off to the first aid department. Filming went on, concentrating on sequences for which he was not needed. But when they were finished and Williams had still not returned, director Gerald Thomas became concerned. 'This is ridiculous,' he said. 'He's been gone for ages. He wasn't hurt that badly.' And he went, himself, to the first aid room. There he found Williams lying on a table with his trousers down, while an elderly nurse slapped handfuls of Savlon on the affected area and gently massaged it in. 'Oh lovely, lovely', moaned Williams softly.

'Come on Kenny. That's enough of that', said Thomas. 'There's work to do.'

'Slave driver', said Williams, reluctantly getting off the table and pulling up his trousers.

Terry Scott had some infectious warts on his backside. 'They need to be burnt off', said the doctor.

'Later', said Terry. 'I'm just off to make *Carry On Camping*.'

'They really ought to be seen to', said the doctor. 'They'll get more and more painful.'

'I'll be all right', said Terry. Then he discovered just what an important part his backside played in the film. 'I had scenes in which it was set on fire, butted by a bull, had a thistle stuck up it, was slapped, and had shotgun pellets picked out of it', he said. 'But the most painful bit of all was that I had to ride a tandem. I'm supposed to look miserable for a big part of that film. Believe me, after riding that tandem, it wasn't difficult.'

You can fool some of the people all of the time. After making *Carry On Up The Khyber*, Bernard Bresslaw was in a pantomime at Newcastle upon Tyne. He went into an Indian restaurant, when the show was over, for a late meal, and was instantly recognised by Muhamid the proprietor. 'Ah, Mr Bresslaw', he cooed. 'How I love them Carry Ons . . . especially *Carry On Up The Khyber*. It was so good to see scenes of my home country again. Tell me, did you enjoy my country?' The film was made in North Wales.

Part Three

The Comedy and The Cast

There were so few films around that week
I thought: 'Oh my God, if I'm not careful
I could end up having to review a Carry On'.
Film critic overheard at a magazine screening
of a non-Carry On film (*Network*) at the
Century Theatre, Soho Square, London
on 11 November 1976.

If on screen you see the front of a home and somebody opens a door and there's a field behind it, that's American humour. If, when the door is opened, there's a field with a lavatory in it, that's French humour. If there's a field with a lavatory and somebody sat on it, using it, that's a Carry On film.

(Jim Dale)

One or two of the excerpts under *Carry On Sergeant*, *Carry On Constable*, *Carry On Regardless* and *Carry On Cruising* did not reach the screen having been trimmed during shooting, for time or story reasons, or cut by the Censor. They are included here in full, however, with the Censor's and the maker's permission, as good examples of Carry On humour.

The number of excerpts from each film is not necessarily an indication of that film's quality or success. Some films depended, more than others, on situation and visual comedy. *Carry On Nurse*, the most successful film of the series, is an example.

How They Carried On

Here, in chronological order, is a list of all the Carry On films so far made:

1958 Carry On Sergeant / 99
      Carry On Nurse / 101

1959 Carry On Teacher / 103
      Carry On Constable / 104

1961 Carry On Regardless / 105

1962 Carry On Cruising / 109

1963 Carry On Cabby / 111
      Carry On Jack / 112

1964 Carry On Spying / 114
      Carry On Cleo / 116

1965 Carry On Cowboy / 118

1966 Carry On Screaming / 121
      Carry On . . . Don't Lose Your Head / 122

1967 Carry On . . . Follow That Camel / 125
      Carry On Doctor / 127

1968 Carry On Up The Khyber / 129
      Carry On Camping / 132

1969 Carry On Again Doctor / 134
      Carry On Up The Jungle / 136

1970 Carry On Loving / 139
      Carry On Henry / 140

1971 Carry On At Your Convenience / 143
      Carry On Matron / 145

1972 Carry On Abroad / 147

1973 Carry On Girls / 148

1974 Carry On Dick / 150

1975 Carry On Behind / 153

1976 Carry On England / 155

1978 That's Carry On
      (a film omnibus of favourite scenes) / 159

How The Stars Carried On

Twenty-eight Carry On films have so far been made. Of these, the best known members of the team have appeared in:

Kenneth Williams / **24**
Joan Sims / **23**
Charles Hawtrey / **23**
Sidney James / **19**
Kenneth Connor / **16**
Peter Butterworth / **15**
Hattie Jacques / **14**
Bernard Bresslaw / **14**
Jim Dale / **10**
Barbara Windsor / **9**
Terry Scott / **7**
Jack Douglas / **6**

The cast lists in the following sections are taken from those kindly provided by the makers of the films.

Carry On Sergeant **Well, he did say he was my mother for the next few weeks! Recruit Charlie Sage (Bob Monkhouse) thought his bride Mary, who followed him to the training camp, was asleep in this room. Instead, as he has just found out, it belongs to his squad sergeant (William Hartnell). So this is what they mean by the kiss of death!**

Carry On Sergeant

Carry On stars Kenneth Williams, Kenneth Connor, Charles Hawtrey, Hattie Jacques and Terry Scott made their début in this opening film of the series. Some interesting names in small roles include: Edward Judd as FIFTH STOREMAN, Jack Smethurst, now well-known as a star of the hit television series *Love Thy Neighbour*, as FIRST RECRUIT, James Villiers as EIGHTH RECRUIT and playwright Henry Livings as THIRTEENTH RECRUIT. Of the regulars Connor was the first to make an appearance, playing HORACE, a hypochondriac who, when asked: 'How you doing?' replies 'Dying, thanks'. He shares a railway carriage with newlywed CHARLIE SAGE (played by Bob Monkhouse) who, because of a mix-up, is on his way to do National Service without having had a honeymoon. HORACE has turned up all the heat in the carriage. Unable to stand the stifling atmosphere any longer, CHARLIE opens a window. This was Connor's first speech.

HORACE Oh! Please, please . . . the draught.
CHARLIE But it's stifling in here.
HORACE Please, my eardrums are very thin. Very weak. The least suspicion of a draught and I'm finished . . . catch a cold.
    CHARLIE closes the window.
HORACE Coo! Thanks, mate.
    CHARLIE takes out a cigarette.
HORACE Ah, don't!
CHARLIE Now what?
HORACE Please, do you mind not smoking? It affects me. I got a weak stomach.
CHARLIE Now, look here . . .
HORACE Have a catarrh pastille. (offers CHARLIE an open tin)
CHARLIE I haven't got catarrh.
HORACE You don't know you're living, mate.
CHARLIE You going to hospital?
HORACE Into the army.
CHARLIE The army?
HORACE Yeah.
CHARLIE Huh, so am I. How did you pass the medical—influence?
HORACE Medical, huh! It's a farce, a criminal farce. A1! Me! A-flaming-one! Army doctors, huh! I tell you, mate, two of everything you should have two of, and you're in!

At the Army camp, Monkhouse, Connor, Hawtrey, and Williams share a barrack room with Norman Rossington, playing a failed recruit called HERBERT BROWN:
HERBERT Here's my excused-marching chit. My excused webbing chit. Excused handling of firearms chit. Chit for . . .
HORACE (awed) Blimey . . . you're just a heap of chits.

    CHARLIE SAGE's un-honeymooned wife MARY (played by Shirley Eaton) turns up at the Army camp and a friendly NAAFI girl (played by Dora Bryan) arranges for them to have a night of love in an empty room.

Unfortunately, she gives them the wrong directions, so that the room they independently head for is that of the fierce SERGEANT GRIMSHAWE (played by William Hartnell). MARY arrives first . . .
MARY pushes door to. It does not close completely. The room is very dimly lit. She sees a bed against the far wall. A shape in it, lying on its back. A happy smile suffuses her.
MARY Darling . . .
No response but a most unromantic snore. She smiles. Advances to the bed.
MARY Darling—don't pretend you're asleep—darling . . .
The snore breaks into a mumble which sounds vaguely desiring.
MARY (advancing) Oh darling—don't tease . . .
She's at the bed. The shape stirs. She smiles very tenderly and touches it on the shoulder. It stirs again, mumbles deliciously.
MARY (passionate) Darling . . .
The shape sits up into what light there is. The shape is GRIMSHAWE—wearing a nightgown. A moment of nightmare. Then MARY strangles a scream and rushes off . . . GRIMSHAWE blinks. This *must* be a dream. He looks suspiciously at the door . . . loses interest . . . and collapses back into sleep.

But a moment later . . . CHARLIE goes to door of GRIMSHAWE's room.

Taps on it. No reply. He smiles to himself.

CHARLIE (tenderly) Bashful . . .

He taps again. A creak of bed-springs within, CHARLIE smiles more confidently. Footsteps within. CHARLIE tries to look his most handsome and masterful. The door opens.

CHARLIE Mary!

It's GRIMSHAWE in a nightshirt. A close-shot of CHARLIE—love frozen in his veins. A close-shot of GRIMSHAWE: indescribable reaction.

CHARLIE (gulping) Sorry sergeant! I—was looking for the . . . !

GRIMSHAWE (exploding) Never mind what you were looking for! What the blazes do you mean by calling me Mary ? ! ?

CHARLIE (half-fainting) In this light—you remind me of my mother . . .

Enter Eric Barker as CAPTAIN POTTS, spying JAMES BAILEY (Kenneth Williams).

POTTS You.

BAILEY (pleasantly) Yes ?

POTTS Who are you ?

BAILEY James Bailey, BSc, (Econ).

POTTS What's your number ?

BAILEY I'm not proud of it. It was given to me. But I earned the degree.

POTTS Your rank.

BAILEY That's a matter of opinion.

POTTS (patting his pips) Look at my shoulders, man!

BAILEY You have nothing to complain of. Look at the suit they gave me.

ANDY tries to hide his guitar before a barrack-room inspection. Another rookie, MILES HEYWOOD (Terence Longden) grins.

MILES Why didn't you take up the harmonica, Andy ?

ANDY 'Cos rock's for pluckin'— not for suckin'. . .

He's struck with the natural rhythm of this phrase. Repeats it, on the beat, clapping his hands in time.

ANDY Hey—that could be a song!

I might work that up . . .

MILES Do.

CAPTAIN POTTS grants CHARLIE seven days' leave to have a honeymoon.

POTTS You'll have to work hard.

CHARLIE (delighted, relieved) Oh I will, sir . . . I will . . .

POTTS (completing) . . . when you come back.

CHARLIE Oh, yes sir . . . of course . . .

HORACE is supposed to be shinning up a rope in the gymnasium. He tugs it as if testing it. CORPORAL COPPING (Bill Owen) sees him.

COPPING It's fixed all right. Go on up.

HORACE (gulp) What—all the way up there ?

COPPING Sure. You'll like it. The air's purer.

HORACE (faintly) I've got vertigo.

COPPING This should suit you, then. That's vere to go.

Cast:

Sergeant Grimshawe	William Hartnell	Third Storeman	Alexander Harris
Charlie Sage	Bob Monkhouse	Fourth Storeman	Pat Feeney
Mary	Shirley Eaton	Fifth Storeman	Edward Judd
Captain Potts	Eric Barker	Sixth Storeman	Ronald Clarke
Norah (NAAFI girl)	Dora Bryan	Seventh Storeman	David Williams
Corporal Copping	Bill Owen	Sage Senior	Martin Wyldeck
Horace Strong	Kenneth Connor	Mary's Mum	Helen Goss
Peter Golightly	Charles Hawtrey	Sergeant O'Brien	Terry Scott
James Bailey	Kenneth Williams	Sergeant Matthews	John Mathews
Miles Heywood	Terence Longden	Sergeant Russell	Edward Devereux
Herbert Brown	Norman Rossington	Sheila	Leigh Madison
Captain Clark (medical		First Recruit	Jack Smethurst
officer)	Hattie Jacques	Second Recruit	Brian Jackson
Andy Galloway	Gerald Campion	Third Recruit	Don McCorkindale
Gun Sergeant	Cyril Chamberlain	Fourth Recruit	Leon Eagles
First Specialist	Gordon Tanner	Fifth Recruit	Malcolm Webster
Second Specialist	Frank Forsyth	Sixth Recruit	Patrick Durkin
Third Specialist	Basil Dignam	Seventh Recruit	Bernard Kay
Fourth Specialist	John Gatrell	Eighth Recruit	James Villiers
Fifth Specialist	Arnold Diamond	Ninth Recruit	Hayden Ward
Sixth Specialist	Martin Boddey	Tenth Recruit	Graydon Gould
Medical Corporal	Ian Whittaker	Eleventh Recruit	Jeremy Dempster
Recruit with sprained		Twelfth Recruit	Terry Dickenson
elbow	Bernard Kay	Thirteenth Recruit	Henry Livings
Stores Sergeant	Anthony Sagar	Fourteenth Recruit	Terry Skelton
First Storeman	Alec Bregonzi	Fifteenth Recruit	Michael Hunt
Second Storeman	Graham Stewart		

Produced by	Peter Rogers	Director of Photography	Peter Hennessy
Directed by	Gerald Thomas	Art Director	Alex Vetchinsky
Screenplay by	Norman Hudis from *The Bull Boys* by R. F. Delderfield	Production Manager	Frank Bevis
		Editor	Peter Boita
Additional material by	John Antrobus		
Music composed and conducted by	Bruce Montgomery	Made in the spring of 1958. Shooting began:	
Music played by	the Band of the Coldstream Guards	24 March. Pinewood Studios and Queen's Barracks, Guildford, Surrey.	

Carry On Nurse

Carry On regular Joan Sims made her début here as the clumsy, accident-prone NURSE DAWSON.

Among those playing visiting friends to the bedridden were: Jill Ireland, now the wife of Hollywood superstar Charles Bronson, and a star in her own right in films like *From Noon Till Three;* June Whitfield, now one of Britain's top comedy actresses in TV series like *Happy Ever After* and stage hits such as *A Bedful of Foreigners;* Michael Medwin, now a successful stage and film producer in partnership with Albert Finney.

Carry On Nurse The Bore War! For building worker Percy Hickson (Bill Owen) the most painful part of breaking a leg is a visit from his wife Marge (Irene Handl). That really makes him feel ill! To hear her talk you'd think she was the one suffering. So here is that moment of conjugal agony: when the conversation is more fractured than his injury; when the weight on his mind is heavier than the weights on his leg; when even time weighs heavily, and he hangs on in a blank mental clinch, waiting to be saved by the bell. Get well soon, Percy!

Two gags on the same theme: commotion in men's ward. Nurses tidying everything. Patient TED (Terence Longden) turns to nurse GEORGIE (Susan Stephen).
TED What's going on?
GEORGIE Matron's round.
TED I don't care if she's triangular.
MATRON is played by Hattie Jacques.

And later: SISTER (Joan Hickson) and patient PERCY (Bill Owen).
SISTER It's Matron's round.
PERCY Well, mine's a pint.

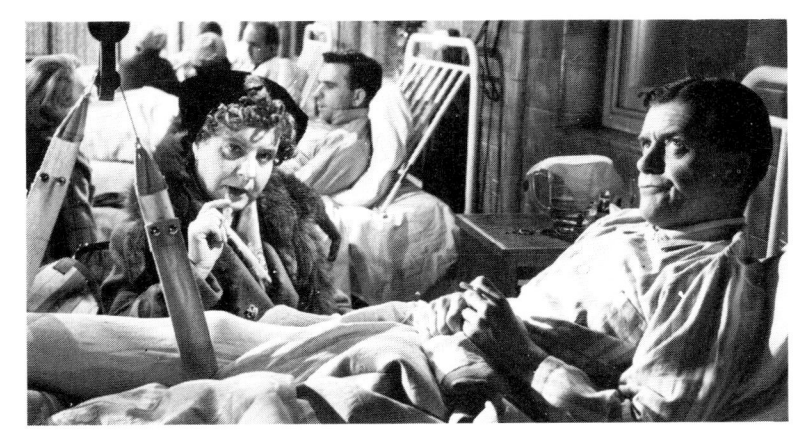

Patient OLIVER (Kenneth Williams) meets patient BERNIE (Kenneth Connor):
OLIVER You've made rather a mess of your hand. Industrial injury?
BERNIE Er, er pardon?
OLIVER Hurt it at work?
BERNIE Oh, yeah, yeah . . . yeah, I'm a boxer.

Saleswoman arrives in ward with trolley.
BERNIE Got any fruit bars.
SALESWOMAN No, but I've got a sliced nut.

BERNIE Come to the right place to have it mended haven't you.

Patient TED (Terence Longden) and Staff Nurse DOROTHY (Shirley Eaton).
TED I want a bath
DOROTHY Suppose you fall with that drain in you? No, Mr York. Back to bed, please.
TED But it's been six days now. I've been picked up twice by radar.

An 'in' joke: a patient called 'the COLONEL' (Wilfred Hyde White) is putting on race bets with nursing orderly MICK (Harry Locke).
COLONEL Half a dollar to win, Rambler . . .
(Rambler was the name of a real horse, running on the day this scene was shot. Punter Wilfrid Hyde White substituted it for the name in the script, which was Bloody Mary. Later that day, Rambler won his race by eight lengths, at 100–8, at Nottingham.)

Cast:

Dorothy Denton	Shirley Eaton	Mrs Rhoda Bray	Hilda Fennemore
Bernie Bishop	Kenneth Connor	Perkins	Martin Boddy
Hinton	Charles Hawtrey	Nightie Nightingale	Rosalind Knight
Matron	Hattie Jacques	Rose Harper	Marita Stanton
Ted York	Terence Longden		(Constantinou)
Percy Hickson	Bill Owen	Miss Winn	Leigh Madison
Jack Bell	Leslie Phillips	New Nurse	Stephanie Schiller
Stella Dawson	Joan Sims	Fat Maid	Christine Ozanne
Georgie Axwell	Susan Stephen	Wow-of-a-Nurse	Shane Cordell
Oliver Reckitt	Kenneth Williams	Civilian Saleswoman	Lucy Griffiths
The Colonel	Wilfrid Hyde White	Stephens	John van Eyssen
	(guest star)	Mick	Harry Locke
Frances James	Susan Beaumont	First Ambulance Man	Anthony Sagar
'Norm'	Norman Rossington	Second Ambulance Man	Fred Griffiths
Jill Thompson	Jill Ireland	Porter	Charles Stanley
Sister	Joan Hickson	Anaesthetist	John Horsley
Helen Lloyd	Ann Firbank		
Mrs Marge Hickson	Irene Handl	Produced by	Peter Rogers
Mrs Jane Bishop	Susan Shaw	Directed by	Gerald Thomas
'Ginger'	Michael Medwin (guest	Screenplay by	Norman Hudis
	appearance)	Based on an idea by	Patrick Cargill and
Bert Able	Cyril Chamberlain		Jack Searle
Henry Bray	Brian Oulton	Music composed and	
Alec Lawrence	Edward Devereux	conducted by	Bruce Montgomery
John Gray	Frank Forsyth	Director of Photography	Reg Wyer BSC
Tom Mayhew	John Mathews	Art Director	Alex Vetchinsky
George Field	Graham Stewart	Production Manager	Frank Bevis
Andrew Newman	David Williams	Editor	John Shirley
Jackson	Patrick Durkin		
Meg	June Whitfield	Made in the autumn of 1958. Shooting began:	
Mrs Alice Able	Marianne Stone	3 November. Pinewood Studios.	

Carry On Nurse **Hitting a man when he's down. Boxer Bernie Bishop (Kenneth Connor) has broken his right wrist in a fight. Now he is involved in a dirtier fight—for his future. That's his manager, Ginger (Michael Medwin) and his sparring partner, Norm (Norman Rossington) visiting him in hospital, boxing clever and setting Bernie up for a double cross—well below the belt. For, in his mind, Ginger is giving Bernie's career the KO. Though Bernie does not know it, the flowers Ginger has brought mark its funeral. Ginger, you see, is a smash and grab merchant. His boxers smash—and he grabs. And when they can't smash anymore . . . nine, ten and out!**

Carry On Teacher

Leslie Phillips starred in three Carry On films in a row. This, which had the smallest cast of any in the series, was his second.

Richard O'Sullivan, now a television comedy star in series like *Robin's Nest*, had the leading role among the pupils, one of whom was played by Carol White, later the co-star of the famous television play about the homeless, *Cathy Come Home*, and films like *Poor Cow*.

BEAN (Charles Hawtrey) I read one of his books once. Free expression. You know what that means—sex in the cycle shed.

Schools inspectors FELICITY WHEELER (Rosalind Knight) and ALISTAIR GRIGG (Leslie Phillips) question gym mistress SARAH (Joan Sims).
FELICITY Are you satisfied with your equipment, Miss Allcock?
SARAH Well! I've had no complaints so far.
ALISTAIR Do you find that mental relaxation follows physical activity?
SARAH Oh, always!
ALISTAIR Splendid. That's all, thank you.
FELICITY I have one more question. Do you favour the Swedish method?
SARAH Well, I always say it's the same the whole world over.

Schoolboy BILLY (George Howeil) to English master EDWIN MILTON (Kenneth Williams) and schoolgirl IRENE (Jane White).
BILLY Didn't you know sir? Girls in Italy sort of . . . earlier. Something to do with the climate.
IRENE Not only in Italy, there's a girl down our street . . .
MILTON I'm not interested in the girl down your street.
IRENE Well, you're in the minority. Only last Saturday night . . .
MILTON Be quiet. This has nothing to do with *Romeo and Juliet*.
IRENE Oh! But it has, sir. She's fourteen.

English master MILTON (Kenneth Williams) and music master BEAN (Charles Hawtrey).
MILTON All right! It's already my Herculean task to coax anything like audibility from these children. If in addition I have to cope with an orchestra which makes a lullaby sound like the climax to '1812' . . .
BEAN You can hear a pin drop during their quiet passages!
MILTON And I'd rather!

Science master ADAMS (Kenneth Connor) during a school concert: 'If music be the food of love, belt up!'

Carry On Teacher A lesson in love. Acting headmaster William Wakefield (Ted Ray) exhorts science master Gregory Adams (Kenneth Connor) to obey his chemical reactions where schools' inspector Felicity Wheeler (Rosalind Knight) is concerned—a lady who has accentuated Mr Adams' interest in biology!

Carry On Teacher Hey, this is the teachers' study, not a box room! This scene of hit and Misses began when pupils put alcohol in the teachers' tea. Gym mistress Sarah Allcock (Joan Sims) and schools inspector Felicity Wheeler (Rosalind Knight) are fighting fit to teach each other a lesson after a misunderstanding about science master Gregory Adams (Kenneth Connor). That's him, with mathematics mistress Grace Short (Hattie Jacques), watching the girls knuckle down. Cause of this petticoat punch-up: Miss Wheeler thinks Mr Adams is a knockout!

Cast:

William Wakefield	Ted Ray	Irene	Jane White
Gregory Adams	Kenneth Connor	Boy	Larry Dann
Michael Bean	Charles Hawtrey		
Alistair Grigg	Leslie Phillips	Produced by	Peter Rogers
Sarah Allcock	Joan Sims	Directed by	Gerald Thomas
Edwin Milton	Kenneth Williams	Screenplay by	Norman Hudis
Grace Short	Hattie Jacques	Music composed and	
Felicity Wheeler	Rosalind Knight	directed by	Bruce Montgomery
Alf	Cyril Chamberlain	Director of Photography	Reginald Wyer, BSC
Robin Stevens	Richard O'Sullivan	Art Director	Lionel Couch
Billy Haig	George Howell	Production Manager	Frank Bevis
Harry Bird	Roy Hines	Editor	John Shirley
Penny Lee	Diana Beevers		
Pat Gordon	Jacqueline Lewis	Made in the spring of 1959. Shooting began:	
Sheila Dale	Carol White	9 March. Pinewood Studios and Drayton	
Atkins	Paul Cole	Secondary School, West Ealing, London.	

Carry On Constable

Sid James joined the Carry On series as POLICE SERGEANT WILKINS and got one of his first laughs with the instruction to a constable: '. . . and look in on Mrs Bottomley at Number 24. She complains of suspicious activities in the rear of her premises.'

Among those taking part were Freddie Mills, ex-light-heavyweight champion of the world, playing a crook (he also appeared in *Carry On Regardless*, next in the series); Robin Ray, now a television and radio authority on classical music, playing a store's assistant manager, and playwright John Antrobus as Fifth Citizen.

Carry On Constable No, it's not the Bow Street Runners! Nor the Flying Squad! But they are policemen. In fact this shower (played by Leslie Phillips, Kenneth Connor, Kenneth Williams and Charles Hawtrey) is going flat out on flat feet from nothing more shiver-making than a shower. Though it is a cold shower. A very, very cold shower. Well, they are supposed to be the boys in blue! They would throw in the towel, except they might land in the cooler.

Kenneth Connor as CONSTABLE: Rank must hold a few privileges, even if they appear to be meaningless.

CONSTABLE CHARLIE CONSTABLE fancies POLICEWOMAN GLORIA PASSWORTHY (Joan Sims) and plights his troth thus:
CHARLIE My name's Charlie—Charles actually.
GLORIA It's against regulations for us to be that familiar. Didn't you learn *anything* at your college?
CHARLIE (eager, correct) Oh yes—Policewoman Passworthy. What constitutes an obstruction—and parking regulations—and the rules of evidence—and—(very proud) I also know how to manipulate my truncheon.
GLORIA That's a great comfort to us all, I'm sure.

INSPECTOR MILLS (Eric Barker) versus SPECIAL CONSTABLE GORSE (Charles Hawtrey)
MILLS Why is your uniform torn?
GORSE I fell down a flight of stairs, sir.
MILLS How? Quick!
GORSE Oh yes, ever so quick, sir. I was on a scooter.

INSPECTOR MILLS versus CONSTABLE POTTER (Leslie Phillips):
MILLS You once ran off to Gretna Green with a firework heiress, didn't you?
POTTER Yes, sir. But she fizzled out.

Cast:

Wilkins	Sid James	Honoria	Diane Aubrey
Inspector Mills	Eric Barker	Eric	Ian Curry
Charlie Constable	Kenneth Connor	First Shop Assistant	Mary Law
Gorse	Charles Hawtrey	Miss Horton	Lucy Griffiths
Benson	Kenneth Williams	Third Citizen	Eric Corrie
Potter	Leslie Phillips	Passerby (thief)	Peter Bennett
Gloria	Joan Sims	Cliff	Jack Taylor
Laura	Hattie Jacques	Shorty	Eric Boon
Sally	Shirley Eaton	Girl with dog	Janetta Lake
Thurston	Cyril Chamberlain	Young Woman	Dorinda Stevens
Mrs May	Joan Hickson		
Distraught Woman	Irene Handl	Produced by	Peter Rogers
Herbert Hall	Terence Longden	Directed by	Gerald Thomas
Harrison	Jill Adams	Screenplay by	Norman Hudis
First Crook	Freddie Mills	Based on an idea by	Brock Williams
Store Manager	Brian Oulton	Music composed and	
Criminal-looking Man	Victor Maddern	directed by	Bruce Montgomery
Suspect	Joan Young	Director of Photography	Ted Scaife BSC
Deaf Old Lady	Esma Cannon	Art Director	Carmen Dillon
Agitated Woman	Hilda Fenemore	Production Manager	Frank Bevis
Vague Woman	Noel Dyson	Editor	John Shirley
First Citizen	Tom Gill		
Fourth Citizen	Frank Forsyth	Made in the autumn of 1959. Shooting began:	
Fifth Citizen	John Antrobus	9 November. Pinewood Studios and the streets of	
Assistant Manager	Robin Ray	Ealing, London.	
Matt	Michael Balfour		

Carry On Regardless

Curvy Liz Fraser, who was to add to the sex-appeal of the next two films in the series, made her Carry On début in this one. She later appeared in *Carry On Behind*. Fenella Fielding, later to star in *Carry On Screaming*, first appeared here, as did Tom Clegg who went on to play the principal monster in *Screaming*, as well as other roles in *Cleo*, *Loving*, *Spying* and *Cowboy*.

Among small parts played by performers now well known were those of a 'wolf' at a wine tasting event (Nicholas Parsons) and a 'raffish customer' (Patrick Cargill). There was also a role for gobble-degook-talker Stanley Unwin, as a landlord.

PENNY PANTING (Fenella Fielding) has lured SAM TWIST (Kenneth Connor) to her room to make her husband jealous, and is trying to explain:
PENNY Please . . . Don't make it hard for me . . .
SAM (sitting cautiously) I'm finding it a bit hard already . . . to understand.

This scene was cut by the censor:

GABRIEL DIMPLE (Charles Hawtrey) stands in for DELIA KING (Liz Frazer) when she fails to turn up for an assignment from Helping Hands, an agency run by BERT HANDY (Sid James) designed to help people in any way they wish. The assignment is to sit in the bedroom of MRS RILEY (Eleanor Summerfield) while her husband is away, and write down everything she says in her sleep. But GABRIEL does not

Carry On Regardless Brief encounter! The chap with the briefcase is Sam Twist (Kenneth Connor) who works for an agency that offers to do anything (gulp!) for anyone. The lady, in brief, is Penny Panting (Fenella Fielding) who has got Sam along to make her husband jealous. Now, as you can see, it's a case of Twist or bust.

know that when he arrives at the door of her flat:

MRS RILEY *Where* have you been? Come *in*! I'm *dying* to get to bed!

Before he knows where he is, she's yanked him into her flat where she does a double-take:

MRS RILEY AAAGH! Who are you?

GABRIEL (still grabbed) *Madam*—let me *go*!

MRS RILEY Not until you give me an explanation.

GABRIEL Of what?

MRS RILEY Your presence.

GABRIEL I was *sent*, by Helping Hands. (referring to paper) Flat 43. Mrs Riley.

MRS RILEY (astonished) There's been a mistake!

GABRIEL I agree.

MRS RILEY (decisive) But never mind! *Stay*!!

GABRIEL Why?

MRS RILEY I'm in the mood.

GABRIEL Are you...?

MRS RILEY I *know* I am.

GABRIEL Oh, do you...?

MRS RILEY That's why I'm so keen to get to bed.

GABRIEL Mrs Riley!!!

MRS RILEY There are nights when I *know* it's going to happen—at its most effective.

GABRIEL You don't say...

MRS RILEY I've *got* it!

GABRIEL I should think you *have!*

MRS RILEY What does it matter *what* you are?

GABRIEL It takes all sorts to make a world—yes...

MRS RILEY Mr Pimple...

GABRIEL Dimple.

MRS RILEY You'll be able to do your part from the wardrobe!

GABRIEL You flatter me, madam. You... EH?!

MRS RILEY Of course! Oh, what a *relief!* I—I don't want to *waste* my mood.

GABRIEL No—of course not...

MRS RILEY And with you in the wardrobe—we can observe the proprieties *and* achieve the result we both want so much.

GABRIEL M-Madam—I think I ought to warn you—I've led rather a sheltered life and... *WHOOP!* For he's dragged by her towards the bedroom, protesting wildly.

GABRIEL I don't quite understand ... I mean... You see... They are in the bedroom.

MRS RILEY (a little testily) What d'you mean you don't understand?

GABRIEL Madam—what possible good can I be to you in the wardrobe?!

MRS RILEY Plenty—with a notebook.

GABRIEL A *notebook*?!

MRS RILEY Do you have one?

GABRIEL No madam I do *not*. One way and another, I seem to be singularly ill-equipped for this job. I really think I'd better go... *WHOOP!* (he's grabbed again).

MRS RILEY *Don't!* I'm *desperate!*

GABRIEL I'm sorry, madam, but there's clearly been the most awful mistake.

MRS RILEY Oh, not too awful really—though I *did* ask for a *woman.*

GABRIEL A *woman*?!

MRS RILEY Well—If you were in my shoes—wouldn't you? (GABRIEL yammers) Oh *really*—man—woman—what difference does it make so long as you use your ears?

GABRIEL (wriggling a finger in each) I can't be *hearing* right!

MRS RILEY Oh *do* help me! I do it every single night. And the awful thing is—I don't *know* what comes out. That's why I need a Helping Hand.

GABRIEL And an 'elpful ear?

MRS RILEY Exactly!

GABRIEL Preferably a woman?

MRS RILEY Naturally.

GABRIEL But you'll settle for me?

MRS RILEY In this emergency—yes. My husband's away for three days —and I may not be so hot the other two nights—so you *will* get into the wardrobe won't you?

GABRIEL Mrs Riley, I have to confess that I have not comprehended a word you've said —but my imagination *boggles!*

MRS RILEY Not—*understood?* Didn't—anyone *tell* you?

GABRIEL No. They did *not*.

MRS RILEY Oh. (giggles) That's embarrassing.

GABRIEL To say the least.

MRS RILEY You must think...

GABRIEL Oh I *do!*

MRS RILEY Poor man. (advancing) I must explain.

GABRIEL From a distance! (she halts. He's still ultra-suspicious) WELL?...

LILY DUVEEN (Joan Sims) at a wine-tasting—and well out of her depth.

ORGANISER: You're a lover of the grape, Miss Duveen?

LILY No—ectually *no*.

ORGANISER Oh.

LILY I never know hawat to do with the pips, you see. Flick away—collect in the palm of the hend—or *spit*—quaite a social problem, don't you faind?

And later:

WAITER For you, madam—a soupçon.

LILY Oh rahly—what sort of soup?

GABRIEL (Charles Hawtrey) is supposed to help a woman with her caged birds but is sent, in error, to a strip club:

GABRIEL Ah! Hello.

MANAGER What d'you want?

GABRIEL Your birds. Oh, I can't wait! Tell me—what sort are they?

MANAGER (cautious) What sort d'you like?

GABRIEL Blue tits.

MANAGER EH?

GABRIEL Got any?

MANAGER No. My place is centrally heated.

DELIA KING (Liz Frazer) calls on a young bachelor, LEONARD BEAMISH, on behalf of the agency Helping Hands. But BEAMISH is expecting a date from a Marriage Bureau. (Note the similarity, between this scene and the one in *Carry On Loving*, although by two different writers.)

BEAMISH (soulful) Isn't it wonderful. We're the same religion.

DELIA EH?!

BEAMISH I mean isn't it clever of the agency to take care of things like that?

Carry On Regardless Just a tick, girls! Bert Handy (Sid James), owner of a do-anything-go-anywhere agency, has been mistaken at a hospital for a visiting eminent doctor. When the nurses line up for a 'physical', Bert puts the stethoscope to his own ticker first! He's heart-searching how far he goes with those helping hands!

Carry On Regardless Sorry mate, we only go to Piccadilly Circus—not Bertram Mills! Francis Courtenay (Kenneth Williams) of the Bert Handy do-anything-go-anywhere agency, is looking after a pet chimpanzee for the day. And it's no tea party getting him on a bus! Not that the conductor has a pet aversion. It's just the law of the asphalt jungle. The chimp does not turn a hair. He knows that when the conductor shouts: 'Have your furs ready please' . . . he's ready.

DELIA I didn't know they did.
BEAMISH Oh, but they *do*.
DELIA *Do* they?
BEAMISH Oh, definitely.
DELIA I can't think *why*. Your personal beliefs don't concern *me*. The important thing is to get on the job and—*enjoy* it.
She rises and takes her coat off. He gapes up at her.
BEAMISH D-don't you want to *talk* —even a *little?*
DELIA (puzzled smile) *Talk?* We both know what I'm here to do. What's there to *talk* about? (finally discards her coat).
BEAMISH (gasping) You sound—more—more experienced than I imagined . . .
DELIA (airily) Oh, I've had plenty of variety since joining the agency.
BEAMISH (screech) VARIETY?!
DELIA (nod) That was all I joined for.
BEAMISH You mean—you do this all the time?!
DELIA (nod) Two-three times a day. Different *types* of job of course . . .
BEAMISH (hollow) Of course . . .
DELIA (laughing) People hire me to do the *strangest* things.
BEAMISH (croak) Do they?
DELIA (merry nod) But *I* don't mind. You must take the rough

with the smooth, that's what I always say.

Under his temporarily speechless gaze, she discards the jacket of her costume.
BEAMISH What—what're you doing?!
DELIA (laughing) Stripping for action. I like to be *comfy* when I'm working.

He springs up, spluttering.
DELIA *You* don't have to do *anything*. Leave it *all* to me.
BEAMISH (weakly) I—think you'd better go . . .
DELIA Go? But I haven't *done* anything for you yet!
BEAMISH AND I DON'T WANT YOU TO! There's been a dreadful mistake. (mopping brow)

DELIA There's *no* mistake. There *can't* be. We've got a *system.* (checking card with dignity) Mr Beamish . . .

BEAMISH (gulp) Now look, I—I may be *shy*, but I'm not *totally* without knowledge of the world. And I think it's *monstrous* of you to work through an apparently reputable organisation and inflict yourself on respectable bachelors! With *flowers*, too!

DELIA (consulting card) You *specifically* asked for flowers! I've got the instructions here!

BEAMISH And I've got the letter here!

DELIA ⎫
BEAMISH ⎬ (Together) Show me!

They swap. They read. Dialogue slows.

BEAMISH (slowly) Helping *Hands* . . . ?

DELIA *Marriage* Agency . . . ?

They look at each other.

DELIA (small voice) I—thought you wanted somebody to tidy your flat—give it the woman's touch— ready for . . .

BEAMISH . . . for a tea-party I'm

giving my aunt . . . in *two weeks time.*

DELIA (faintly) The right job . . . but . . . a fortnight early . . . (gulp). Oh *dear*. And *you* thought I . . .

BEAMISH (very small voice) Yes, I—beg your pardon.

DELIA That's quite all right. I'd better go.

BEAMISH (faint hope, quite tender) I—wish you wouldn't . . .

DELIA (quiet) I'd better.

BEAMISH Can't you stay?

DELIA Well—perhaps for a little while—just to arrange the flowers.

Cast:

Bert Handy	Sidney James
Sam Twist	Kenneth Connor
Gabriel Dimple	Charles Hawtrey
Lily Duveen	Joan Sims
Francis Courtenay	Kenneth Williams
Mike Weston	Bill Owen
Delia King	Liz Fraser
Montgomery Infield-Hopping	Terence Longden
Penny Panting	Fenella Fielding
Miss Cooling	Esma Cannon
Frost-faced Sister	Hattie Jacques
Landlord	Stanley Unwin
Mrs Riley	Eleanor Summerfield
Mr Panting	Ed Devereaux
Mad Woman	Ambrosine Phillpotts
Park Keeper	Cyril Chamberlain
Matron	Joan Hickson
Trevor Trelawney	Terence Alexander
Referee	Norman Rossington
Club Manager	Sydney Tafler
Bird Woman	Molly Weir
Sister	June Jago
Sinister Man	Eric Pohlmann
Martin Paul	Jerry Desmond
Mr Delling	Jimmy Thompson
Wine Organiser	Howard Marion Crawford
Bus Conductor	Tony Sagar
Taxi Driver	Fred Griffiths
Wine Waiter	Bernard Hunter
Young Connoisseur	David Lodge
Wine 'Wolf'	Nicholas Parsons
Raffish Customer	Patrick Cargill
Bystander	Michael Nightingale
Testy Old Man	Kynaston Reeves
Houseman	Fraser Kerr
Fanatic Patient	Douglas Ives
Pretty Probationer	Maureen Moore
Shop Assistant	Ian Whittaker
Mata Hari	Betty Marsden
Massive Mickey McGee	Tom Clegg
Lefty	Freddie Mills
Trudi Trelawney	Julia Arnall
Dynamite Dan	Joe Robinson
MC	Jack Taylor
Auntie Acid	Lucy Griffiths
Army Officer	Cyril Raymond
Club Reception Man	George Street
Advertising Man	Ian Wilson
Photographer	Michael Ward
Chinese Lady	Madame Yang
Capable Old Lady	Nancy Roberts
Formidable Lady	Judith Furze
First Railway Policeman	Jack Taylor
Second Railway Policeman	David Williams
Distracted Manager	David Stoll
First Member of philosophers' club	Victor Maddern
Man in health club	Carl Conway
Old Man in Ruby Room	Charles Julian
Second Member of philosophers' club	Denis Shaw
Helen Delling	Carol Shelley
Leonard Beamish	Ian Curry

Produced by	Peter Rogers
Directed by	Gerald Thomas
Screenplay by	Norman Hudis
Music composed and directed by	Bruce Montgomery
Associate Producer	Basil Keys
Director of Photography	Alan Hume BSC
Art Director	Lionel Couch
Editor	John Shirley

Made in the winter of 1961. Shooting began 2 January. Pinewood Studios and Ealing, London.

Carry On Cruising

This was the first Carry On film made in colour. Lance Percival had a starring role as a ship's chef. The part was originally intended for Charles Hawtrey but was given to Percival after Hawtrey had a disagreement about his star status. Dilys Laye also starred in this Carry On . . . and carried on, with roles in *Spying*, *Doctor*, and *Camping*.

Carry On Cruising **Tablet d'hote! This tittersome twosome are cooking up a cure for the ship's chef. They are First Officer Marjoribanks (Kenneth Williams) and ship's doctor Arthur Binn (Kenneth Connor). The chef (Lance Percival) suffers from chronic** seasickness, so when he heaves into sight, this pair plan to stick a large hypodermic needle up his rear, after popping a couple of particularly nasty tablets down his hatch. If the chef has any sense, he'll stay seasick! It's more pleasant.

CAPTAIN CROWTHER (Sid James) is inspecting his new officers before the SS *Happy Wanderer* sets sail on a Mediterranean cruise. Before him are LEONARD MARJORIBANKS (Kenneth Williams), first officer, and ARTHUR BINN (Kenneth Connor), in a cap too large for him.
CROWTHER Who *are* you?
BINN Ship's doctor.
CROWTHER Impossible!
BINN I've got certificates to prove it. I'm certified, I am.
CROWTHER In that hat you look it.
MARJORIBANKS Ha-ha. *Wit*. They were right. Ha-ha-ha.
CROWTHER Shut up!
MARJORIBANKS Sir.
CROWTHER consults list.
CROWTHER Binn?
BINN No. That's just it.
CROWTHER Eh?
BINN The reason I *took* this job. Lately, I *haven't* bin regular. I prescribed myself exercise and a sea voyage—and here I am.
MARJORIBANKS (kindly) Say 'Sir'.
BINN Say 'Ah'. (steps from rank, approaches MARJORIBANKS) I don't like that fleck of green in your eye . . .

MARJORIBANKS anxiously feels his eye.
CROWTHER Never mind the eye!
BINN (naval) Aye-Aye!
MARJORIBANKS (hurt) Aye-*Aye*.
CROWTHER (to Binn) Where've *you* sprung from?
BINN Consolidated Marmalade. I was their Factory Medical Officer, y'see and . . .
CROWTHER Where is Doctor *Jepson*?
BINN Consolidated Marmalade. Jammy job . . . 'cept when they're overcome by the fumes.
CROWTHER *Who*?
BINN The workers. Hours at a stretch over a vat of seventy thousand steaming oranges . . . Gives 'em the pip so to speak.
MARJORIBANKS (yanking down his eye) *This* eye? Are you sure?
BINN (quick look) Green as grass. Probably too much chlorophyll in your toothpaste.
MARJORIBANKS (impressed) Affecting my eye-tooth?
BINN Very likely. It's all linked-up . . .

Enter WILFRED HAINES (Lance Percival) the new ship's cook.
CROWTHER What's happened to Norrington—our regular ship's cook?
HAINES (shrugs) Perhaps he got fed up. (sudden laugh)
MARJORIBANKS Oh, *excellent*. Fed up! (appreciative laugh)
BINN Cook! Fed up! (laughs)
CROWTHER *Belt up!*

CROWTHER coaches a steward (Brian Rawlinson)
CROWTHER . . . All you need to be a good steward is *tact*. Like—give you an example—take a steward I knew, years ago. Happened to walk in on a lady standing in her bath. What did he do? Said: 'Excuse me, *sir*', and left. *Tact*, see?
STEWARD That's *clever*, sir! I'll remember. Thank you.
CROWTHER Go ahead then. You'll be all right.
CROWTHER watches benignly as STEWARD knocks on cabin door, and enters. Within—HONEYMOON

COUPLE in embrace.
STEWARD 'Allo—'al*lo!* And which of you two fellas takes sugar?
CROWTHER creeps away guiltily.

Ship's bar.
DRUNK Have one wi' me. It's all free . . .
BINN Thanks, I need it.
DRUNK (blearily sympathetic) Love, eh?
BINN Well—yes . . . How did you know?
DRUNK (dramatic shrug) That's why I drink. To f'*get* her.
BINN Forget who?
DRUNK (gloomily) Bless'd 'f I c'n r'm'mber . . .

MISS BRIDGET MADDERLEY, a game little spinster, played by Esma Cannon, enters the bar. TURNER (Jimmy Thompson) turns to serve her:
TURNER Hallo there, madam. First time I've seen you in here.
MISS MADDERLEY I don't usually drink—but I've just been through such a *shocking* experience . . .
TURNER (soothing) And what d'you think you'd like to get over it?
MISS MADDERLEY That. (indicates bottle) Such an enigmatic label.
TURNER (demurring) Vodka—neat?
MISS MADDERLEY Oh yes—I do like things *tidy.*

Some minutes later:
MISS MADDERLEY Who makes this stuff?
TURNER The Russians, madam.
MISS MADDERLEY That explains it.
TURNER Explains what?
MISS MADDERLEY Their space programme. I'm halfway to the moon already. Fill her up—and two shots of Redex!
FLO What's your first name?
CROWTHER Wellington.
FLO Mother frightened by a boot, eh?

And later:
FLO Oh, it's *wonderful!* You're so *human*—mature—yet *modest!* Why have I wasted my time on mere *boys?* Wellington—*you* are my Waterloo!
CROWTHER (croaking) Flo—ebb a little!

CROWTHER . . . A Captain must *understand* his men. So I'm going to try the psychological approach. I don't claim to be a Jung man . . .
MARJORIBANKS (flattering) So long as you're young in heart, sir.

A COOK opens the door of a huge refrigerator. Head down, deep in thought, chef HAINES (Lance Percival) strides as if to enter it. COOK stops him.

HAINES Kindly let me pass.
COOK Into the fridge, Chef?
HAINES (blank. Then realises, jovially) Nearly gave you a chance to lead the lads in a song, then, didn't I?
COOK Song, sir?
HAINES Freeze a jolly good fellow!

BINN I'm a plain, simple man.
FLO Agreed . . . You look plain— and you act simple.

BINN What's your job?
FLO Typist.
BINN Shorthand?
FLO No. Both the same length.

BINN Hallo, hallo—what's afoot?
MARJORIBANKS It's that peculiar-shaped thing at the end of your leg.

MISS MADDERLEY . . . Why should I say it again, when you've already wheedled it out of me right here on deck.
CROWTHER I've never wheedled on deck in my life!

CHEF HAINES makes a cake with ingredients from all parts of the world. CAPTAIN CROWTHER samples it:
CROWTHER Excellent. Reminds me of everywhere I've ever been! (Gets full taste) Including Port Said . . .

Cast:

Captain Crowther	Sidney James	Table Tennis Player and	
Leonard Marjoribanks	Kenneth Williams	Shapely Miss	Jill Mai Meredith
Arthur Binn	Kenneth Connor	Kindly Seaman	Alan Casley
Glad Trimble	Liz Fraser	Bridegroom	Evan David
Flo Castle	Dilys Laye		
Bridget Madderley	Esma Cannon	Produced by	Peter Rogers
Wilfred Haines	Lance Percival	Directed by	Gerald Thomas
Sam Turner	Jimmy Thompson	Screenplay by	Norman Hudis
Drunk	Ronnie Stevens	From a story by	Eric Barker
Jenkins	Vincent Ball	Music composed and	
Tom Tree	Cyril Chamberlain	conducted by	Bruce Montgomery
Very Fat Man	Willoughby Goddard		and Douglas Gamley
Young Officer	Ed Devereaux	Director of Photography	Alan Hume BSC
Steward	Brian Rawlinson	Art Director	Carmen Dillon
Young Man	Anton Rodgers	Production Manager	Bill Hill
Cook	Anthony Sagar	Editor	John Shirley
Handsome Passer-by	Terence Holland		
Cook	Mario Fabrizi	Made in the winter of 1962. Shooting began	
Bridge	Marian Collins	9 January. Pinewood Studios.	

Carry On Cabby

This was not intended to be part of the Carry On series, but was made as a separate film with the title *Call Me A Cab*. As it contained most of the Carry On crowd, however, it was decided after shooting to make it part of the series.

Jim Dale joined the team with this film, playing an anxious father-to-be, and went on to appear in the next eight. After an absence of just over a year and two Carry Ons, he returned for *Carry On Again Doctor* in 1969, his last appearance. He turned down the Tarzan-like role of Jungle Boy in the next film, *Carry On Up The Jungle*.

Esma Cannon gave her fourth consecutive Carry On performance and Charles Hawtrey was back. Bill Owen returned for his last Carry On appearance.

Peter Gilmore, later to achieve television fame as the star of the sea-going series *The Onedin Line*, appeared in his first Carry On as a thuggish crook. Amanda Barrie, later to have the name part in *Carry On Cleo*, made her début as a sexy taxi-driver. Peter Byrne, well known as Sergeant Crawford of the TV series *Dixon of Dock Green*, played a bridegroom who gets involved with taxi-driving Charles Hawtrey.

Talbot Rothwell took over from Norman Hudis as the Carry On scriptwriter, and wrote the next nineteen.

Kenneth Williams was absent for the first time, but the film gave Hattie Jacques her favourite Carry On part, as the neglected and defiant wife of a taxi firm owner (played by Sid James).

Not being originally intended as a Carry On, the film was made in black and white.

TED (Kenneth Connor), SMILEY (Bill Owen).

TED Don't laugh too much, you might strain something. And you don't want to have to wear one of them belts, do you?
SMILEY I already do. The old woman give it me for Christmas.
TED That's what I like to see. A marriage based on mutual truss.

Wife PEGGY (Hattie Jacques) complains that her husband CHARLIE (Sid James) is totally obsessed with his taxi business. SALLY (Liz Fraser), whose boyfriend TED (Kenneth Connor) is CHARLIE'S right-hand man, agrees:
SALLY ... Ted's just the same. Put me and an old engine side by side and I'll give you one guess which he'd start to strip down. They've got cabs on the brain, both of them.
PEGGY Yes. Even when we do get a chance to talk, it's always cabs, cabs, cabs. He can't even get into bed now without saying: 'Where to?'

Cast:

Charlie	Sidney James	Punchy	Darryl Kavann
Peggy	Hattie Jacques	Car Salesman	Peter Jesson
Ted	Kenneth Connor	Tubby	Don McCorkindale
Pintpot	Charles Hawtrey	Geoff	Charles Stanley
Flo	Esma Cannon	Bride	Marion Collins
Sally	Liz Fraser	Chauffeur	Frank Forsyth
Smiley	Bill Owen		
Len	Milo O'Shea	Producer	Peter Rogers
'Battle-axe' Woman	Judith Furse	Directed by	Gerald Thomas
Aristocratic Lady	Ambrosine Phillpotts	Screenplay by	Talbot Rothwell
Molly	Renee Houston	Based on an original	
Small Man	Jim Dale	idea by	S. C. Green and
Anthea	Amanda Barrie		R. M. Hills
Dumb Girl	Carole Shelley	Music composed and	
Sarge	Cyril Chamberlain	conducted by	Eric Rogers
Allbright	Norman Chappell	Associate Producer	Frank Bevis
Dancy	Peter Gilmore	Director of Photography	Alan Hume BSC
Man in tweeds	Michael Ward	Art Director	Jack Stephens
District Nurse	Noel Dyson	Editor	Archie Ludski
Business Man	Michael Nightingale		
Clerk	Ian Wilson	Made in the spring of 1963. Shooting began	
Bridegroom	Peter Byrne	25 March.	

Carry On Jack

Originally called 'Carry On Sailor', but changed after shooting, this was the first in the series to use period costume. Counting *Carry On Spying*, with its exotic Middle East outfits, six costume Carry Ons followed consecutively, with another four being made, along with Carry Ons of a more contemporary setting, between 1968 and 1974. A suggestion from Jim Dale to make a Carry On about Camelot was turned down by producer Peter Rogers because it is not a theme which interests him.

Carry On Jack also introduced more realistic violence into the series, including a flogging. Bernard Cribbins, Juliet Mills, Donald Houston and Percy Herbert were drafted into this film with fewer than usual of the Carry On regulars—Sid James, Kenneth Connor, Joan Sims and Hattie Jacques were absent. Cecil Parker guest starred.

Carry On Jack **Back seat drivers! While Midshipman Poop-Decker (Bernard Cribbins) takes a forced stroll mid ship and sea, frightened but silent, it is the banished Captain Fearless (Kenneth Williams) the fella with the festering foot, who is doing all the shiver me timbers back-biting. What is he saying? Why, 'Don't Carry On' of course! But perhaps the exercise and the sea air will do them good. Drop in anytime, mates!**

NELSON (Jimmy Thompson) lying on the deck minus arm and eye, with HARDY (Anton Rodgers) bending over him.
NELSON ... Kiss me, Hardy.
HARDY I beg your pardon, sir?
NELSON Kiss me, Hardy.
HARDY Are you mad? What will they say at the Admiralty?
NELSON They'll only be jealous.
HARDY Well, I don't know. It may not be good for you. You're very weak.

Rather uncomfortable he bends down and kisses NELSON. NELSON gives a groan and expires. HARDY looks at him disapprovingly:
HARDY I told you so.

SALLY (Juliet Mills) takes ALBERT (Bernard Cribbins) to her bedroom.
SALLY What's the matter?
ALBERT I was just remembering ... before I left home my mother warned me that things like this might happen to me. I must write and thank her.
SALLY My mother always told me to be good. I hope I am. You'd tell me, wouldn't you?

Press gang leader HOWETT (Donald Houston) and his men spot WALTER SWEETLEY (Charles Hawtrey) alone in a bar.
HOWETT Evenin' friend. You a sailor?
WALTER Me? No. I'm a cesspool cleaner.
HOWETT I wondered why there wasn't anybody else around. Wouldn't you like to go to sea?
WALTER Like to go to see what?

SALLY and CAPTAIN FEARLESS (Kenneth Williams) face a milkless cow.
SALLY Steady sir. Don't you see why? It's had no fodder.
FEARLESS I don't care if it had no mother, I want my milk.

FEARLESS I hardly expect you to understand these things, Sweetley, but I can only make an estimate based upon existing knowledge of prevailing winds, currents, tides and, er, so on ...
WALTER Oh, I do understand those things, sir. It's like when they ask me for an estimate for cleaning out a cesspit. I have to know how long, wide and deep it is ...
FEARLESS Yes, well, it's not quite the same, Sweetley. And then we've had to keep tacking with the wind. It's no use working against it, is it?
WALTER Same in my job, sir. Work against the wind and it's horrible!

Cast:

Captain Fearless	Kenneth Williams
Albert Poop-Decker	Bernard Cribbins
Sally	Juliet Mills
Walter Sweetley	Charles Hawtrey
First Officer Howett	Donald Houston
Angel	Percy Herbert
Carrier	Jim Dale
Spanish Governor	Patrick Cargill
First Sea Lord	Cecil Parker (guest star)
Hook	Ed Devereaux
Patch	Peter Gilmore
Ned, and Clown	George Woodbridge
Ancient Carrier	Ian Wilson
Nelson	Jimmy Thompson
Hardy	Anton Rodgers
Town Crier	Michael Nightingale
Second Sea Lord	Frank Forsyth
Coach Driver	Barrie Gosney
Third Sea Lord	John Brooking
Spanish Captain	Jan Muzurus
Spanish Secretary	Viviane Ventura
First Woman at Dirty Dick's	Marianne Stone
Second Woman at Dirty Dick's	Dorinda Stevens
Girls at Dirty Dick's	Rosemary Manley
	Sally Douglas
	Jennifer Hill
	Dominique Don
	Marian Collins
	Jean Hamilton

Produced by	Peter Rogers
Directed by	Gerald Thomas
Screenplay by	Talbot Rothwell
Music composed and conducted by	Eric Rogers
Associate Producer	Frank Bevis
Director of Photography	Alan Hume BSC
Art Director	Jack Shampan
Editor	Archie Ludski

Made in the autumn of 1963. Shooting began 2 September. Pinewood Studios.

Carry on Jack The moment of truth—and what a grisly picture it makes! No, not this one! But the one in the head of Midshipman Poop-Decker (Bernard Cribbins). After being put adrift in an open boat by the rest of the ship's crew, this fearful foursome thought they had landed at Littlehampton. Now Poop-Decker realises they are in Spain, and the horrors of the Inquisition fill the space where his mind would be if he were not out of it! He sees pictures of them being questioned, with white-hot pokers held before their eyes—known as the eye-level grill. Suffering with him are: Sally (Juliet Mills), a publican's daughter searching for her lost lover; Walter Sweetley (Charles Hawtrey), a press-ganged cesspool cleaner; Captain Fearless (Kenneth Williams), who was the ship's cowardly captain.

Carry On Jack Cor, strike a light—a touch of black comedy! Not-Very-Able Seaman Walter Sweetley (Charles Hawtrey) was making a fire on deck, to sterilise instruments to operate on the captain's septic leg, when suddenly his career was booming. For sparks from the fire set off all the cannons, which destroyed a fleet of attacking ships! Sweetley, a former cesspool cleaner, never believed that one day he would be a big shot.

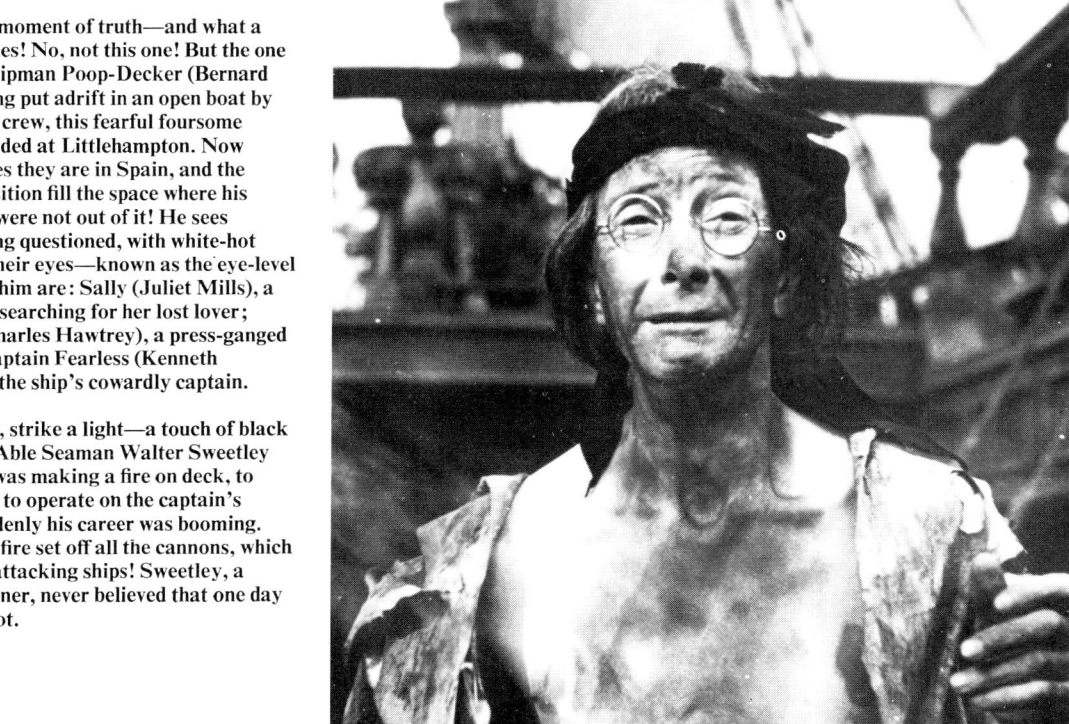

Carry On Spying

Barbara Windsor joined the Carry On team, playing a trainee spy. Her first words, prophetically, highlighted her personal attributes which were to be made much of in future films. Reporting with name and number to spy trainer DESMOND SIMKINS (Kenneth Williams) she declared: 'Agent Daphne Honeybutt. 36–28–36. Oh, no, sorry, that's my . . .', she giggles, then corrects herself 'Daphne Honeybutt. 4–7–11.' Her next speech, in which she agrees to be treated like a man when on missions, would have robbed the Carry Ons of a lot of fun if she had carried it out: 'Of course, sir. Don't worry. I'm quite prepared to forget my sex.'

Jim Dale as British agent CARSTAIRS, 'our man in Vienna', appeared as six different characters: An Austrian railway ticket collector; a Viennese customs official; an old, blind match-seller; a sexy woman of the streets; a waiter; an Arab.

Carry On Spying **Here's a juicy little scene. Foreign spy The Fat Man (Eric Pohlmann) has gone to an Algerian 'funhouse' feeling fruity. So Daphne Honeybutt (Barbara Windsor) is giving him all the fruit he can take! Daphne, the peach of the British secret service, and an agent with a lot worth investigating, is getting ready to put the squeeze on The Fat Man because he is the only one who can give her what she wants. That's right! A stolen British formula. And, as you see, she's already got him wide open. Has The Fat Man bitten off more than he can chew? Or will Daphne reveal too much?**

Secret Agent SIMKINS (Kenneth Williams) shows trainee-agent DAPHNE (Barbara Windsor), and others, how to do a fast draw. He opens his jacket to show his holster, then buttons it again.
SIMKINS See? All ready to get off a slick draw like this.
His hand goes like lightning to the inside of his jacket and with a triumphant cry he whips out his revolver. All very smooth, except he's holding it by the barrel . . .
SIMKINS Oh, dear. I wish they'd make these things with the barrel at the right end.
DAPHNE That was wonderful, Mr Simkins! I'm sure I'll never get my draws off as slickly as that!

FAT MAN Come, perhaps you will be a little more co-operative, my little flower.
DAPHNE Not blooming likely!

SIMKINS and trainee agent JAMES BIND (Charles Hawtrey) face a difficult situation in Algiers:
SIMKINS Right. I'm all ready. When he answers say something really rude to him. Something to make him rush out angrily.
JAMES Well, let's see. The rudest word I know is . . . manure.
SIMKINS No, no. Do it like the Arabs do. You know, insult his father. They hate that.

JAMES Oh yes, I know. (he knocks at the door and a tough face peers out of hatch angrily) Oh, hallo. I just wanted to say that your father was the illegitimate son of a flea-picker's daughter.
DOORMAN (smiles) Ah! You knew my father!
JAMES Oh. Of all the rotten luck!

JAMES passes a fruit machine, stops, goes back, gets out a coin,

puts it in, and pulls the handle.
SIMKINS dashes back.
SIMKINS Oh come on, we haven't got time for that now!
JAMES (excitedly as machine stops) Three oranges! Three oranges! He looks at the big slot for his winnings. The machine clacks loudly three times—and three oranges roll out . . .
SIMKINS Serves you jolly well right!

Carry On Spying Walls have ears! In fact, here's a cell carpeted with wall-to-wall spies. What you might call a thick pile. But though they are down on their knees and up to their ears in it, British agent Desmond Simkins (Kenneth Williams) and trainee-agents Harold Crump (Bernard Cribbins) and James Bind (Charles Hawtrey) leave no stone untapped. Instead of going up the wall, they use it to knock out a message, in morse, to the chap in the next cell. And they get a reply. 'Stop that tapping. I'm trying to sleep.' Some people! You give them the chance to be involved in murder, terror and danger—and they don't want to know!

Cast:

Simkins	Kenneth Williams	Funhouse Girls	Virginia Tyler
Daphne	Barbara Windsor		Judi Johnson
Harold Crump	Bernard Cribbins		Gloria Best
James Bind	Charles Hawtrey	Amazon Guards	Audrey Wilson
The Chief	Eric Barker		Vicky Smith
Lila	Dilys Laye		Jane Lumb
Carstairs	Jim Dale		Marian Collins
Cobley	Richard Wattis		Sally Douglas
The Fat Man	Eric Pohlmann		Christine Rodgers
Milchmann	Victor Maddern		Maya Koumani
Dr Crow	Judith Furse		
The Headwaiter	John Bluthal	Produced by	Peter Rodgers
Madame	Renee Houston	Directed by	Gerald Thomas
Doorman	Tom Clegg	Screenplay by	Talbot Rothwell and
First Thug	Jack Taylor		Sid Colin
Code Clerk	Gerton Klauber	Music composed and	
Second Thug	Bill Cummings	conducted by	Eric Rogers
Native Policeman	Norman Mitchell	Songs: *Too Late*	by Alex Alstone and
Professor Stark	Frank Forsyth		Geoffrey Parsons
Algerian Gent	Derek Sydney	*The Magic of Love*	by Eric Rogers
First Guard	Anthony Baird	Associate Producer	Frank Bevis
Cigarette Girl	Jill Mai Meredith	Director of Photography	Alan Hume BSC
Second Guard	Patrick Durkin	Art Director	A. Vetchinsky
Cloakroom Girl	Angela Ellison	Editor	Archie Ludski
Scrawny Native	Hugh Futcher		
Elderly Woman	Norah Gordon		

Made during the winter of 1964. Shooting began 3 February. Pinewood Studios.

Carry On Cleo

An element of death and blood-thirstiness entered the Carry Ons with this film (see Part One of the book for additional comments), to be intensified in *Carry On Cowboy* which came next. In a setting like that of Rome's militaristic empire, this added touch of reality was necessary to give point to the comedy which, in turn, defused the more unpalatable aspects of those times. But I still cannot quite get over Sid James, even as a MARK ANTONY under the influence of CLEOPATRA's sex appeal, playing something of a cowardly baddy by plotting with CLEO to invite CAESAR to her boudoir, while he hides under the bed ready to kill him.

In the canon of Carry On, however, *Cleo* is one of the best, providing, for me, Kenneth Williams' most outstanding, and definitive, performance in a Carry On, as Caesar, and one of Kenneth Connor's most entertaining portrayals as HENGIST POD, Ancient-Briton-manufacturer-of-square-wheels-turned-CAESAR's-bodyguard. In addition, writer Talbot Rothwell never excelled this script for the audacity, cleverness and profusion of the puns, the swagger and cheekiness of the *double entendres*, or the absurd logic of the plot. He also, except in *Carry On Up The Khyber*, never equalled *Cleo* as a send-up of history, historical characters, or types of characters.

Warren Mitchell played the part of SPENCIUS, partner in the firm of Markus and Spencius, who were in the slave-selling business. Wanda Ventham had a few moments in the slave-market scene, bidding for handsome, young ancient (young ancient?) Briton, Jim Dale. Sheila Hancock, as SENNA, wife of HENGIST POD, and Jon Pertwee as a soothsayer with better vision than the best TV set, also appeared in their first Carry On.

Close shot of a slab of rock hanging over the cave entrance on which are carved the words:
HENGIST POD, WHEELMAKER
NARRATOR Here in a modest thirty-flints-a-week council cave lived a very simple Briton called Hengist Pod and his wife, Senna. ... HENGIST, a gentle soul, wears a simple off-the-pig fur, with matching bootees.
    HENGIST (Kenneth Connor)

introduces a new neighbour, HORSA (Jim Dale) to his wife:
HENGIST Oh, this is our next door neighbour, dear, Mister ...
HORSA Horsa. Son of Ethelred.
HENGIST Not Ethelred the Unready?
HORSA Oh no, my dad was always ready. So my mum said.

CAESAR ... A nice little thing. Where did we capture her?
BILIUS At the settlement they call Bristol, sir.
CAESAR (eyeing her) Oh yes, I should have guessed ...

HENGIST AND HORSA outside HENGIST'S CAVE
HORSA There's no prettier sight than a young couple courting.
HENGIST Yes. Makes you feel like getting a club and having a bit of a bash yourself.
HORSA Was it like that with you and Senna?
HENGIST Just about. Except that she had the club.
HORSA I had my eye on a mate in Bristol. Gloria her name was. Beautiful. With lovely long, strong hair. Man, I could have dragged that girl anywhere.

MARK ANTONY We've just had word from Egypt. Ptolemy's raised an army and is marching on Alexandria!
CAESAR Oh dear! And what about Cleopatra? Is she mustered?
MARK (grinning) Well, I have heard one or two stories.

Carry On Cleo **Flaming heck! Charles Hawtrey, as Caesar's father-in-law Seneca, tunes in to some real hot news, in a vision by the local soothsayer (Jon Pertwee), which forecasts the assassination of Caesar. The flashy set on which they are watching this vision is on hire from Roman Rentals.**

Carry On Cleo **Another close shave— thank goodness he brought a blade! The others may be saying that, but the chap with the sword wants to cut and run! The object is to escape from Cleopatra's palace after an unsuccessful stab by Cleo at assassinating Caesar. That's Caesar's bodyguard Hengist Pod (Kenneth Connor) out in front, dressed as Caesar to fool Cleopatra. That's Caesar (Kenneth Williams) behind, dressed as his bodyguard. Bringing up the rear, escaped English slave Horsa (Jim Dale). The unseen terror, cutting them off, is Sosages (Tom Clegg), Cleopatra's enormous bodyguard. Life is never simple is it?**

HORSA We'll have to chance it. Look, if anyone in there asks, say we're . . . eunuchs.
HENGIST Eh—oh well, what have we got to lose?

CAESAR Infamy! Infamy! They've all got it in fer me!

HENGIST (down on knees) No, no, please sir. I plead for mercy! I plead for my life! I plead for forgiveness!
MARK What a miserable little pleader. Take him away!

CAESAR . . . With him beside me who will dare attempt my life again? He's impregnable! Aren't you?
HENGIST Oh no, sir. It's just that Senna didn't *want* any kids just yet.

MARK ANTONY (Sid James) returns from Egypt to CAESAR (Kenneth Williams) in Rome:
MARK It's an amazing country. You should see the pyramids they've built. And the sphinx!
CAESAR Yes, well, that's because they have no drains, of course. But how did everything go?

Later:
MARK You know you wanted me to get rid of Cleopatra and put Ptolemy on the throne?
CAESAR Yes?
MARK Well, I did it the other way round.
CAESAR Oh well, anybody can make a mistake, I suppose.
MARK Not by accident! I did it because, frankly, I thought she'd make a much better queen than he would.
CAESAR Well, she's the right sex of course.
Later:
CAESAR Tell me more. What's she like, this Cleopatra?
MARK You should see her! Hair as black as ebony, face like an ivory goddess, a neck like a swan's . . .
CAESAR Yes, yes, go on!
MARK Feet like sculptured marble . . .
CAESAR Oh, don't miss out all the best bits!
Later:
MARK . . . She's absolute perfection! They call her the Siren of the Nile!
CAESAR I hope she doesn't go off.

They do tend to in these hot countries, you know.
MARK Don't worry. She's got a deep frieze running all round the walls of her palace.

CAESAR, aboard his galley, bound for Egypt, feels seasick and cannot face the meal being served by the handmaiden GLORIA
GLORIA You are not well, my Lord.
CAESAR Just a little sic transit, Gloria.

CAESAR takes a round medallion on a chain from his neck and puts it on HENGIST:
CAESAR In recognition of your great service to me. Centurion Pod, I hereby confer on you the Imperial Order of the Bath.
MARK (pointing at medallion) Don't lose that—it's the plug.

CLEO I have a poisonous asp.
MARK (with a look behind her) Oh, I wouldn't say that.
CLEO I have! Look!
She goes to a box, opens it, and takes out a small snake by the tail.
CLEO One bite from that is enough!
MARK Let's see.
He takes it from her, bites a bit off, makes a face and spits it out.
MARK You're right! One bite's enough for anyone! Revolting!

MARK and CLEO (Amanda Barrie) plot to assassinate CAESAR.
MARK Look, I can't do anything till we get him away from that bodyguard of his. That's where you come in.
CLEO Where have I been, then?
MARK You haven't been anywhere! You're there! Try and use your nut for a change! What you have to do is get Caesar *alone!*
CLEO Oh, is that what he's come for? Money!
MARK Alone! On his tod!
CLEO Oh, you should have said.
MARK Just get him to go into your bed-chamber, where I'll be waiting, and we'll do it!
CLEO Do what?
MARK Oh blimey, there must be an easier way to make a killing.

With HENGIST and his father-in-law SENECA (Charles Hawtrey), CAESAR questions CLEOPATRA'S bodyguard, SOSAGES (Tom Clegg), about his meeting with the queen:

SOSAGES flaps his arms chicken-fashion and makes a soundless crowing.

HENGIST He's going to lay an egg.

SENECA No, No, no! He means at cock crow!

SOSAGES nods.

CAESAR Yes, but what cock? The morning one or the evening one?

SENECA Morning cock or evening cock?

SOSAGES makes 'asleep' motion.

SENECA Evening cock.

CAESAR Thanks cock, I'll be ready.

CLEO ... So you are the great Caesar?

CAESAR Ah, you recognised me!

CLEO I have seen your bust!

CAESAR I wish I could say the same.

HENGIST I'm trying to find a clean pitcher.

SENECA Oh, never mind that. You're in Egypt now. They only have dirty pitchers here.

SENECA Oh, I say! An Arab, eh? I've heard they're very intense lovers!

MARK Well, naturally. They do everything in tents ...

HENGIST I can't relax! I told you— I'm not used to this sort of thing.

CAESAR What sort of thing?

HENGIST Well ... you know. Making passionate love and all that.

CAESAR What? But you've been married for ten years!

HENGIST That's what I say! I'm not used to it!

Cast:

Mark Antony	Sidney James	Gloria's Bridesmaid	Judi Johnson
Julius Caesar	Kenneth Williams	Vestal Virgins	Gloria Johnson
Hengist Pod	Kenneth Connor		Joanna Ford
Seneca	Charles Hawtrey		Donna White
Calpurnia	Joan Sims		Jane Lumb
Horsa	Jim Dale		Vicki Smith
Cleopatra	Amanda Barrie	Seneca's Servant	Thelma Taylor
Sergeant Major	Victor Maddern	Heckler	Norman Mitchell
Gloria	Julie Stevens	Dusky Maiden	Sally Douglas
Senna Pod	Sheila Hancock	Pretty Bidder	Wanda Ventham
Soothsayer	Jon Pertwee	Willa Claudia	Peggy Ann Clifford
Agrippa	Francis de Wolff	Guard (Caesar's palace)	Mark Hardy
Archimedes	Michael Ward	Narration by	E. V. H. Emmett
Brutus	Brian Oulton		
Sosages	Tom Clegg	Produced by	Peter Rogers
Virginia (head Vestal		Directed by	Gerald Thomas
Virgin)	Tanya Binning	Screenplay by	Talbot Rothwell
Bilius	David Davenport	From an original idea by	William Shakespeare
Galley Master	Peter Gilmore	Music composed and	
Messenger	Ian Wilson	conducted by	Eric Rogers
Hessian Driver	Brian Rawlinson	Associate Producer	Frank Bevis
Markus	Gertan Klauber	Director of Photography	Alan Hume BSC
Spencius	Warren Mitchell	Art Director	Bert Davey
Caveman	Michael Nightingale	Editor	Archie Ludski
Sixth Companion	Peter Jesson		
Cleo's Handmaidens	Christine Rodgers		
	Gloria Best		
	Virginia Tyler		

Made in the summer of 1964. Shooting began 20 July. Pinewood Studios.

Carry On Cowboy

Bernard Bresslaw and Peter Butterworth joined the Carry On team with this film. Angela Douglas, who played ANNIE OAKLEY, went on to star in *Screaming, ... Follow That Camel* and *Up The Khyber*. A brief one-speech part for Margaret Nolan, as a secretary in a passionate embrace with her boss (the Commissioner for Internal Affairs), blossomed five years later into a succession of larger roles in *Henry, At Your Convenience, Matron, Girls* and *Dick*. Percy Herbert,

(above right)
Carry On Cowboy **They've garter go! Scandalised after scanning this thighful eyeful of scanties, Judge Burke (Kenneth Williams) of Stodge City decides: 'Can-can? Cannot-cannot!' The girls (played by The Ballet Montparnesse) have been imported by a gang of gunslingers and aim only to please. As you see, they are even bending over backwards to give the judge a frill! Though, in the end, he is the one who is led a merry dance.**

who was Angel the brutal bo'sun in *Carry On Jack*, returned as an ambitious, gun-toting barman, and Jon Pertwee made his second Carry On as a sheriff with bad hearing and defective eyesight.

Of all the Carry On films, *Cowboy* is the most realistically violent, the one where scenes of killings and foul deeds have the thinnest coating of comedy. Most of the comedy is reserved for other scenes. Even one of the most beloved Carry On stars, Sid James, plays the baddy (see Part One of the book for additional comments).

Gerald Thomas, who has directed all of the Carry On films, says that this was the most enjoyable to make . . . the most interesting, the most exciting, the most entertaining. It is the only Carry On film to have exceeded its shooting schedule. It was one day late, caused by heavy rain on the first day of production, which Thomas was never able to make up.

JUDGE BURKE (Kenneth Williams), DOC WESTON (Peter Butterworth) and SAM HOUSTON (Sydney Bromley) in the saloon.

SAM Now Judge, there hasn't been any shootin' in Stodge City since the day you ran Jesse James out of town.

DOC Oh yes, what a day that was. You know Judge, I never credited you with either the guts or the courage to do that.

JUDGE (modestly) Oh, I don't know. I'm sorry I had to get tough with Jessie though. She was a nice girl.

SAM I never did get to know exactly what she done that was so wrong.

JUDGE Old Ben was a friend of mine, Sam. And she killed him.

DOC Yes, but it was his own fault.

He was ninety-two and I warned him not to marry her.

JUDGE *How* she did it is immaterial.

Saloon owner BELLE ARMITAGE (Joan Sims) points a derringer at gunslinger THE RUMPO KID (Sid James)

BELLE I don't allow any shooting at my place.

RUMPO Lady, I wouldn't dream of shooting at your place.

BELLE I'm not afraid to use this, you know.

RUMPO Okay.

He shrugs and draws his gun and hands it to her. BELLE looks down at the long barrel admiringly.

BELLE Ooh, haven't you got a big one.

RUMPO I'm from Texas, ma'am. We all got big ones down there.

SAM I—er—I was just helpin' the hired girl get the stock in.

RUMPO Oh yeah. Well, I certainly hope I didn't stop you getting it in.

JUDGE It was Rumpo and his gang. They ran their horses right over you!

KNUTT (Jim Dale) What a terrible thing to do!

JUDGE Oh, it's an old Western trick. They call it nagging someone to death.

Indian Chief BIG HEAP (Charles Hawtrey) gets drunk and sings:
Oh, there was a Red Indian's daughter,
Who everyone called Running Water,
Till an arrow from high
Punctured her main supply,
Now her water don't run as it oughter.

BIG HEAP . . . I say, did you hear the one about the Indian who couldn't get a room in the hotel?

RUMPO No.

BIG HEAP He hadn't got a reservation!

Carry On Cowboy **Stand and deliver! Notorious gunslinger the Rumpo Kid (Sid James) gets everything he wants in Stodge City, and now he aims to get nubile new arrival Annie Oakley (Angela Douglas). What he doesn't know is that Annie also aims to get him—with a bullet, 'cause he done shot her daddy. And Annie knows that nothing puts a man off his guard quite like a pair of flashing thighs. Though, being a gunman, Rumpo can also admire a set of 38s . . . or 36s . . . or 34s . . . or . . . Looks like another staring tale of the Old West.**

KNUTT I think it's got a lot to do with you. They got away with forty cows.
RUMPO Bullocks.
KNUTT I know what I'm talking about.

JUDGE Yes, you may as well admit you stole those cattle, Rumpo. We've got you by the shorthorns.

The door opens and BELLE glides in. KNUTT jams his revolver up against her back.
KNUTT Hold it right there!
BELLE I hope that's your gun, Marshal.

BELLE Maybe it's because I go for you, Marshal honey. Don't you feel it? That certain something between us?
KNUTT looks down . . .
KNUTT Yes. It's my hot water bottle.

JUDGE I happen to be her lawyer. And since her husband died I've been handling everything.

Carry On Cowboy Warriors? No, worriers! Where there's a quill there's a way, thought gunslinger the Rumpo Kid (Sid James) and his buckskinned bucko Charlie (Percy Herbert), all tricked out as Indians to set a trap for the new sheriff just arriving by stagecoach. They have even pow-wowed redskinny Chief Big Heap (Charles Hawtrey) into sending his braves against the stage. But all this Indian corn fails, as the new sheriff appears to know his oats with a gun. Well, you could knock 'em down with a feather. It's the best stage performance they've seen for years! (Psst! The real sharpshooter aboard is a woman, Annie Oakley. Who put that daughter on the stage . . .?)

Cast:

The Rumpo Kid	Sidney James	Dancing Girls	The Ballet Montparnesse
Judge Burke	Kenneth Williams		
Marshall P. Knutt	Jim Dale	Cowhand	Hal Galili
Big Heap	Charles Hawtrey	Drunk	Norman Stanley
Belle	Joan Sims	Mexican Girl	Carmen Dene
Annie Oakley	Angela Douglas	Minnie	Andrea Allen
Little Heap	Bernard Bresslaw	Polly	Vicki Smith
Doc (Stodge's doctor)	Peter Butterworth	Jane	Audrey Wilson
Charlie	Percy Herbert	Jenny	Donna White
Sheriff	Jon Pertwee	Sally	Lisa Thomas
Sam	Sydney Bromley	Bridget	Gloria Best
Dolores	Edina Ronay	Stage Coach Driver	George Mossman
Clerk	Lionel Murton		
Curly	Peter Gilmore	Produced by	Peter Rogers
Josh	Davy Kaye	Directed by	Gerald Thomas
Fiddler (commissioner)	Alan Gifford	Screenplay by	Talbot Rothwell
Stage Coach Guard	Brian Rawlinson	Music composed and conducted by	Eric Rogers
Bank Manager	Michael Nightingale		
Short	Simon Cain	Associate Producer	Frank Bevis
Kitikata	Sally Douglas	Director of Photography	Alan Hume BSC
Mex	Cal McCord	Art Director	Bert Davey
Slim	Garry Colleano	Editor	Rod Keys
Old Cowhand	Arthur Lovegrove		
Miss Jones	Margaret Nolan		
Blacksmith	Tom Clegg		
Perkins	Larry Cross		
Trapper	Brian Coburn		

Made in the autumn of 1965 at Pinewood Studios, Chobham Common in Surrey and Black Park, Fulmer, Bucks.

Carry On Screaming

Charles Hawtrey was, originally, not cast for a part in this one. The role of Dan Dann, the attendant at a men's public convenience, who claims to have knowledge about the mysterious disappearance of several girls, was first given to Sydney Bromley, who played rancher Sam Houston in *Carry On Cowboy*. Hearing that Hawtrey would not be in the film, C. H. B. Williamson, a show-business writer, put a short piece in the magazine *Today's Cinema* regretting this and wondering if it would affect the film's success. When some executives at Anglo Amalgamated Films, backers and distributors of the Carry Ons at that time, read the piece, they got on to producer Peter Rogers suggesting that Hawtrey ought to be brought in. To appease the distributors and to publicly deny the piece in *Today's Cinema*, Rogers gave Hawtrey the part of Dan Dann.

The squeaky voice of the smaller monster, Odbodd Junior, played by Billy Cornelius, was done by the director, Gerald Thomas, during dubbing. Once Thomas' youngest daughter, Samantha, discovered this, she began to insist, as he kissed her goodnight: 'Do the monster and I'll go to sleep.'

Sid James, having been absent from *Carry On Jack* and *Carry On Spying*, since he joined the series in 1959, also missed this one. Harry H. Corbett starred, his only appearance in a Carry On. Fenella Fielding made it her second and Jon Pertwee his third.

Description of opening scene . . .
Exterior. Bleak stretch of country. Night. A touch of the eeries. A potential Dracula Development Area. Wooded stretches, windswept hills and a forbidding-looking turreted mansion lurking behind high walls in the near distance. The wind moans. An owl hoots mournfully. A hound howls dismally. Everybody's happy.

DETECTIVE SERGEANT BUNG (Harry H. Corbett) and his wife EMILY (Joan Sims) are arguing, as usual.
EMILY . . . Do you realise you haven't taken me out anywhere for years?
BUNG Don't be silly. We were out a couple of months ago. Had a lovely time.
EMILY You call that lovely? To my poor dear mother's funeral?
BUNG Well *I* enjoyed it.

BUNG and DETECTIVE CONSTABLE SLOBOTHAM (Peter Butterworth) investigate:

BUNG . . . We can't afford to leave any stone unturned. What's the name of this road, Slobotham?
SLOBOTHAM Er . . . Avery Avenue, sir.
BUNG Well, like I said, we must explore avery avenue.

BUNG and SLOBOTHAM visit the mansion of the mysterious DR WATT (Kenneth Williams)
BUNG First of all, your name please, sir?
WATT Doctor Watt.
SLOBOTHAM Doctor who, sir?
WATT No, Watt. Who's my uncle. Or was. I haven't seen him for ages.
SLOBOTHAM We appear to be at loggerheads, sir
WATT Oh no, this is Bide-a-Wee. Loggerheads is about five miles down the road.
SLOBOTHAM No, I mean about your name, sir.
WATT Watt.
SLOBOTHAM (much louder) Your name!
BUNG Watt's his name!

SLOBOTHAM That's what I'm trying to find out, sir!
BUNG Excuses, excuses, always excuses! Just put his statement down! I didn't hear or see anything suspicious in this vicinity tonight!
WATT You too, eh? I'm so glad it wasn't just me who didn't.

ALBERT (Jim Dale), boyfriend of a missing girl, receives a mysterious note:
ALBERT (reading) If you want to know what happened to Doris Mann, I can tell you. I am the cloakroom attendant at the one by the park and you can see me any time at my convenience.
BUNG Let me see that!
He snatches the piece of paper and studies it.
SLOBOTHAM Do you think it's genuine, sir?
BUNG I don't know. Unusual notepaper . . . perforated at both ends . . . could be! Come on!
And when they get there:
SLOBOTHAM I'm a police detective and I must warn you that I shall take down anything you say.
ATTENDANT All right. Trousers.

Lavatory attendant DAN DANN (Charles Hawtrey) about his job: 'Well, there's something to be said for it. I live in a man's world.'

Carry On Screaming **And something's afoot. Detective sergeant Sidney Bung (Harry H. Corbett) and his assistant, detective constable Slobotham (Peter Butterworth) are looking for a man with six toes as part of their investigation into why girls are mysteriously disappearing in Hocombe Woods. The foot belongs to Jim Dale, playing Albert Potter, boyfriend of one of the girls.**

The pavement forms the ceiling of MR DANN's office, and part of it is clear glass. A pair of female feet and legs cross it. Attendant Dann looks up:

ATTENDANT Ah, Mrs Peabody. (calling up) Mornin' Mrs Peabody!... Nice woman. Her husband's a customer of mine.
BUNG Very interesting, but...
ATTENDANT I know all of 'em that go past 'ere, you know. Intimately, you might say.
BUNG Yes, I can see that business here is definitely looking up!

BUNG meets VIRULA (Fenella Fielding), DR WATT's slinky daughter. She kisses him:

VIRULA Forgive me. But I just had to do that.
BUNG Oh, that's all right, miss. We're here to be of service to the public.
VIRULA But I don't think you are experienced in the ways of love.
BUNG Oh, I wouldn't say that. You know what they say. If you want to know the way, ask a policeman.

The evil DR WATT and his daughter VIRULA kidnap beautiful girls and turn them into dummies for shop windows.

VIRULA Come Father, there is work to do.
WATT Oh dear. No rest for the wicked.

SLOBOTHAM is captured by DR WATT and VIRULA:

WATT Well, if he's Sergeant Bung's assistant I suppose he'll have to go, too.
VIRULA Why not do what they did to your friend Dracula. Drive a spike through his heart.
WATT No, I don't think so. I don't really feel like driving tonight.

WATT Aha! You thought you'd beaten me, didn't you? Ha, ha, ha! But you'll never get away. Oh no! You think this spray is for greenfly, don't you? But it isn't, see! It's filled with petrifying liquid. And it works. I've tried it on my rhubarb with amazing results.

Cast:

Detective-Sergeant Bung	Harry H. Corbett	Mrs Parker	Marianne Stone
Dr Watt	Kenneth Williams	Rubbatiti	Denis Blake
Albert	Jim Dale		
Dan Dann	Charles Hawtrey	Produced by	Peter Rogers
Virula	Fenella Fielding	Directed by	Gerald Thomas
Emily Bung	Joan Sims	Screenplay by	Talbot Rothwell
Doris Mann	Angela Douglas	Music composed and	
Sockett	Bernard Bresslaw	conducted by	Eric Rogers
Det-Con Slobotham	Peter Butterworth	Song 'Carry On	Myles Rudge and Ted
Dr Fettle	Jon Pertwee	Screaming' by	Dicks
Vivian (window dresser)	Michael Ward	Associate producer	Frank Bevis
Odbodd	Tom Clegg	Director of Photography	Alan Hume BSC
Odbodd Junior	Billy Cornelius	Art Director	Bert Davey
Cabby	Norman Mitchell	Editor	Rod Keys
Mr Jones (shop manager)	Frank Thornton		
Desk Sergeant	Frank Forsyth	Made in the spring of 1966 at Pinewood Studios,	
Policeman	Anthony Sagar	with location shooting at Windsor, Berkshire and	
Girl	Sally Douglas	Fulmer, Bucks.	

Carry On ... Don't Lose Your Head

Like the next film, *Carry On ... Follow That Camel*, this was not made as a Carry On and, though it contained most of the Carry On team and looked and behaved like a Carry On film, it did not bear the Carry On name for more than two years. It was simply called: *Don't Lose Your Head*. The reason for the absence of the Carry On prefix was that producer Peter Rogers had changed his backers and distributors, leaving Anglo Amalgamated Films and going over to Rank. But Rank, while liking the idea of backing a money-making series, did not like the idea of taking over a title which had become associated with a rival. So the team was kept, but the words Carry On were dropped. A Carry On film (*Carry On Doctor*) was not made for Rank for another year, by which time the film industry had become used to the Peter Rogers–Rank Organisation association.

Carry On ... Don't Lose Your Head
You must think I'm a right blockhead— trying to sell me life insurance at a time like this! The French Revolution. Another aristocrat, the Duc de Pommfrit (Charles Hawtrey) is about to get it in the neck. But keep your hair on! Here is a gay blade sharper than Madame Guillotine. He is Sir Rodney Ffing, known as 'The Black Fingernail' (Sid James) with an idea to prevent the Duc's problems coming to a head. While pretending to sell life insurance, Sir Rodney provides it, by popping a snuff box in the runner of the guillotine. Yes, an idea not to be sniffed at.

It was more than a year after that, however, before *Dont Lose Your Head* and *Follow That Camel* were brought into the Carry On fold. One of the reasons—apart from the fact that they were *really* Carry On films—was that the words Carry On had ·become to mean something distinctive in the minds of the public and had a selling value.

Peter Gilmore, who had by now become a Carry On regular, played the part of the French Revolution leader ROBESPIERRE, and Julian Orchard had the small part of a rake who is supposed to be looking at Joan Sims' locket but is really admiring her bosom.

SIR RODNEY FFING—pronounced 'Effing'—(Sid James) and LORD DARCY PUGH (Jim Dale) are bored English aristocrats:
DARCY Definitely the same old round.
RODNEY The same old people.
DARCY Same old girls.
RODNEY Same old tea parties.
DARCY Same old concerts.
RODNEY Same old balls.

SIR RODNEY to LE DUC DE POMMFRIT (Charles Hawtrey) as he lies beneath the guillotine during the French Revolution:
RODNEY . . . I represent Lloyds of London, and I was just wondering whether I could interest you in a little life insurance.
POMMFRIT I don't think so, thank you. Not today.
RODNEY It's a very good policy,

Your Grace. It covers accidental death by drowning, shooting, stabbing, poisoning, hanging . . .
POMMFRIT Beheading?
RODNEY Oh no. Well, we can't take too many risks, you know.
(Psst! It was really a ruse to rescue him)

An Englishman known as the BLACK FINGERNAIL is rescuing aristocrats from the guillotine. ROBESPIERRE (Peter Gilmore) turns to his chief of secret police, CITIZEN CAMEMBERT (Kenneth Williams):
ROBESPIERRE It seems that the English have struck again.
CAMEMBERT Ah yes, Citizen Robespierre. But then they say it's the one thing the English are good at—striking.

Sir Rodney (disguised as a woman) is thought to be a French aristocrat and is questioned by CITIZEN BIDET (Peter Butterworth), CAMEMBERT's assistant:
BIDET We secret police have ways of making people talk.
FIRST SOLDIER Shall we use the thumbscrew?
BIDET No. No, we'll wait till Citizen Camembert gets here. If there's any screwing to be done, he'll do it. He's practically screwed up the Revolution already.

SIR RODNEY, still disguised as a woman, escapes. CITIZEN CAMEMBERT takes a coach in pursuit. At a road barrier:
FIRST GUARD Halt. Who goes there?
CAMEMBERT appears at coach window
CAMEMBERT Listen. Has anyone passed out within the hour?
FIRST GUARD Only the sergeant. He's sleeping it off now.
CAMEMBERT I'm looking for a woman.
FIRST GUARD Oh, nothing doing out here, chum. Ha, you want to try Montmartre.
CAMEMBERT Mon . . . I don't mean that. Oh, how I loathe these peasants. Give me the aristocracy any time.

BIDET It's about the girl. It's like you said, sir. I spent half the night working on her . . . to get information out of her.
CAMEMBERT And what did you find out?
BIDET Nothing.
CAMEMBERT Nothing! Nothing at all?
BIDET No. She kept mum.
CAMEMBERT I'm not interested in her financial arrangements with her mother. What about the Black Fingernail?
BIDET Oh well, there was this silver locket. It appears he gave it to her.
CAMEMBERT Oh, what's in it? A lock of his hair?
BIDET No. A set of his teeth.
CAMEMBERT A set of . . . set of his

teeth! Fancy keeping their teeth in a a silver locket. I ask you! Isn't that just typical of these damn aristocrats. A glass of water isn't good enough.

BIDET Mind you, sir, it'll help us find him. All we've got to do is to look for a man who talks like that. (he talks as though he hasn't any teeth)

CAMEMBERT A man that talks like that. That's no good. You know what these plutocrats are like. He's probably got a second set.

DOWAGER Ah, Sir Rodney, I must congratulate you. A perfectly splendid charity ball.

RODNEY Thank you, Lady Binder.

DOWAGER Now, do tell me, what is it all in aid of?

RODNEY SFA.

DOWAGER Oh come. It must be in aid of something.

RODNEY SFA. Stranded French Aristocrats.

DOWAGER Oh, of course. A very worthy cause. And you've done them proud tonight. But then, you've always had magnificent balls . . . And I wouldn't miss one of them.

BIDET fancies CAMEMBERT's bit of stuff, DESIREE (Joan Sims), and makes his desires obvious. But she does not fancy him:

DESIREE Cammy, I'd be very much obliged if you'd ask this underling to take his hot sticky eyes off me.

BIDET Underling! There'll be no more of that sort of talk. In our glorious New Republic all are equal! Equality, fraternity . . . liberty.

DESIREE I don't care about the equalities and the fraternities . . . but I'm not having the liberties.

Taking Desiree with him, CAMEMBERT goes, disguised as an aristocrat, to England to try and find the BLACK FINGERNAIL. But DESIREE finds the journey . . . painful:

DESIREE It's all these hump-backed bridges and these English roads. I shan't be able to sit down for a week.

CAMEMBERT I do wish you wouldn't be so vulgar! Kindly remember you're supposed to be an aristocrat.

DESIREE Well, don't they have bottoms, then?

CAMEMBERT Of course they do, but they don't refer to them as such. Down here they're called country seats.

DESIREE Oh, what do they call them in London?

CAMEMBERT Surely you've heard of the London derrière?

BIDET Psst!

CAMEMBERT What?

BIDET Psst!

CAMEMBERT Don't be ridiculous. I've only had a couple.

CAMEMBERT All men talk nonsense in their cups, Bidet. It's what we call coq-au-vin.

DESIREE Oh, why can't we get back home? I'm fed up with this country. All they seem to want you to do is talk about their parents.

CAMEMBERT What do you mean?

DESIREE Well, I've had dozens of men come up to me and say: 'What about a bit of "How's your father?"'

CAMEMBERT captures the girl that SIR RODNEY loves:

RODNEY . . . Who knows what's happening to her in there! Death . . . or even a fate worse than death.

POMMFRIT Oh, I shouldn't worry. I haven't tried death, but I've tried the other thing. It's not half as bad as they say.

POMMFRIT Well, there we are . . . the Chateau Neuf. Or, as you would call it, Number Nine.

RODNEY It's well named. Won't be easy to take.

Carry On . . . Don't Lose Your Head
Hold on a minute you seconds, this is my darkest hour! Who says the Carry Ons don't give you your actual deep, meaningful drama? Suffering a black moment at first light, a bird called Desiree (Joan Sims) gives out with her own dawn chorus. For she is watching her lover and the man she loves (Desiree is French, so they are not the same man) fight to the death. But though Desiree is crying for duel control, all she gets is this dual control from the fight's seconds—Citizen Bidet (Peter Butterworth) and Lord Darcy (Jim Dale). The off-picture combatants are Kenneth Williams as Citizen Camembert, Head of the Secret Police during the French Revolution, and Sid James as English nobleman Sir Rodney Ffing. Gets you right there, doesn't it?

124

Cast:

Sir Rodney Ffing	Sidney James	Girls	Monica Dietrich
Citizen Camembert	Kenneth Williams		Anna Willoughby
Lord Darcy	Jim Dale		Penny Keen
Duc de Pommfrit	Charles Hawtrey		Christine Pryor
Citizen Bidet	Peter Butterworth		June Cooper
Desiree Dubarry	Joan Sims		Karen Young
Jacqueline	Dany Robin	Guard	Hugh Futcher
Robespierre	Peter Gilmore		
Landlady	Marianne Stone	Produced by	Peter Rogers
Henri	Michael Ward	Directed by	Gerald Thomas
Malabonce (executioner)	Leon Greene	Screenplay by	Talbot Rothwell
Sergeant	David Davenport	Music composed and	
Captain of Soldiers	Richard Shaw	conducted by	Eric Rogers
Second Lady	Valerie Van Ost	Song 'Don't Lose Your	Bill Martin and Phil
First Lady	Jennifer Clulow	Head' by	Coulter
Third Lady	Jacqueline Pearce	Choreographer	Terry Gilbert
Rake	Julian Orchard	Production Manager	Jack Swinburne
Bald-headed Dowager	Joan Ingram	Director of Photography	Alan Hume BSC
Dowager	Elspeth March	Art Director	Lionel Couch
Soldier	Billy Cornelius	Editor	Rod Keys
Messenger	Nikki van der Zyl		
Little Man	Ronnie Brody	Made in the summer–autumn of 1966. Shooting	
Princess Stephanie	Diana Macnamara	began 12 September. At Pinewood Studios,	

Made in the summer–autumn of 1966. Shooting began 12 September. At Pinewood Studios, Waddesdon Manor, Clandon Park and Clivedon.

Carry On . . . Follow That Camel

American comedian Phil Silvers was invited to star in this one—his first British film—in the hope of boosting sales in the United States. (It did not help much.) This film was not originally a Carry On. See under *Carry On Don't Lose Your Head*.

Singer Anita Harris appeared in this one as an Oriental dancer. She turned up for the next film too, *Carry On Doctor*, as a love-lorn nurse. Julian Holloway, son of comedian and actor Stanley Holloway, made his début in the Carry On series (for the film was always a Carry On comedy in everything but name) playing a ticket collector on a train who takes advantage of the beautiful LADY JANE PONSONBY (Angela Douglas) in an empty compartment. First class too! So that's what you pay extra for! Julian Orchard returned for his second Carry On.

During the making of the film a catch-phrase adopted by performers and crew was 'Mustapha Leke'. This is the name of the prophet worshipped by the fierce SHEIKH ABDUL ABULBUL (Bernard Bresslaw) who, claims the sheikh, has ordained the massacre of all legionnaires in the area. ABDUL's followers repeatedly fall to their knees, bowing their heads low in homage, chanting: 'Mustapha Leke . . . Mustapha Leke . . .'. Off the set it was often used as an exit line, with the appropriate salaam, of course.

Carry On . . . Follow That Camel Mind if I cut in! The chap slashing about in the desert is following the call of Mustapha Leke. That is the name of a prophet who has ordained that all French Foreign Legionnaires must die. So Sheik Abdul Abulbul (Bernard Bresslaw), aided by his lieutenant, Riff (Larry Taylor), urges his men to take Fort Zuassantneuf, confident that this will come to pass, for such things are cut and dried in the desert. (The Legionnaires won).

BERTRAM OLIPHANT WEST (Jim Dale) and his manservant SIMPSON (Peter Butterworth) try to join the French Foreign Legion. But BURGER (Kenneth Williams) the Legion's commandant at Sidi-Bel-Abbes thinks they are spies:

BO WEST Spies! How dare you, sir! We are English gentlemen.
BURGER Don't talk to me about your English gentlemens. I have seen what you scribble on the walls of your English gentlemens.

SERGEANT NOCKER (Phil Silvers) after watching exotic dancer CORKTIP (Anita Harris)
NOCKER Hold it, baby. How about giving us the dance of the two veils?
CORKTIP You mean seven veils.
NOCKER Why bother with preliminaries?

BURGER to LADY JANE PONSONBY (Angela Douglas) who has followed Bo West to Africa:
BURGER . . . Out here, it's different. These hot-blooded Arabs, once they get you out amongst the sand dunes, ooh!
JANE Oh, do tell me, what do they do?
BURGER Oh, I cannot tell you. But there's an old Arab saying: 'There's many a good fiddle played on an old dune.'

SHEIKH ABDUL ABULBUL (Bernard Bresslaw) is the sworn enemy of the French Foreign Legion:
ABDUL The infidels will all perish when the second crescent of the moon enters the third phase of Orion.
NOCKER When is that?
ABDUL Tuesday.
   He goes on: (Doesn't he!)
ABDUL First the accursed Legionnaires at Fort Zuassantneuf. And then the infidels at Sidi-Bel-Abbes. It has been ordained by the prophet Mustapha Leke.

BURGER and CAPTAIN LE PICE (Charles Hawtrey) discuss ZIGZIG (Joan Sims) who owns a café full of Eastern promise:
BURGER Zigzig. Er, it's a strange name.
LE PICE It is an old Arabic word for serving woman. Meaning: 'She who handeth it out on a platter.'

Marching across the burning desert, exhausted, without water, SIMPSON (Peter Butterworth) looks up at the ever-circling, ever-waiting vultures:
SIMPSON To hell with you! To hell with all of you! Go on, do your worst. (exclaims) Oh!! (puts hand quickly to eye) Blimey, one of 'em did!
   BURGER and his men are too late to save the distant garrison of Zuassantneuf from the hordes of SHEIKH ABDUL. Now, besieged there themselves, they check the fort's remaining supplies:
BURGER Figs. Dates. Sennapods. Cascara . . .
NOCKER They couldn't have been regular troops, sir.

And later:
NOCKER . . . They've got indigestion tablets, glucose tablets, salt tablets, the pill . . . and . . . the pill? What d'you suppose they used that for?
BURGER I can't conceive! . . .

Well how would you look if somebody said you were going to be shot? Director Gerald Thomas explains a scene to Phil Silvers and Kenneth Williams during the making of *Carry On . . . Follow That Camel* **at Camber Sands, Sussex. Williams admits to 'having a go' at Silvers about his need of a prompt board, but on set all differences were forgotten. In the scene, Silvers as Sergeant Nocker, and Williams, as Commandant Burger, of the French Foreign Legion, are holed up in the fort—in more ways than one. For Williams is peppered with bullets during an Arab attack. When Silvers gives him water, it spurts out of the bullet holes. Don't anybody dare call the Commandant a little squirt! He's the fountainhead. Or is that what they mean by being liquidated?**

Cast:

Sergeant Nocker	Phil Silvers	Harem Girls	Carol Sloan
Commandant Burger	Kenneth Williams		Gina Gianelli
Bo West	Jim Dale		Dominique Don
Captain Le Pice	Charles Hawtrey		Anne Scott
Zigzig	Joan Sims		Margot Maxine
Lady Jane Ponsonby	Angela Douglas		Patsy Snell
Simpson	Peter Butterworth		Zorenah Osborne
Sheikh Abdul Abulbul	Bernard Bresslaw		Karen Young
Corktip	Anita Harris		Gina Warwick
Corporal Clotski	John Bluthal		Angie Grant
Sir Cyril Ponsonby	William Mervyn		Sally Douglas
Captain Bagshaw	Peter Gilmore		Helga Jones
Ticket Collector	Julian Holloway		
Riff	Larry Taylor	Produced by	Peter Rogers
Raff	William Hurndell	Directed by	Gerald Thomas
Manager of Algerian		Screenplay by	Talbot Rothwell
hotel	David Glover	Music composed and	
Doctor	Julian Orchard	conducted by	Eric Rogers
Ship's Officer	Vincent Ball	Belly Dance arranged by	Julie Mendez
Lawrence	Peter Jesson	Production Manager	Jack Swinburne
Spiv	Gertan Klauber	Director of Photography	Alan Hume BSC
Riffs at Abdul's tent	Richard Montez	Art Director	Vetchinsky
	Frank Singuineau	Editor	Alfred Roome BGFE
	Simon Cain		
Butler	Michael Nightingale	Made in the spring of 1967 at Pinewood Studios	
Hotel Gentleman	Harold Kasket	and Camber Sands, Sussex.	
Bowler	Edmund Pegge		

Carry On Doctor

This was Frankie Howerd's first Carry On film. Two years later he starred in another: *Carry On Up The Jungle*. Sid James, who had suffered a heart attack earlier in the year, returned in a smaller, less strenuous, role than usual, comfortably and appropriately playing a patient, CHARLIE ROPER. Barbara Windsor was back for her second Carry On appearance after *Carry On Spying*, made three and a half years earlier. Hattie Jacques returned after four and a half years, having starred in *Carry On Cabby*. Singer Anita Harris turned in her second consecutive Carry On acting performance and Julian Orchard his third. Dandy Nichols, later brilliant as the wife in the TV series *Till Death Us Do Part*, made her Carry On début as MRS ROPER, Sid's nagging wife. Derek Guyler, as a surgeon who leaves a watch inside a patient, and Peter Jones, as a deaf chaplain with a flat battery, also appeared in their first Carry On. A name worth noting is that of Penelope Keith, winner, in 1977, of the 1976 Variety Club Show Business Personality of the Year award and of the British Academy Award for the best light entertainment performer. In 1967 when this film was made she played a part listed merely as 'Plain Nurse'.

Patient KEN BIDDLE (Bernard Bresslaw) to NURSE CLARKE (Anita Harris):
BIDDLE I dreamt about you last night, Nurse.
NURSE CLARKE Did you?
BIDDLE No, you wouldn't let me.

Cheery DR KILMORE (Jim Dale) keeps the patients happy:
KILMORE Did you hear about the pregnant bed-bug?
BIDDLE No.
KILMORE She's having a baby in the spring.

DR TINKLE (Kenneth Williams) and MATRON (Hattie Jacques) examine Biddle:
MATRON I've seldom seen a better appendectomy scar, Doctor.
BIDDLE There's only one thing I don't get, Doctor. Why have I got two other scars? (He points to his

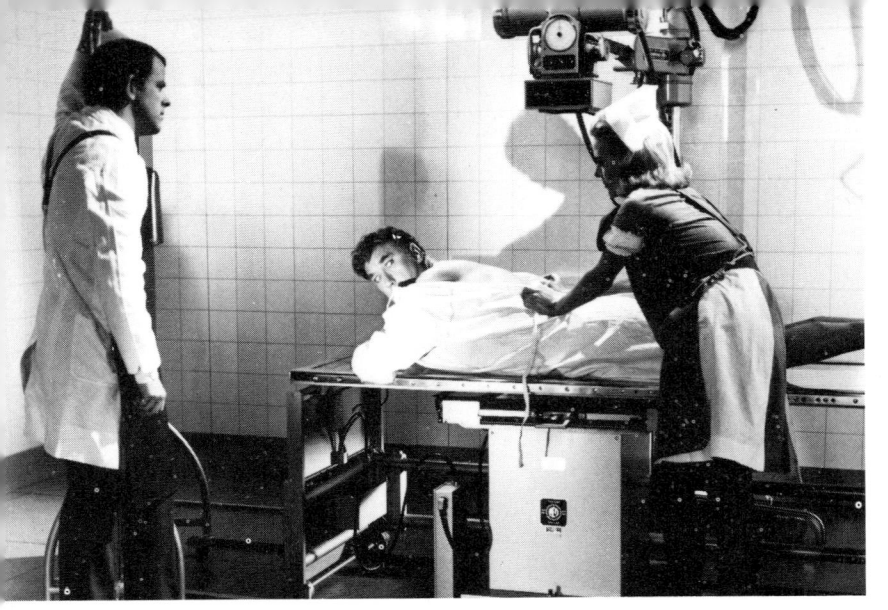

Carry On Doctor What's going on back there? Remember, this is X-ray, not X-certificate! Patient Francis Bigger (Frankie Howerd), about to have the base of his spine X-rayed, watches the birdie (Nurse Parkin—Valerie Van Ost). Bigger doesn't trust hospitals. Bottoms up it may be, but there's nothing going down that hatch! Radiologist Simmons (Julian Holloway) will soon be able to see right through him, however, and note that, despite the back chat, he's a nice chap at base. Here—watch it!

stomach) One here and one here.
DR TINKLE My dear man, an appendix is smaller than a golf ball. And you know how difficult they are to find sometimes.

And later:
Dr Tinkle points at Biddle's foot:
DR TINKLE How long's that cast been on?
MATRON Eight days, Doctor.
DR TINKLE Then, Mr Biddle, in that case, I think it's high time you had it off.
BIDDLE I've been lying here thinking the same thing.

Patient CHARLIE ROPER (Sid James):
MATRON It's certainly a very puzzling case, Doctor.
DR TINKLE It's an enigma. That's what it is, Matron ... an enigma.
ROPER I am not having another one of those!

Patient FRANCIS BIGGER (Frankie Howerd) is having the base of his spine X-rayed. Radiologist SIMMONS (Julian Holloway) goes into action:
SIMMONS Right. Smile please.
BIGGER Smile? What with?
SIMMONS Oh, I'm terribly sorry. Force of habit. You see, before this I used to be a top portrait photographer.
BIGGER Er ... did you? Well, you've reached the bottom now, haven't you?

Visitor CHLOE (Joan Sims) hands some flowers to NURSE CLARKE:
NURSE CLARKE ... Would you like me to put those in a vase for you?
CHLOE Oh yes, thank you so much. Mr Bigger's very fond of fresh flowers, especially chrysanthemums. He's never without a pot by his bed.

DR TINKLE is visited in his room by NURSE SANDRA MAY (Barbara Windsor) who feels she owes him something:
SANDRA Oh, have you forgotten you saved my life?
DR TINKLE All I did was treat you for tonsillitis. It was nothing.
SANDRA You can't kid me. Why, you came to visit me in my room every night for months afterwards.
DR TINKLE That was merely professional courtesy. You were in no danger.
SANDRA No? Then why did you keep giving me the kiss of life?

Enter small boy with chamber pot stuck on his head:
MOTHER They was playing soldiers ...
AMBULANCEMAN SAM He must've been one of the Jerries.
DR KILMORE examines the boy:
DR KILMORE Poor little feller!
MOTHER Never mind 'Poor little feller'. What about his poor grandad? He's bedridden. He relies on that.

MATRON fancies DR TINKLE and pleads her case:
MATRON Young chickens may be soft and tender, but the older birds have more on them.
DR TINKLE True. And take a lot more stuffing.

DR KILMORE is the victim of a misunderstanding—which gets into the newspapers:
ROPER (reading) It says here ... 'He tried to peep at one nurse sunbathing in the semi-nude ... half stripped another. And attacked a third in her bath.' I wonder what he has for breakfast!
BIDDLE defends DR KILMORE:
BIDDLE That's a load of rubbish. Dr Kilmore's not like that.
SMITH We saw him rip her skirt off, didn't we?
BIDDLE Not on purpose. It was an accident.
ROPER That's what I tried to tell my old woman, but I still had to marry her.

DR KILMORE tries to cheer up the patients—again:
DR KILMORE Did you hear about the little boy who swallowed half-a-crown?
ROPER No.
DR KILMORE Two days later his mother phoned the hospital to see how he was and they said, 'There's still no change.'

DR TINKLE ... It's my duty to keep myself fit and strong. You may not realise it, but I was once a weak man.
MATRON Well, once a week's enough for any man.

Cast:

Francis Bigger	Frankie Howerd	Patient	Pat Coombs
Charlie Roper	Sidney James	Second Orderely	Gertan Klauber
Barron	Charles Hawtrey	Simmons	Julian Holloway
Dr Tinkle	Kenneth Williams	Nurse in bath	Jenny White
Dr Kilmore	Jim Dale	Nurse	Helen Ford
Nurse Sandra May	Barbara Windsor	Night Porter	Gordon Rollings
Chloe Gibson	Joan Sims	Tea Orderly	Simon Cain
Ken Biddle	Bernard Bresslaw	Plain Nurse	Penelope Keith
Matron	Hattie Jacques	Women's Ward Nurse	Cheryl Molineaux
Nurse Clarke	Anita Harris	Female Instructor	Alexandra Dane
Mr Smith	Peter Butterworth	Grandad	Bart Allison
Sister Hoggett	June Jago	Nurse	Jane Murdoch
Sir Edmund Burke	Derek Francis	Small Boy	Stephen Garlick
Mrs Roper	Dandy Nichols		
Chaplain	Peter Jones	Produced by	Peter Rogers
Surgeon Hardcastle	Deryck Guyler	Directed by	Gerald Thomas
Mrs Barron	Gwendolyn Watts	Screenplay by	Talbot Rothwell
Mavis	Dilys Laye	Music composed and	
Henry (ambulance man)	Peter Gilmore	conducted by	Eric Rogers
Sam (ambulance man)	Harry Locke	Production Manager	Jack Swinburne
Mum	Marianne Stone	Art Director	Cedric Dawe
Mrs Smith	Jean St. Clair	Director of Photography	Alan Hume BSC
Nurse Parkin	Valerie Van Ost	Editor	Alfred Roome, BGFE
Fred (Biddle's visitor)	Julian Orchard		
Man from Cox & Carter	Brian Wilde		
Patient	Lucy Griffiths		

Made at Pinewood Studios in the autumn of 1967.

Carry On Up The Khyber

This was one of the most successful Carry On films in every way; one of the best scripts, one of the biggest money-spinners, and among the two or three favourites of most of the Carry On team, including producer Peter Rogers and director Gerald Thomas.

The final scenes in which the British Governor, SIR SIDNEY RUFF-DIAMOND (Sid James), his wife LADY JOAN (Joan Sims) and their guests calmly get on with their dinner and their trivial talk, to the background accompaniment of a small orchestra, while Rajah Kenneth Williams, tribal leader Bernard Bresslaw and Indian troops are blowing the building to pieces around them with artillery, is a superb send-up, not only of Hollywood films depicting similar scenes, but of the feeling of superiority, the feeling of rightness, with God on your side, the coolness and the phlegm which all true Britishers were expected to possess at this time in history—about 1895. The scenes are nicely pointed up by Peter Butterworth as a missionary, a normal sort of chap, who is scared out of his wits and thinks they are mad.

Terry Scott, who played a sergeant in the first Carry On film in 1958, was promoted to sergeant-major for his second Carry On ten years later. Roy Castle, made his only Carry On appearance so far, as did comedian Cardew Robinson. Wanda Ventham had her second Carry On role, and Angela Douglas her fourth and, to date, last. Johnny Briggs, had one scene as a soldier. Note also Valerie Leon, now known for her 'Hi Karate' television commercial.

Exterior. Streets. India: A Ceremonial Procession approaching, watched by a crowd.
NARRATOR India—1895. The most precious gem in the far flung belly of the great British Empire. Here the British rulers and their memsahibs enjoy the life of luxury and ease. Matched only by that of the Indian rajahs.

SIR SIDNEY RUFF-DIAMOND (Sid James) and LADY JOAN RUFF-DIAMOND (Joan Sims) are seated in a howdah on an elephant. Onlookers are waving in the background.
NARRATOR None more so than Her Majesty's Governor of the North West Frontier Province, Sir Sidney Ruff-Diamond.

Close-up of the elephant's rump. A nameplate on its rump reads: GB. The elephant passes wind.

Indian rajah, the KHASI OF KALABAR (Kenneth Williams) and his daughter PRINCESS JELHI (Angela Douglas) discuss SIR SIDNEY RUFF-DIAMOND:

JELHI You don't like this man, my Father?
KHASI Light of my Darkness, there is no mountain in all India high enough from which to adequately show my contempt of him.

CAPTAIN KEENE (Roy Castle) The Third Foot and Mouth never wear anything under the kilt. It's part of our glorious tradition. Look at our motto: 'Always ready for action'.

SIR SIDNEY I will go and see the Khasi personally. This calls for a spot of top-level diplomatic bluff. The sort of thing that made our Empire what it is. We're not called John Bull for nothing.

SIR SIDNEY I've got to go to the Khasi.
LADY JOAN Well, you should have gone before tiffin. You know it's very bad . . .
SIR SIDNEY The Khasi of Kalabar.
LADY JOAN Oh! Oh!

SIR SIDNEY . . . Tell Shorthouse to call me an elephant.
LADY JOAN He needn't bother. I will. You're an elephant.

KHASI Your Excellency, your presence enriches my humble home. May the benevolence of the god Shivou bring blessings on your house.
SIR SIDNEY And on yours.
KHASI And may his wisdom bring success in all your undertakings.
SIR SIDNEY And in yours.
KHASI And may his radiance light up your life.
SIR SIDNEY And up yours.

KHASI I see Your Excellency is admiring my trophies.
SIR SIDNEY Yes, they're really

Curry on . . . sorry . . . Carry On Up The Khyber . . . or The British Position in India **Underpants. That is what this top level, political confrontation is about. The scene is the North-West Frontier of India in 1895, and the British Governor, Sir Sidney Ruff-Diamond (Sid James) has put on his best gear to visit the local bigwig, the Khasi of Kalabar (Kenneth Williams), for a below the belt discussion about the underpants of one, Private Widdle (Charles Hawtrey) of the ferocious Highland regiment, The Third Foot and Mouth. You see, the Khasi is keen to be rid of the British but is terrified of The Third Foot and Mouth who are so fearless that they disdain to**

something to be proud of. Camera pans to take in a tiger skin and trophies displayed on the wall.
KHASI Come and take a closer look. It has taken me many years to collect them.
SIR SIDNEY Very impressive, very, very impressive. I . . . I would even go as far as to say you're a bit of a shot.
KHASI I hope I heard you correctly.

LADY JOAN wants the KHASI to make love to her:
KHASI Oh, but you drive an impossible bargain, dear lady. I do not make love.
LADY JOAN You don't?
KHASI No. I am extremely rich. I have servants to do everything for me.

wear anything under their kilts apart from what they have been endowed with by nature. It's a real swinging regiment. But the Khasi has discovered an awful truth. Private Widdle wears underpants. British domination is threatened. The Third Foot and Mouth has put its foot in it. What is more, it is soon to be revealed that Sergeant-Major McNutt (Terry Scott) and Captain Keene (Roy Castle), who have accompanied the Governor, also have a big secret under their kilts. No wonder the Khasi's attitude is one of: 'Knickers!' In those historic words: Winter drawers on for the reign of the British in India . . .

Missionary BELCHER (Peter Butterworth) stands on his dignity:
BELCHER Do you expect me, a missionary to . . . lend myself to such carryings on? My job is to save fallen women.
KEENE I realise that, Mr Belcher.
BELCHER Good! Save me the one with the big ear-rings.

LADY JOAN has dropped a photograph—which the KHASI wants—down her bosom. But warrior chief BUNGHIT DIN (Bernard Bresslaw) is impatient:

Carry On Up The Khyber **One point to us! If this lot look happy enough to be in a laxative commercial, it's because they've got the British on the run! Appropriately, the ribald rajah with the rigid digit is called the Khasi of Kalabar (Kenneth Williams). On the right, with the teeth all ready to be armed-up-to, is tribal leader Bunghit Din (Bernard Bresslaw). They are fighting the disgraced Highland regiment, The Third Foot and Mouth, who recently revealed that they wear drawers. To which the tribesmen replied: 'Up your kilts! We're coming through!' Or words to that effect. They're certainly going at it tooth-and-nail in this picture!**

BUNGHIT DIN Why waste time? Let us take it from her by force.
KHASI That would be unpardonable. In India the cow is sacred.

BROTHER BELCHER chats up BUSTI, an Indian beauty:
BELCHER Well . . . oh . . . what pretty ear-rings! Are they rubies?
BUSTI No! They are mine.

KHASI . . . They will die the death of a thousand cuts.
JELHI Oh, no! Oh, that's horrible.
KHASI Nonsense, child. The British are used to cuts.

LADY JOAN You haven't mentioned the dress.
KHASI Sari.
LADY JOAN Oh, there's no need to apologise.
She runs her finger along the neckline of her sari.
LADY JOAN It's a nice little fringe.
KHASI No, no, no. The garment is called a sari.
Lady Joan laughs.
LADY JOAN Oh yes, of course. Silly me. The sari with the fringe on top!

SIR SIDNEY Under a flag of truce, eh? I wonder what that means?
MAJOR SHORTHOUSE Well sir, it's a piece of white material stuck on a pole . . .
SIR SIDNEY I know what it *is!*

Attacked by the Khasi and hordes of Burpa warriors:
CAPTAIN KEENE What are we going to do?
SIR SIDNEY Do, Captain. We're British, we won't do anything.
MAJOR SHORTHOUSE Till it's too late.

BUNGHIT DIN It is a typical exhibition of the British Phlegm.
KHASI I spit on their British Phlegm.

As the Burpa tribesmen shell the British Governor's residency:
BUNGHIT DIN (to himself) That will teach them to ban turbans on the buses.

As the residency windows are shattered by the attack, plaster falls from the ceiling:
LADY JOAN Oh, I say. The wind seems to be a little strong tonight.

SIR SIDNEY Whose?

SIR SIDNEY We used to know a missionary feller when we were in the Solomon Islands. You remember, dear?
LADY JOAN Oh yes, a splendid man. He went down very well with the natives.
MISSIONARY BELCHER Oh really?
SIR SIDNEY Yes, they ate him.

Through the heavy shellfire from the Indian cannons, as the residency is shot away from around them, the governor, his lady and friends continue, unruffled, with their dinner.
KHASI This is ridiculous! What must one do to arouse these idiots?
BUNGHIT DIN I do not know, Highness.
KHASI A thing like that leaves them unmoved. But put the tea in the cup before the milk, and they go berserk.
BUNGHIT DIN It is like their Sir Francis Drake finishing his bowls.
KHASI Oh, don't talk bowls to me. Kill them! Kill them all!

Cast:

Sir Sidney Ruff-Diamond	Sidney James
The Khasi of Kalabar	Kenneth Williams
Private James Widdle	Charles Hawtrey
Captain Keene	Roy Castle
Lady Joan Ruff-Diamond	Joan Sims
Bunghit Din	Bernard Bresslaw
Brother Belcher	Peter Butterworth
Sergeant-Major Macnutt	Terry Scott
Princess Jelhi	Angela Douglas
The Fakir	Cardew Robinson
Major Shorthouse	Julian Holloway
Ginger	Peter Gilmore
Stinghi	Leon Thau
Wife Number One	Wanda Ventham
Busti	Alexandra Dane
Chindi	Michael Mellinger
Belcher's Indian Girl	Dominique Don
Khasi's Major Domo	Derek Sydney
Burpa Guard	Steven Scott
Bunghit Din's Servant	David Spenser
Wife Number Two	Liz Gold
Wife Number Three	Vicki Woolf
Wife Number Four	Anne Scott
Wife Number Five	Katherina Holden
Wife Number Eight	Lisa Noble
Wife Number Ten	Tamsin MacDonald
Wife Number Eleven	Eve Eden

Wife Number Thirteen	Barbara Evans
Sporran Soldier	Johnny Briggs
Bagpipes Soldier	Simon Cain
Burpa at door grill	Larry Taylor
Burpa in crowd	Patrick Westwood
Burpa on rooftops	John Hallam
Hospitality Girls	Angie Grant, Josephine Blain, Vicki Murden, Carmen Dene, Valerie Leon, June Cooper, Karen Young, Sue Vaughan

Produced by	Peter Rogers
Directed by	Gerald Thomas
Screenplay by	Talbot Rothwell
Narrator	Patrick Allen
Music composed and conducted by	Eric Rogers
Choreographer	Julie Mendez
Production Manager	Jack Swinburne
Art Director	Vetchinsky
Director of Photography	Ernest Steward BSC
Editor	Alfred Roome

Made in the spring of 1968 at Pinewood Studios and in North Wales.

Carry On Camping

This was the first Carry On to dare a flash of bare breast (Barbara Windsor's) and there have been bare boobs (quick glimpses to full exposure), often Barbara Windsor's, in every Carry On since. The tradition-setting scene occurred when Barbara was doing exercises at a camping site and her bra popped off. No wonder it was a box office winner.

But the Carry Ons are not all broad comedy, puns and *double entendres*. There is a well observed, cleverly written scene about a jaded marriage in this film. It involved Terry Scott as PETER POTTER, a bullied, suburban husband whose wife, HARRIET (Betty Marsden), never waited for replies to the questions she asked or listened to anything he said. So, in his unassuming way, he challenged her, sending her up with outrageous replies, spoken in a casual manner.

For example: Potter arrives home from the office (complete with bowler hat, sober suit, brief case, umbrella) to find his wife checking their camping equipment. They always have camping holidays because she likes them:
HARRIET Had a good day?
POTTER Oh, not bad. Got drunk at lunchtime, went to a strip club . . . and finished up in bed with a popsie.
HARRIET Oh look, there's a hole in this tent flap . . .
And later:
HARRIET Did you have a good day?
POTTER Not bad. No, no. Another chap came into the office with a pound of opium. Then we smoked it and we spent the afternoon in a harem.

HARRIET Oh Peter, I've been thinking. We ought to try Devon again this year. We had such a marvellous time there last time. And so on . . .

Sid Boggle (Sid James) and his girlfriend Joan Fussey (Joan Sims) are watching—and arguing about—a nudist film:
SID Oh, you wouldn't think anything of it if we were walking around like that all the time. Free, unfettered, unashamed.
JOAN Oh no! I suppose you'd rather we sat here all stark naked?
SID Wouldn't bother me.
JOAN It would if your ice lolly fell in your lap.

PETER (Terry Scott) and HARRIET POTTER (Betty Marsden) are getting ready for a camping holiday:
HARRIET We mustn't forget to take a good supply of toilet paper this time, you know what happened last year.

Carry On Camping . . . or Let Sleeping Bags Lie **They're living hand to mouth on a camping holiday! You've heard of the ground-to-air missile—well here's a ground-to-air Miss. She is Anthea Meeks (Dilys Laye). What you might call a hand-maiden. Certainly a maiden, as for most of the film she keeps boyfriend Bernie Lugg (Bernard Bresslaw) at arm's length. But Anthea has decided, at last, that she's a big girl now, and ready to be swept off her feet. In fact she's up in arms at all the time she's wasted!**

POTTER Yes. We had nothing to write to your mother on.

CHARLIE MUGGINS (Charles Hawtrey) meets a farm girl leading a cow:
CHARLIE What's a nice girl like you doing with an old cow?
FARM GIRL I'm taking her to the bull.
CHARLIE To the bull. Oh! Couldn't your father do that?
FARM GIRL No, it has to be the bull.

Farmer to daughter who is pregnant by an unknown man:
FARMER All that money I spent on a posh education trying to make a lady out of you, and you haven't even got the manners to ask: 'With whom am I having the pleasure?'

DR SOAPER (Kenneth Williams), Headmaster of the Chayste Place Finishing School for Young Ladies is teaching his girls how to erect a tent:
DR SOAPER Get your frames up first, then canvas later. And there's bedding and bunks by the coach. No, no Barbara! Tent up first. Bunk up later.

SID and BERNIE (Bernard Bresslaw) are on a camping holiday at the same camp as Dr Soaper's young ladies. They especially have eyes for BABS (Barbara Windsor) and FANNY (Sandra Caron):
BERNIE Frustrated? What do you mean, you feel frustrated?
SID What did Fiddler say to you yesterday when you asked him for some eggs?
BERNIE He said he was not getting any.
SID Exactly. Six days we've been here now, and those birds are dead ready to be friendly.
BERNIE Oh, they're friendly all right. Mr Fiddler says they're just not laying.
SID Not the bloomin' chickens. I mean . . . Babs and . . . (indicates shape of woman with his hands) . . . the other.
BERNIE Fanny.
SID Yeah, that's it.

SID and BERNIE's regular girlfriends, JOAN and ANTHEA (Dilys Laye) are looking at postcards on sale at a monastery:

JOAN Oh, I like this one of the monks doing their laundry.

ANTHEA Oh, lovely!

BERNIE I suppose that's where they get rid of their dirty habits.

JOAN That is not very funny, Bernie. Has Sid got a ... Well, where is he? Where's Sid?

BERNIE Oh, he's just crept into the crypt for a ... smoke.

Carry On Camping Hands, knees ... and oops-a-daisy! There's a case to answer for here. The one in the hands of teenage schoolgirl Fanny (Sandra Caron) to be precise. Coach driver Jim Tanner (Julian Holloway) tripped over the case at a hostel, while taking the Chayste Place Finishing School for Young Ladies on a camping holiday, and accidentally ripped off the nightie of schoolgirl Babs (Barbara Windsor). At that moment, Matron Miss Haggerd (Hattie Jacques) rumbled into sight. So while Babs' appearance may be brief, Jim's breath is in short pants too!

Cast:

Sid Boggle	Sidney James
Charlie Muggins	Charles Hawtrey
Joan Fussey	Joan Sims
Dr Soaper	Kenneth Williams
Peter Potter	Terry Scott
Babs	Barbara Windsor
Miss Haggerd	Hattie Jacques
Bernie Lugg	Bernard Bresslaw
Jim Tanner	Julian Holloway
Anthea Meeks	Dilys Laye
Joshua Fiddler	Peter Butterworth
Harriet Potter	Betty Marsden
Sally	Trisha Noble
Mrs Fussey	Amelia Bayntun
Store Manager	Brian Oulton
Farmer's Daughter	Patricia Franklin
Farmer	Derek Francis
Man in cinema	Michael Nightingale
Jane	Elizabeth Knight
Scrawny Man	George Moon
Fanny	Sandra Caron
Pat	Valerie Shute
Joy	Georgina Moon
Verna	Vivien Lloyd
Hilda	Jennifer Pyle
Norma	Lesley Duff
Betty	Jackie Poole
Hefty Girl	Anna Karen
Girl with cow	Sally Kemp
Store Assistant	Valerie Leon
Commentator	Peter Cockburn
Lusty Youths	Michael Low
	Mike Lucas
Sally G-String	Gilly Grant
Produced by	Peter Rogers
Directed by	Gerald Thomas
Screenplay by	Talbot Rothwell
Music composed and conducted by	Eric Rogers
Production Manager	Jack Swinburne
Art Director	Lionel Couch
Director of Photography	Ernest Steward BSC
Editor	Alfred Roome

Made in the autumn of 1968 at Pinewood Studios and in a flooded field several hundred yards away.

Carry On Again Doctor

This was Jim Dale's tenth and last Carry On film. After this he decided to aim his career in other directions, later working with Sir Laurence Olivier at the National Theatre in London, and now spending much of his time in Hollywood starring in films for the Walt Disney company. He also starred in the Tony Richardson romp, *Joseph Andrews* released in 1977.

Patsy Rowlands made her début into the Carry On series playing MISS FOSDICK, secretary to a senior surgeon (played by Kenneth Williams). She also played Kenneth Williams' secretary in *Carry On At Your Convenience*. Wilfrid Brambell had a guest spot in *Carry On Again Doctor* as a patient with a roving eye (and two roving hands) for a pretty nurse.

DR CARVER (Kenneth Williams) and DR STOPPIDGE (Charles Hawtrey) talk shop:
CARVER She's a rather wealthy private patient of mine. I took her appendix out the other day.
STOPPIDGE I hope you both had a nice time.

DR NOOKEY (Jim Dale) tends patient MRS BEASLEY (Patricia Hayes):
MRS BEASLEY Doctor, I never told you about the rheumatism in my right leg.

NOOKEY Well, there's nothing to worry about, Mrs Beasley, it's just old age.
MRS BEASLEY But my left leg's as old. I don't get no rheumatism in that.

DR CARVER and wealthy MRS MOORE (Joan Sims)
MRS MOORE Be honest now. Do I look like a woman of forty?
CARVER You really feel as young as that?
MRS MOORE No, that's what I am!

And later:
MRS MOORE ... Oh, they told me you were a wonderful surgeon.
CARVER Well, I suppose I am a cut above the rest!

And later:
CARVER For many years now... I've had a dream. A dream of something that would bring hope and comfort to millions of suffering people. The 'Frederick Carver Foundation'.
MRS MOORE What's that? Some sort of corset?
CARVER No, no! A private clinic!

DR NOOKEY and model GOLDIE LOCKS (Barbara Windsor):
NOOKEY Do you realise we've known each other for what... four whole weeks now?
GOLDIE Yeah. Do you think that's a record?
NOOKEY Well, I don't know. It's the longest I've been out with a girl without... well, getting somewhere.
GOLDIE What do you mean, without getting somewhere? We went to Bognor last Sunday.

DR NOOKEY is banished to a medical mission on a remote Pacific island and meets the resident orderly, GLADSTONE SCREWER (Sid James), who tells him about the island:
NOOKEY Marvellous! Rain for nine months, hurricanes for three.
GLADSTONE Yeah. That's why the natives call these islands 'Orlpice na

Carry On Again Doctor When nobody wants you ... hic! Because of machinations by superiors in England, Dr James Nookey (Jim Dale) has been banished to a medical mission on a tropical island which is so primitive there are not even eight gramophone records. So he tries to keep his spirits up by getting plenty of spirits down—encouraged by Sid James as the mission's orderly, Gladstone Screwer, a liberal-minded twister who lives off the fat of the land, including five overweight wives. Because Screwer does not want a new boss spoiling his easy life he is plotting to have luckless Jim shipped back to England as drunk and incompetent. Go on ... one more for the road!

Fa-Fah'. All rain and wind.

And later, DR NOOKEY meets some island women:

NOOKEY Your wives?
GLADSTONE Only these five here. Come on, I'll introduce you. Here we are. There's Monday . . . Tuesday . . . Wednesday . . . Thursday. And last but definitely not least . . .
NOOKEY Friday.
GLADSTONE That's it.
NOOKEY Well, I'll be damned! At least you've got no problem with what to do with your spare time.
GLADSTONE Well, I don't know. There's not much doing at the weekend.

DR NOOKEY checks the laboratory equipment:

NOOKEY It's a good skeleton. Did the last doctor leave it here?
GLADSTONE That is the last doctor.

Suddenly the native drums start up. GLADSTONE listens, and a look of horror crosses his face:
NOOKEY Well . . . well, what's up?
GLADSTONE Manchester United, six—Chelsea, one. Arsenal, five—Wolves, nil.

NOOKEY is shown a liquid, allegedly prepared by a witch doctor on the island, which can make people lose excess weight almost overnight. He sees the profits from such a discovery back in the civilised world:
NOOKEY . . . Gladstone, how does he make that stuff?

GLADSTONE Oh, a little juice from the banyan tree. Powdered parrot droppings; little gnat's milk.
NOOKEY D'you think I could make it?
GLADSTONE Oh no. There's a definite art to it. Have you ever tried to milk a gnat?

NOOKEY sets up a luxury clinic in England, but GLADSTONE follows him. Complains MATRON (Hattie Jacques):
MATRON Look, all he seems to think about is whiskey and sex.
NOOKEY Well, where he comes from they can't get soda.

Cast:

Gladstone Screwer	Sidney James	Nurse Willing	Elizabeth Knight
Dr Frederick Carver	Kenneth Williams	Stout Woman	Alexandra Dane
Dr Ernest Stoppidge	Charles Hawtrey	Henry	Peter Gilmore
Dr James Nookey	Jim Dale	Miss Armitage	Pat Coombs
Mrs Ellen Moore	Joan Sims	Mrs Beasley	Patricia Hayes
Goldie Locks	Barbara Windsor	Lord Paragon	William Mervyn
Matron	Hattie Jacques	Old Lady in headphones	Lucy Griffiths
Miss Fosdick	Patsy Rowlands	Porter	Harry Locke
Male Patient	Peter Butterworth (guest appearance)	Night Sister (women's ward)	Gwendolyn Watts
Mr Pullen (patient)	Wilfrid Brambell (guest appearance)	Deirdre (posh secretary)	Valerie Leon
		Porter	Frank Singuineau

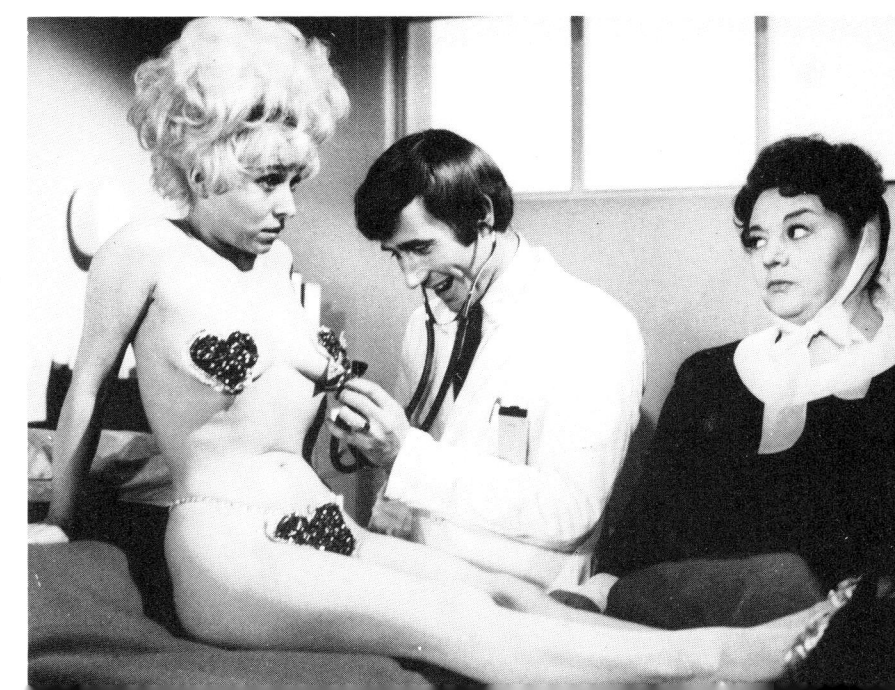

Carry On Again Doctor . . . or Where There's A Pill There's A Way . . . or The Bowels Are Ringing . . . or If You Say It's Your Thermometer I'll Have To Believe You, But It's A Funny Place To Put It **Say aaahhh! Only this time it's the doctor, not the patient, saying it! Doctor James Nookey (Jim Dale) was sighing over a pin-up picture on a calendar in the casualty department of Long Hampton Hospital when (oh, lucky Nookey!) there was that very pin-up peach, Miss Goldie Locks (Barbara Windsor), being carried in on a stretcher after falling off a large packet of Bristol's Bouncing Baby Food while posing for an advertisement. But if Nookey has got Miss Locks in his stethoscopic sights, Matron (Hattie Jacques) has got his thoughts pretty well diagnosed . . . for now and the immediate future. (Oh, unlucky Nookey!)**

Out-Patients Sister	Valerie Van Ost	Trolley Nurse	Yutta Stensgaard
Patient in plaster	Billy Cornelius	Waiter	George Roderick
X-ray Man	Simon Cain	Night Nurse	Jenny Counsell
Hospital Board Member	Elspeth March	Stunt Orderly	Rupert Evans
Nurse	Valerie Shute		
Patient	Ann Lancaster	Produced by	Peter Rogers
Scrubba	Shakira Baksh (Miss Guyana in 1967 Miss World contest)	Directed by	Gerald Thomas
		Screenplay by	Talbot Rothwell
		Music composed and conducted by	Eric Rogers
Men's Ward Nurse	Georgina Simpson		
Berkeley Matron	Faith Kent	Production Manager	Jack Swinburne
Mr Bean	Frank Forsyth	Art Director	John Blezard
Patient	Donald Bissett	Director of Photography	Ernest Steward BSC
New Matron	Ambrosine Phillpotts	Editor	Alfred Roome
Patient	Bob Todd		
Plump Native Girl	Heather Emmanuel	Made in the spring of 1969 at Pinewood Studios.	

Carry On Up The Jungle

Originally to be called 'Carry On Jungle Boy', the title was changed after shooting. Frankie Howerd returned and Kenneth Connor made his first Carry On for five years (since *Carry On Cleo*) having not appeared in the previous eight. Jim Dale turned down the part of Jungle Boy, which went to Terry Scott. The idea to feature a group of beautiful, but tough, Amazon girls, first used in *Carry On Spying*, was again included and Valerie Leon, appearing in her fourth consecutive Carry On film, played their leader. Twenty-three year old Jacki Piper became the latest Carry On glamour girl, though she begins the film as a dowdy secretary/maid, but blossoms in the heat and primitiveness of the jungle. Cor! She went on to have roles in *Carry On Loving*, *Carry On At Your Convenience* and *Carry On Matron*. Note Nina Baden-Semper, later a star of the hit television series *Love Thy Neighbour*, in a small part as a member of a cannibal tribe.

One of the funniest Carry On scenes occurs in this film when LADY EVELYN BAGLEY (Joan Sims) is at a table with BILL BOOSEY (Sid James), PROFESSOR TINKLE (Frankie Howerd) and CLAUDE CHUMLEY (Kenneth Connor), having a meal. A snake crawls up between her legs and reacting not unpleasantly, LADY EVELYN assumes that one of the men is caressing her. As they all have their hands beneath the table she looks at them in turn. BILL BOOSEY winks and she mouths the words: 'Naughty boy.' But when he puts his hands in his pockets and the caressing continues, she turns to PROFESSOR TINKLE, who smiles:

TINKLE Is there something wrong, my dear?
EVELYN No! No, no, no, it's . . . it's quite all right.
TINKLE laughs.

TINKLE Er . . . a little more?
EVELYN I don't mind.
TINKLE Of course!
He then pours her some wine.
As the caressing is going on, Lady Evelyn turns with a frown to Chumley, whom she does not like.
CHUMLEY Lovely, isn't it? (Meaning the wine)
EVELYN I . . . can't say I'm enjoying it, Mr Chumley.
She then slaps the surprised Chumley across the face and stands up. As the caressing still goes on, the truth dawns and she runs off screaming.
BOOSEY I wonder what's up with her?
TINKLE Well, I don't know. But whatever it is, it's certainly rubbed her up the wrong way.
Fade out.

A strange assortment of people trek through the jungle. They are on a twin mission: to find the rare oozulum bird and to find the missing husband and son of LADY EVELYN BAGLEY. Suddenly big game hunter BILL BOOSEY (Sid James) freezes, looks at PROFESSOR TINKLE (Frankie Howerd) and the rest of the party, then points at the ground ahead:
BOOSEY See all that? Elephants!
TINKLE (affronted) Well, I didn't think it was ours.

CLAUDE CHUMLEY (Kenneth Connor), TINKLE's assistant, finds a glove lost by LADY EVELYN (Joan Sims):

CHUMLEY It's a great pleasure to be of service, ma'am. After all, we have travelled together a thousand miles now.

EVELYN Yes, I know that, Mr Chumley. But I shall not be requiring a thousand mile service. Thank you.

EVELYN . . . I am a bit disappointed we've not seen any monkeys so far.
BOOSEY Oh, you won't. They're very busy. It's the mating season.
EVELYN Oh, I see. Would they come if I threw them some peanuts, d'you think?
BOOSEY Would you?

Then:
EVELYN That is a very big one you have there, is it not, Mr Boosey?
BOOSEY Eh? Oh, this!
He holds up the rifle.
BOOSEY Yes. Well, er . . . I'm going hunting, you see. I'll see if I can bag something for supper.
EVELYN I see. Game?
BOOSEY Any time. If you are.

TINKLE You don't find golden crested tits here in Africa. An occasional black one, maybe.

PROFESSOR TINKLE watches, with growing passion, as LADY EVELYN takes a shower:
TINKLE (to himself) That's enough. You're getting too excited. Take something, man, take something. What?
He turns to a first aid box, opens it and takes out a bottle.
TINKLE (to himself) No!
He puts it back and takes out another bottle.
TINKLE (to himself) What's this? (reading label) 'Pickett's Muscular Elixir. Eases Stiffness'. Just the thing!

PROFESSOR TINKLE discusses BILL BOOSEY:
TINKLE My dear Lady Bagley, we must face up to it, the man is simply not a gentleman. I understand . . . he sleeps in his vest!

EVELYN Oh, but sleeping in just a vest . . . displays a sense of individuality, surely.
TINKLE It displays a great deal more than that.

EVELYN Night draws on, you know.
TINKLE Oh, how sensible of you to bring a pair.

BOOSEY . . . if there's one thing that drives a lion stark raving mad, it's being disturbed when he's with a lioness.
EVELYN Oh, do they charge?
BOOSEY Oh, no. They do it for love.

EVELYN But what I wanted to know was . . . if one came in close contact with a snake, could it harm one?
TINKLE Oh, that would depend on the snake. You see, there's a brown one, the African viper, which is very deadly . . .
EVELYN Oh, no, no, this one was definitely green.
TINKLE Ah!
EVELYN And it sort of moved . . . (She waves her hand backward and forward) . . . like that.
TINKLE Ah, that would be the vindscreen viper. Quite harmless.

TINKLE No, don't tell me. I'm flabbergasted. My ghast has never been so flabbered.

EVELYN You would need to be . . . very circumspect.
TINKLE Oh, I was, when I was a baby.

Carry On Up The Jungle **Honestly, sometimes I could explode! Big game hunter Bill Boosey (Sid James) feels he is a voice crying in the wilderness. The party of travellers he is guiding now look as if they need jungle potty training! For even when the smallest room stretches beyond the horizon on all sides, members of his party manage to take the same relief road, as it were, at the same time and, in the dark, scare the shakes out of each other! No need to spend a penny for big-shot Bill's thoughts. Even the look of his native helper Upsidasi (Bernard Bresslaw) says: 'Oh dear, what can the matter be . . .'**

BOOSEY Leave the tents and stores. We'll travel with bare essentials.
TINKLE What? I'm not baring my essentials.

African guide UPSIDASI (Bernard Bresslaw) warns of an attack by Nosha warriors:
UPSIDASI Boss. Boss, there are many Noshas coming.
BOOSEY How many?
UPSIDASI Oh! As many as teeth in a mouth of a crocodile.
BOOSEY Well, how many's that?
UPSIDASI Don't know. Nobody ever stopped long enough to count them.

Captured by the Noshas, the expedition stands before the Nosha idol Tum Tum.
WITCH DOCTOR (chanting) Tum Tum! Tum Tum!
NOSHA WARRIORS (chanting) Tum Tum! Tum Tum!
TINKLE Tum Tum?
UPSIDASI That their god, Boss.
TINKLE Oh, I see. The head of the corporation.

And later:
CHUMLEY What's that big pot?
TINKLE Probably flatulence.
CHUMLEY No, that stewing pot.

TINKLE They can't possibly do this

Carry On Up The Jungle . . . or The African Queens . . . or Stop Beating About The Bush . . . or Show Me Your Waterhole And I'll Show You Mine

You'd be grinning too if you were Tonka, King of Lovers, Master of Women, Father of Countless, the only man among a tribe of 400 women—especially when Leda (Valerie Leon), on the left, is a sample of those women. Charles Hawtrey plays Tonka, who is really the longtime missing Sir Walter Bagley. As you may guess from her expression, that is Sir Walter's wife, Lady Evelyn (Joan Sims) on the right, who has just found him in this passion paradise after worrying about him for years. Oh mate, wait until she gets you home!

to us. After all, we are . . . British subjects.

BOOSEY They've got no taste, these people. They'll eat anything.

TINKLE Oh, the indignity of it all! I, Professor Tinkle, ornithologist, trussed like a chicken!

BOOSEY Just keep hoping they don't like stuffing.

They are rescued by LEDA (Valerie Leon) and her all-woman tribe from the province of Afrodisia. LEDA explains:

LEDA . . . there are no men in Afrodisia, only women.

CHUMLEY No men!

LEDA For some reason, for the last hundred years we have borne nothing but girl children. The last man died ten years ago.

CHUMLEY I can guess what of.

LADY EVELYN's long-lost husband, SIR WALTER, is found to be the chief of this all-woman tribe, and is now called: Tonka, King of Lovers, Master of Women and Father of Countless. The role is played by Charles Hawtrey who explains the system to the expedition:

BOOSEY Do you mean we get lumbered with just one woman?

WALTER That's right. Until tomorrow, then you have an automatic divorce, and marry another one.

TINKLE Another one!

WALTER That's right. And then, the following day, another and so on and so on . . .

TINKLE Yes. Well, after two weeks of that it'll *need* sewing on.

But the men soon revolt against this mass mating:

BOOSEY I tell you one thing we can do. We can go on strike.

LEDA Strike? What is the meaning of this?

TINKLE We down tools.

But LEDA is not that easily beaten:

LEDA We have ways of making people work . . . Like this for example. Fresh oysters from our lake.

BOOSEY Oysters. They're no good.

LEDA They're known to be highly beneficial.

BOOSEY Rubbish! I had a dozen last night and only five of them worked.

Then CHUMLEY cracks:

CHUMLEY I can't go through any more. I've got to get out of here. Let me out! Let me out!

TINKLE Chumley, control yourself. Chumley, Chumle . . . ey . . . ey . . . ey.

CHUMLEY I can't help it, sir, I've come to the end of my tether.

TINKLE Oh, you're lucky. I can't even find mine.

CHUMLEY It's like a factory. An endless belt.

There is only one solution:

CHUMLEY Can't we make a run for . . . Can't we make a crawl for it? Anything will be better than this.

Cast:			
Professor Tinkle	Frankie Howerd	Lubi Lieutenant	Cathi March
Bill Boosey	Sidney James	Nosha Chief	Danny Daniels
Tonka	Charles Hawtrey	Witch Doctor	Yemi Ajibadi
Lady Evelyn Bagley	Joan Sims	Gong Lubi	Verna Lucille
Jungle Boy	Terry Scott		MacKenzie
Claude Chumley	Kenneth Connor	Pregnant Lubi	Heather Emmanuel
Upsidasi	Bernard Bresslaw	Nosha with Girl	Lincoln Webb
June	Jackie Piper	Noshas	Roy Stewart
Leda	Valerie Leon		John Hamilton
Gorilla	Reuben Martin		Chris Konyils
Nerda	Edwina Carroll		Willie Jonah
Lubi Lieutenant	Valerie Moore		Nina Baden-Semper

Produced by	Peter Rogers	Art Director	Vetchinsky
Directed by	Gerald Thomas	Director of Photography	Ernest Steward BSC
Screenplay by	Talbot Rothwell	Editor	Alfred Roome.
Music composed and conducted by	Eric Rogers	Made in the autumn of 1969 at Pinewood Studios.	
Production Manager	Jack Swinburne		

Carry On Loving

This was one of the half-dozen most immediately successful Carry Ons at the box office. Bill Maynard made his début with this one, as did the late James Beck and Bill Pertwee, later best known for their roles in the hit television series *Dad's Army*. Note also Kenny Lynch as a bus conductor, and Lauri Lupino Lane. Sid James and Hattie Jacques played husband and wife in three Carry On films—though for most of this one they are not legally wed. The other two were: *Carry On Cabby* and *Carry On At Your Convenience*.

Reprehending BISHOP to dashing bachelor TERENCE PHILPOT (Terry Scott):
BISHOP ... you've been a guest in that gentleman's house for the weekend and you tell him to his face that his wife makes love magnificently?
PHILPOT Yes. That's right.
BISHOP But ... but ... do you think that's quite correct?
PHILPOT Well, no. Not exactly, no. But he's such a nice chap, I wouldn't like to say anything to offend him.

BUS CONDUCTOR (to snogging couples) Going all the way?

SIDNEY BLISS (Sid James) runs a marriage bureau and outlines the terms to customer BERTIE MUFFET (Richard O'Callaghan):
SID ... two guineas registration. Two guineas for the introduction. And two guineas when you click.
BERTIE Click?
SID Get married. And if you click without getting married, it's four guineas. All right?

MALE CLIENT The first wife died from eating mushrooms.
SID Oh, I'm sorry to hear that.
MALE CLIENT So was she. Second wife died from ... a fractured skull.
SID Fractured skull? How did that happen?
MALE CLIENT Wouldn't eat the mushrooms.

SID watches two girls in mini skirts:
SID (to himself) Oh! If they get any shorter, they'll have two more cheeks to powder.

ESME CROWFOOT (Joan Sims) throws herself at PERCIVAL SNOOPER (Kenneth Williams):
ESME I'm yours. You know it. Take me.
SNOOPER I don't want you. Stop it! Stop it at once!
ESME Oh no, you ... found someone else. I know it. I can feel it.
SNOOPER Well, stop feeling it.

Cast:			
Sidney Bliss	Sidney James	Esme Crowfoot	Joan Sims
Percival Snooper	Kenneth Williams	Sophie	Hattie Jacques
James Bedsop	Charles Hawtrey	Terence Philpot	Terry Scott
		Bertie Muffet	Richard O'Callaghan

Carry On Loving ... or It's Not What You Feel, It's The Way That You Feel It ... or Two's Company But Three's Quite Good Fun Too ... or Love Is A Four Letter Word ... or It's Just One Thing On Top Of Another **Oops, false alarm! Fashionable, randy Terence Philpot (Terry Scott) goes back to the flat of curvy Jenny Grubb (Imogen Hassall) planning a night of lustful developments. A succession of surprises, however, heralded by this false start, and ending with somebody threatening suicide, turn his plans to farce and frustration. The 'falsies', which he discovered under a cushion, belong to one of Jenny's flatmates. Well, they're obviously not hers! You couldn't describe Jenny as a *flat* mate!**

Gripper Burke	Bernard Bresslaw	Barman	Bill Pertwee
Sally Martin	Jacki Piper	Cousin Wilberforce	
Jenny Grubb	Imogen Hassall	Grubb	Colin Vancao
Adrian	Julian Holloway	Window Dresser	Gavin Reed
Mrs Grubb	Joan Hickson	Second	Joe Cornelius
Miss Dempsey	Patsy Rowlands	Maitre d'Hotel	Len Lowe
Gay	Janet Mahoney	Taxi Driver	Fred Griffiths
Aunt Victoria Grubb	Ann Way	Henry	Ronnie Brody
Mr Dreery	Bill Maynard	Bus Conductor	Kenny Lynch
Uncle Ernest Grubb	Gordon Richardson	Mr Thrush	Norman Chappell
Corset Lady	Amelia Bayntun	Mr Roxby	James Beck
Girl (lover)	Valerie Shute	Mrs Roxby	Yutte Stensgaard
Boy (lover)	Michael Grady	Policeman	Robert Russell
Trainer	Tom Clegg	Marriage Bureau Client	Peter Butterworth
Woman	Lucy Griffiths	(Mushrooms)	(guest appearance)
Lavatory Attendant	Harry Shacklock		
Man in hospital	Anthony Sagar	Produced by	Peter Rogers
Bishop	Derek Francis	Directed by	Gerald Thomas
Emily	Alexandria Dane	Screenplay by	Talbot Rothwell
Robinson	Philip Stone	Music composed and	
Violinist	Sonny Farrar	conducted by	Eric Rogers
Mrs Dreery	Patricia Franklin	Production Manager	Jack Swinburne
Grandma Grubb	Hilda Barry	Art Director	Lionel Couch
Pianist	Josie Bradly	Director of Photography	Ernest Steward BSC
Grandpa Grubb	Bart Allison	Editor	Alfred Roome
Wife	Anna Karen		
Aunt Beatrice Grubb	Dorothea Phillips	Made in the spring of 1970 at Pinewood Studios	
Husband	Lauri Lupino Lane	and Ealing.	

Carry On Henry

The original subtitle was 'Anne Of A Thousand Lays' but 'Mind My Chopper' was substituted after filming. The publicity slogan of the film was 'A Great Guy With His Chopper', showing Sid James as HENRY VIII holding an executioner's axe. Sid's costume as HENRY was the one previously worn by Richard Burton in *Anne Of A Thousand Days*.

David Essex, before he became one of Britain's leading pop stars, had a bit part in this one as a page boy, though he never appeared on the screen. His role was cut out during editing.

The Queen gave permission for some filming to take place in the Long Walk at Windsor Castle, and elsewhere, including a scene of HENRY setting out on a hunting trip, during which he forsakes the deer in the woods for another little dear in a barn (Margaret Nolan).

The serious, and unpleasant, aspect of execution was not always successfully blended with the comedy and an unusual feature was that one of the leading players (Joan Sims as QUEEN MARIE) became pregnant after alleged adultery. Usually in a Carry On they either simply talk about carrying on or get interrupted before they go beyond the kissing stage. Other exceptions are *Carry On . . . Follow That Camel* in which Angela Douglas, as Jim Dale's wife, presents

Carry On Henry . . . or Mind My Chopper Without embroidering the facts, this is a meeting in a threadbare cellar to put in the needle against Henry VIII. You're getting the pattern, are you? That's Sir Hampton of Wick (Kenneth Connor) in the middle, leader of a gay band of anti-king rebels. He is cottoning on to a tangled skein to abduct the king, which is being laid before him by Thomas Cromwell (Kenneth Williams). The chap with the needlework is Fawkes (Bill Maynard), quite a guy (if that's the right word), who is also getting the thread of it. Indeed, the whole thing seems to be sewn up . . . ready to have you in stitches.

him with a son who looks just like Kenneth Williams, and *Carry On England* where it is very plain that more than necking is going on.

In *Carry On Henry*, scriptwriter Talbot Rothwell gives the monarch two more wives—MARIE, and BETTINA (Barbara Windsor).

This film is based on a recently discovered manuscript by one William Cobbler which reveals the fact that Henry VIII did in fact have two more wives. Although it was at first thought that Cromwell originated the story, it is now known to be definitely all Cobbler's . . . from beginning to end.

KING HENRY (Sid James) to his lord chancellor, SIR THOMAS CROMWELL (Kenneth Williams) about his latest queen:
HENRY . . . Every time I felt like it, it was 'Oh not tonight dear. I've got a headache, I've got a bellyache . . .'
CROMWELL No wonder Your Majesty did not consummate the marriage.
HENRY Yeah, marvellous, innit? After six months of married life, the only thing I'm having off is her head.

The KING has remarried.
CROMWELL and CARDINAL WOLSEY (Terry Scott) drink to the marriage 'and an early issue'.
WOLSEY To issue!
CROMWELL Issue!
WOLSEY All fall down!

CROMWELL . . . the queen has vowed to remain in her room until she's no longer a virgin.
WOLSEY Poor, dear woman! Perhaps I could do something . . . to get her down. By way of verbal persuasion I mean!
CROMWELL Any kind of persuasion from you would get anybody down.

Eventually the queen—QUEEN MARIE (Joan Sims) comes down to dinner:
WOLSEY A drink, ma'am?
MARIE Thank you.
WOLSEY I can heartily recommend the porter here.
MARIE Really? Then, do send him up to my room later.

HENRY wants the skirt of his latest outfit made shorter, and explains to his tailor:
HENRY We're proud of our royal legs, Moisha. We like the ladies of the Court to marvel at their length.
TAILOR Your Majesty, I make the skirt any higher and . . . they won't be marvelling at the length of the legs.
HENRY Oh, that reminds me. I need

a bit more length on my hose.
TAILOR Ah! Your Majesty is much too modest.

CROMWELL thinks of a new tax:
CROMWELL . . . SET
HENRY SET?
CROMWELL Sex Enjoyment Tax.
HENRY Sex Enjoyment Tax?
CROMWELL Exactly, Your Majesty. Like drinking or smoking. Every time they have one . . .
HENRY Yes, that could bring in quite a bit. Might be a bit difficult to apply, though.
CROMWELL Oh, I don't think so. No man wants to be thought lacking. We give them a form and they submit some sort of . . . weekly return.
HENRY Do you think they'd stand for it?
CROMWELL Oh, stand for it, sit for it, lie down for it, what's it matter, as long as we get the money!

HENRY suspects his equerry, SIR ROGER DE LODGERLEY (Charles Hawtrey) of making the QUEEN pregnant:
HENRY Well, Sir Roger? Have you been dallying with the Queen . . . perhaps?
ROGER Certainly not, Sire.
HENRY Your hand on it.
ROGER Not even a finger on it.

MARIE Thomas Cromwell, you are a cruel man.
CROMWELL Me cruel, ma'am! Why, I'm known as Cromwell the Considerate.
MARIE Considerate! You! What about all those poor martyrs you had burnt at the stake last week? CROMWELL Well, what about them? MARIE You call that being considerate?
CROMWELL Why, of course! Didn't I go round every one of them personally and say 'How do you like your stake?'

The QUEEN is confined to the Tower:
MARIE Oh, Wolsey! What is to become of me? Will I ever look up to see the clear blue of the sky

again? Will I ever again feel the blessed warmth of the sun on my tender skin?

WOLSEY I really couldn't say. The weather report isn't too good.

SIR ROGER, suspected of cohabiting with the QUEEN, is asked to sign a document:

CROMWELL I'll read it to you. It's just a simple little confession: 'Insomuch as I, Roger de Lodgerley, of Bedside Manor, Wilts, hereinafter referred to as the party of the first part, did unlawfully, with malice aforethought, and without taking due precaution, on the night of October 4th last, admire, covet, blandish, cosset, seduce and otherwise get at Marie, spouse to Henry Tudor, hereinafter referred to as the party of the second part. I do now hereby solemnly declare and in witness whereof I do hereby append my signature below, that the resulting issue, hereinafter referred to as the party of the third part, is the direct consequence of the joining together of the party of the first part's and the party of the second part's parts.'

HENRY Wolsey.

WOLSEY Yes, Milord?

HENRY Who is that with the two beauties?

WOLSEY That's your third wife, Sire.

HENRY Oh no, not her. The feller that's just come in with the two beauties.

WOLSEY Feller with two beauties, My Lord? Ooh! I see what you mean. Oh, that's old Charles, the Earl of Bristol and his daughters.

HENRY Oh, so those are Charlie's . . .

HENRY decides to dance with one of the daughters, BETTINA (Barbara Windsor):

HENRY May I have the pleasure?

BETTINA Oh no, I only came here to dance.

And later:

HENRY It's getting chilly in here. Shall we go into the summer house . . . warm up a bit?

BETTINA Oh no! I've heard what happens to girls who go into summer houses with men.

HENRY Good! That should save a bit of time.

BETTINA Oh, but I mustn't. I promised my mother I'd be a good Bett.

HENRY You're the best bet I've seen in years, believe me.

And as they exit:

MARIE Why is he taking her out into the garden?

WOLSEY Oh, I expect just to get a little air, ma'am.

MARIE How many more heirs does he want?

BETTINA Drink inflames the ardour.

HENRY Yes. The more you have, the 'arder it gets.

BETTINA Oh, I can hardly believe it. Little me in the King's arms.

HENRY Well, it's the best boozer in town.

BETTINA Oh, Maj! You're only after one thing.

HENRY Why? What's the matter with the other one?

BETTINA Oh, no! My mother says I mustn't start kissing men. You never know where it will end.

HENRY Believe me, I know where it'll end.

BETTINA No. She says I must save myself until I have a husband.

HENRY Well, that's all right. I'm a husband.

BETTINA That's right . . . you are, aren't you?

HENRY makes BETTINA the QUEEN's lady-in-waiting to keep her in the palace. And when he presents her to the QUEEN:

BETTINA Your Majesty, it is a great honour. The King has done me.

HENRY No, no, no! No full stop. A great honour the King has done me.

BETTINA Oh, that's right. Sorry. It is a great honour the King has done me by making me . . .

HENRY By making me your lady-in-waiting. Dear, oh dear, oh dear!

BETTINA By making me your lady-in-waiting. Dear, oh dear, oh dear.

HENRY and WOLSEY see BETTINA's naked reflection in a mirror:

WOLSEY Those dimpled shoulders! That slender neck! Those shell-like ears!

HENRY Later. I'm going the other way.

HENRY Where's Wolsey? Where is he?

BETTINA Oh, he said he had to go to Canterbury to try a witch.

HENRY To try a witch! Why?

BETTINA Oh, don't ask me. I should've thought they'd be the same as any other girl.

Cast:

Henry VIII	Sidney James	Bidet	Gertan Klauber
Thomas Cromwell	Kenneth Williams	Major Domo	David Davenport
Sir Roger de Lodgerley	Charles Hawtrey	Buxom Lass	Margaret Nolan
Queen Marie	Joan Sims	Physician	William Mervyn
Cardinal Wolsey	Terry Scott	First Plotter	Norman Chappell
Bettina	Barbara Windsor	Farmer	Derek Francis
Lord Hampton of Wick	Kenneth Connor	Fawkes	Bill Maynard
Sir Thomas	Julian Holloway	Second Plotter	Douglas Ridley
Francis, King of France	Peter Gilmore	Warder Number Two	Dave Prowse
Duc de Poncenay	Julian Orchard	Katherine Howard	Monika Dietrich

Serving Maid	Marjie Lawrence	Earl of Bristol	Peter Butterworth
Queen	Patsy Rowlands		(guest appearance)
Guard	Billy Cornelius		
Conte di Pisa	Alan Curtis	Produced by	Peter Rogers
First Warder	Leon Green	Directed by	Gerald Thomas
Royal Tailor	John Bluthal	Screenplay by	Talbot Rothwell
Flunkey	William McGuirk	Music composed and	
Heckler	Anthony Sagar	conducted by	Eric Rogers
Page Boy	David Essex	Production Manager	Jack Swinburne
Henry's Second Wife	Jane Cardew	Art Director	Lionel Couch
Dandy	John Clive	Director of Photography	Alan Hume BSC
Warder	Brian Wilde	Editor	Alfred Roome
Maid	Valerie Shute		
Henry's Courtiers	Peter Rigby	Made in the winter of 1970 at Pinewood Studios,	
	Trevor Roberts	Windsor Great Park and the Long Walk of	
	Peter Munt	Windsor Castle.	

Carry On At Your Convenience

Because the phrase 'at your convenience' may not have the same two-fold meaning abroad that it has in Britain, the film was called *Carry On Round The Bend* in its overseas version.

This was the twenty-second Carry On and the first major mis-judgement by the makers of their audience. It is one of two candidates as the least immediately successful Carry On at the box office and can be said, at present, to be the most unsuccessful, as the other (*Carry On England*) has not yet been on release long enough for the same degree of financial assessment to be made.

Many of the scenes in *Convenience*, much of the dialogue, the location (a lavatory-making factory), the performances, are typical, in some cases vintage, Carry On. Hattie Jacques, for example, is outstanding. So what went wrong? A major theme of the film is labour relations in a factory . . . increasingly a complicated, shifting, inflammatory topic. What the film suffers from is a lack of under-standing, a lack of research which would have told the makers that here was a subject possibly too involved, too serious, too full of hid-den traps for a Carry On. It is out of touch with the feelings of mil-lions of workers about trades unions and treats, in a flippant manner, a subject which workers take seriously.

Designer CHARLES COOTE (Charles Hawtrey) defends his latest toilet bowl against the doubts of factory foreman SID PLUMMER (Sid James) and MR W. C. BOGGS (Kenneth Williams) head of W. C. Boggs and Sons, makers of fine toiletware since 1870.
SID Very slender this pedestal, innit?

BOGGS Mm.
COOTE It's streamlined.
SID What for? Wind resistance? And:
COOTE I can assure you, sir . . . an elephant could safely use that toilet.
SID Not without a much bigger bowl.

Workers CHLOE MOORE (Joan Sims) and MAUD (Marianne Stone) discuss shop steward VIC SPANNER (Kenneth Cope):
CHLOE Oh, oh! Old Tinderbottom's off again. Another bloomin' strike, I suppose.
MAUD Oh no! What's it for?
CHLOE You know our Vic. He never has known what it's for.

SID's wife BEATTIE (Hattie Jacques) thinks their pet budgerigar is about to talk for the first time. She just saw it open and close its beak:
SID A bird opening and closing its beak! We'll have to write to the newspapers about that.
BEATTIE Well, it's a start. Generally he just sits there doing nothing.
SID He's a natural mimic. He's copying you.

But is budgie Joey a 'he' bird or a 'she' bird. Sid wonders:
BEATTIE . . . we know Joey's a 'he' bird don't we?
SID Cock.
BEATTIE He is! The man in the shop said so.
SID Cock bird, not 'he' bird.
BEATTIE Oh well, it's all the same thing. You wouldn't call yourself a cock man, would you?
SID Opportunity'd be a fine thing.

Carry On At Your Convenience When I said let's get down to business Miss Withering, I didn't mean . . .! But Miss Withering (Patsy Rowlands) does not plan to be chained to a desk at a loo factory for the rest of her life. Although, as his secretary, she has long hidden her deep-seated passions for toilet firm chairman W. C. Boggs (Kenneth Williams), today they have overflowed. Love not lavatories is on her mind. And while boss Boggs obviously thinks she has gone clean round the bend, we know that here is one loo chairman who has met his Waterloo.

VIC and his mate BERNIE (Bernard Bresslaw) visit The Whippet Inn, where meals are served by Bunny-type girls in very low-cut costumes:
VIC 'Course, that's nothing, you know. In some places they're completely topless.
BERNIE Cor! Nothing?
VIC Not a stitch.
BERNIE Cor! I bet that's tricky when they're serving the soup.

VIC It's a bit dodgy when they're frying the chips, an 'all.

MR BOGGS is caught in a compromising clinch with his secretary, and tries to explain:
BOGGS It's just she was upset. Worried about her future. And after all, she's not getting any younger.
SID She's not getting any.

Invited by MR BOGGS, on the firm's outing, to have a cockle, the secretary MISS WITHERING (Patsy Rowlands) is cautious:
MISS WITHERING I mean, I've heard that shellfish do very strange things. In a sex way, I mean.
BOGGS Really! (he holds up the carton of cockles and gazes into it) Let's watch them for a bit, then.

Cast:

Sid Plummer	Sidney James
W. C. Boggs	Kenneth Williams
Charles Cooie	Charles Hawtrey
Chloe Moore	Joan Sims
Beattie Plummer	Hattie Jacques
Bernie Hulke	Bernard Bresslaw
Vic Spanner	Kenneth Cope
Miss Withering	Patsy Rowlands
Myrtle Plummer	Jacki Piper
Lewis Boggs	Richard O'Callaghan
Fred Moore	Bill Maynard
Benny	Davy Kaye
Agatha Spanner	Renee Houston
Maud	Marianne Stone
Popsy	Margaret Nolan
Willie	Geoffrey Hughes
Ernie	Hugh Futcher
Barman	Simon Cain
Chef	Leon Greene
Doctor in film	Harry Towb
Hotel Manager	Peter Burton
Roger	Larry Martyn
Bunny Waitress	Shirley Stelfox
Roadhouse Manager	Bill Pertwee
Mr Bulstrode	Philip Stone
Hoopla Girl	Jan Rossini

Produced by	Peter Rogers
Directed by	Gerald Thomas
Screenplay by	Talbot Rothwell
Music composed and conducted by	Eric Rogers
Production Manager	Jack Swinburne
Art Director	Lionel Couch
Director of Photography	Ernest Steward BSC
Editor	Alfred Roome

Made in the spring of 1971 at Pinewood Studios and Brighton.

Carry On Matron

Comedian Jack Douglas joined the team with this one, doing a scene as a father-to-be, and got paid in champagne (see story, Part Two). He has since appeared in the next five Carry On films, nineteen Carry On television shows and two Carry On stage shows. Kenneth Cope came back after *Carry On At Your Convenience* to play a crook dressed as a nurse. Bill Kenwright, the slick Gordon Clegg of *Coronation Street* and the producer of many West End shows, appeared as a reporter.

Carry On Matron . . . or From Here To Maternity . . . or Familiarity Breeds . . . or Womb At The Top . . . or The Preggers Opera **Scene: Night-time. A woman's flat. A couple sit close together on a settee. There are drinks. The woman wears a black negligée and a mischievous expression. The man laughs knowingly and purposefully removes his jacket. What can they be up to? Unless it's a commercial for soap powder and how white his shirt is? No—Hattie Jacques, as Matron, and Charles Hawtrey, as psychiatrist Francis Goode, are there for the reason you thought of first, That's right, they are going to watch television! So that's what he meant by a horizontal hold. (PS: Matron's admirer, chief surgeon Sir Bernard Cutting (Kenneth Williams) did not believe them either). (PPS: But it's true!)**

MATRON (Hattie Jacques) trying to pacify angry unmarried mother MISS WILLING (Wendy Richard):
MATRON . . . You have a beautiful baby there. I wish I had one like it.
MISS WILLING Yes, and if you run into the same bloke as I did, you can have one.

MATRON to receptionist FRANCES KEMP (Gwendoline Watts):
MATRON Poor Sir Bernard! He's only got to read of some complaint and he's convinced he's got it.
FRANCES I wonder if he's read *Gone With The Wind?*

Commissionaire ARTHUR (Derek Francis) to DR PRODD (Terry Scott):
ARTHUR Blimey, she looked upset, Doc.
PRODD I'm not surprised. I've just told her she was pregnant.

ARTHUR What? Is she, really?
PRODD No. But it certainly cured her hiccoughs.

MR TIDEY (Kenneth Connor), expectant father and railway worker, is angry at the delays and false alarms over the birth of his wife's baby:
TIDEY We'd soon be in a right old mess, wouldn't we, if we ran the railways like that.
MATRON I was under the impression that you did.

MRS JENKINS (Amelia Bayntun), who is hard of hearing and the mother of many children, is pregnant again:
PRODD I thought you were going to stop having relations.
MRS JENKINS Oh, I've tried, Doctor. But you know what it is. My husband gets into bed and he says, 'Are you going to sleep, or what?'
PRODD And you say 'What'.
MRS JENKINS Well, that settles it this time. Whether he likes it or not I'm gonna use something from now on.
PRODD You'd better, Mrs Jenkins.
MRS JENKINS What d'you think's the safest, Doctor?
PRODD For you, Mrs Jenkins, a hearing aid.

PRODD Oh yes! I have some good news for you, Mrs Smethurst.
SMETHURST Miss Smethurst.
PRODD Oh! In that case, I have some bad news for you . . . Miss Smethurst.

Chief Surgeon SIR BERNARD CUTTING (Kenneth Williams) believes that a lack of sex is ruining his health, so he corners MATRON in her room:
SIR BERNARD Matron, a man and a woman are here to fulfil one basic function! You know what that is, don't you?
MATRON Well, I . . . I should do after fifteen years in a maternity hospital.
SIR BERNARD That's what's wrong

Carry On Matron **Any fool, including commissionaire Arthur (Derek Francis), can see that there is something funny going on here. Not just funny funny, but funny peculiar. Which is why he has stopped this furtive foursome as they try to leave Finisham Maternity Hospital. They are allegedly Dr Zhivago, an eminent foreign gynaecologist, his ambulance driver, his patient and his nurse. In reality they are the Carter Gang, who have just pulled off their latest sensational burglary: Sid Carter (Sidney James), Freddy (Bill Maynard), Ernie (Bernard Bresslaw) disguised as the happy mother, and Cyril Carter (Kenneth Cope) dressed as your original angel of murky . . . sorry . . . mercy. The baby? That's their loot. Inside the blanket are boxes of contraceptive pills which they plan to sell to underprivileged and overpopulated nations (though any country which is overpopulated is obviously getting its privileges). For students: This kind of theft is called pillfering.**

with me! I need to prove myself as a man!

MATRON Well, the proof of the pudding is in the eating.

SIR BERNARD Exactly! So, will you lay the table, or shall I? Get your cruet out!

But MATRON wants marriage first. SIR BERNARD fights back gamely:

SIR BERNARD But how do we know we're physically suited to each other? I mean, it's like do-it-yourself with wallpaper, isn't it?

MATRON Wallpaper?

SIR BERNARD Yes. You don't just go into a shop and buy enough for the whole room. You tear yourself off a little strip . . . and try it first.

MATRON That may be so. But you're not going to stick me up against the wall!

And as SIR BERNARD presses his advances:

MATRON No, I do not believe in free love! And what's more, I think it's very insulting of you to ask me!

SIR BERNARD Well, you don't believe in paying for it, do you?

Meanwhile railway worker MR TIDEY is still waiting for his wife to give birth:

TIDEY . . . Has she . . . has she had the. . . erm . . .

MATRON No, I'm afraid not, Mr Tidey. You may as well go back to your trains.

TIDEY What again? I can't do that. What'll my mates say? I shall be a laughing-stock.

MATRON Well, in your job you should be used to that.

MRS TUCKER (Maggie Nolan), a sexy young wife, consults DR PRODD:

MRS TUCKER . . . I came to see you three months ago, if you remember, because I was going to get married

. . . and I was a little bit worried about my husband being able to have a baby.

PRODD Yes, that's right. He was a bit older than you wasn't he?

MRS TUCKER Eighty-eight.

PRODD Yes and?

MRS TUCKER Well, if you remember, you suggested it might be a good idea if I were to take in a lodger. You know, someone a little nearer my own age.

PRODD Yes, but purely off the record, of course.

MRS TUCKER Well, it worked. I'm pregnant.

PRODD Really? What about your husband?

MRS TUCKER Oh, he's tickled pink.

PRODD Oh! That's all right then. What about the lodger?

MRS TUCKER Well, that's the trouble. She's pregnant, too.

Cast:

Sid Carter	Sidney James	Mrs Tidey	Joan Sims
Sir Bernard Cutting	Kenneth Williams	Matron	Hattie Jacques
Dr Francis Goode	Charles Hawtrey	Ernie	Bernard Bresslaw

Cyril Carter	Kenneth Cope	Expectant Father	Jack Douglas
Dr Prodd	Terry Scott	Mrs Pullitt	Madeline Smith
Nurse Susan Ball	Barbara Windsor	Mrs Putzova	Marianne Stone
Mr Tidey	Kenneth Connor	Mrs Bentley	Juliet Harmer
Sister	Jacki Piper	Nurse in bath	Gilly Grant
Freddy	Bill Maynard	Shapely Nurse	Lindsay March
Evelyn Banks	Patsy Rowlands	Nurse	Laura Collins
Arthur	Derek Francis		
Mrs Jenkins	Amelia Bayntun	Produced by	Peter Rogers
Jane Darling	Valerie Leon	Directed by	Gerald Thomas
Ambulance Driver	Brian Osborne	Screenplay by	Talbot Rothwell
Frances Kemp	Gwendoline Watts	Music composed and	
Miss Smethurst	Valerie Shute	conducted by	Eric Rogers
Mrs Tucker	Margaret Nolan	Production Manager	Jack Swinburne
Pearson	Michael Nightingale	Art Director	Lionel Couch
Miss Willing	Wendy Richard	Director of Photography	Ernest Steward BSC
Au Pair Girl	Zena Clifton	Editor	Alfred Roome
Reporter	Bill Kenwright		
Jane Darling's Husband	Robin Hunter	Made in the autumn of 1971 at Pinewood Studios.	

Carry On Abroad

Barbara Windsor revealed more in this Carry On than in any previous one—marking a wobble forward in the series, permissively speaking. June Whitfield, who appeared in the second Carry On, the highly successful *Carry On Nurse*, as a girlfriend visiting Leslie Phillips in hospital, returned after fourteen years to play a frigid and nagging wife who blossoms on a continental holiday, eagerly assisted by a hotel-keeper's son (Ray Brooks in his first Carry On). June also starred in the next one, *Carry On Girls*. Scottish comedian Jimmy Logan made his début in the series, as did Sally Geeson, who was appearing at the time as Sid James' daughter in the television series *Bless This House*. Note also David Kernan, now best known as the co-star of the hit show *Side By Side By Sondheim*, as the chap who brings romance to Sally's holiday.

The courier for Wundatours (Kenneth Williams) arrives at the Palace Hotel, on the continental island of Elsbels, with guests for a long weekend, and introduces himself to the manager, PEPE (Peter Butterworth):

STUART ... I'm the representative of Wundatours. Stuart Farquhar.
PEPE Stupid what?
STUART Stuart ... Stuart Farquhar.

Guest VIC FLANGE (Sid James) looks on:
VIC I think he was right the first time.

Carry On Abroad **When it comes to pulling birds, these foreigners are experts! Except that this wench-wrenching is not part of a pick-up, but a punch-up, involving police, tourists and tradesmen on the holiday isle of Elsbels. That's Marge (Carol Hawkins), one of the holiday gals, being hugged and tugged, and behind the cop is Brother Bernard (Bernard Bresslaw), a monk who is so in love with Marge that he prefers her to ... well ... butter. Here he asks the Lord's forgiveness before lending a hand, or rather a fist, and putting the cop into a heavenly sleep. A case of hit and Miss you might say!**

Randy guest BERT CONWAY (Jimmy Logan) to sexy guest SADIE (Barbara Windsor):

BERT For goodness sake, what's wrong with you? Why won't you come to the party with me?

SADIE Because you only want one thing from me.

BERT That's not true. I'm quite happy to have the lot.

SADIE Don't you understand? I don't want just a quick roll in the hay. I need something that's going to last.

BERT Who says it's not going to last? Jings, we don't go home till tomorrow afternoon.

Cast:

Vic Flange	Sidney James
Stuart Farquhar	Kenneth Williams
Eustace Tuttle	Charles Hawtrey
Cora Flange	Joan Sims
Brother Bernard	Bernard Bresslaw
Mrs Sadie Tomkins	Barbara Windsor
Stanley Blunt	Kenneth Connor
Pepe	Peter Butterworth
Bert Conway	Jimmy Logan
Evelyn Blunt	June Whitfield
Floella	Hattie Jacques
Brother Martin	Derek Francis
Lily	Sally Geeson
Georgio	Ray Brooks
Marge	Carol Hawkins
Robin	John Clive
Harry	Jack Douglas
Miss Dobbs	Patsy Rowlands
Moira	Gail Grainger
Nicholas	David Kernan
Tuttle's Mother	Amelia Bayntun
Police Chief	Alan Curtis
Vendor	Gertan Klauber
Stallholder	Brian Osborne
Second Policeman	Hugh Futcher
Madame	Olga Lowe
Fiddler	Bill Maynard
Produced by	Peter Rogers
Directed by	Gerald Thomas
Screenplay by	Talbot Rothwell
Music composed and conducted by	Eric Rogers
Production Manager	Jack Swinburne
Art Director	Lionel Couch
Director of Photography	Alan Hume BSC
Editor	Alfred Roome

Made in the spring of 1972 at Pinewood Studios and Slough, Bucks.

Carry On Girls

Jimmy Logan and Sally Geeson, who were in the previous *Carry On Abroad*, returned. Wendy Richard, one of the stars of the television comedy series *Are You Being Served?* also made her second appearance in a Carry On. She previously played an unmarried mother, MISS WILLING, in *Carry On Matron*. Arnold Ridley, of the television series *Dad's Army* made his Carry On début.

The seaside resort of Fircombe is holding its first bathing beauty contest. CONNIE PHILPOTTS (Joan Sims), owner of the hotel where the girls are staying, has a complaint for contest organiser SID FIDDLER (Sid James):

CONNIE It's your girls I'm talking about. I've heard them all night long, doors banging.

SID Oh blimey, Con, when you get a

Carry On Girls I give you my fullest support! Lady Mayoress Mildred Bumble (Patsy Rowlands) hands over her brassiere for burning and becomes, as it were, a foundation member of the women's rights movement led by Councillor Augusta Prodworthy (June Whitfield). But the voluminous, tent-like garment only brings a look of awe from the councillor and her committee, which says: We've heard of the Big Top, but this is ridiculous!

bunch of young dollies, you've got to expect a bit of banging.

Beauty contestant HOPE SPRINGS (Barbara Windsor) arrives on a motor-cycle. She unzips her jacket . . . revealing an ample bust:

SID Excuse me, I always thought they built the shock absorbers into the bikes.

Mayor FREDERICK BUMBLE (Kenneth Connor) and his wife MILDRED (Patsy Rowlands) first thing in the morning:

MILDRED You're up, then?

BUMBLE Of course I am. Didn't you hear me calling?

MILDRED I had the radio on.

BUMBLE I know you had it on. I can't remember when you had it off.

MILDRED Neither can I.

HOPE I like to think that a man can have a relationship with a woman which isn't just based on sex.

SID I fully agree. She should have money as well.

Carry On Girls **Crash, bang, wobble! This pile of pulchritude is supposed to be a beauty contest. But sex appeal became sock appeal when contestant Hope Springs (Barbara Windsor) accused contestant Dawn Brakes (Margaret Nolan) of stealing a bathing suit. Trying to sort out the settee set-to is contest organiser Sidney Fiddler (Sid James). Still, good looking girls like these are probably used to wrestling on a settee!**

Cast:

Sidney Fiddler	Sidney James	Mildred Bumble	Patsy Rowlands
Hope Springs	Barbara Windsor	Mrs Dukes	Joan Hickson
Connie Philpotts	Joan Sims	Police Inspector	David Lodge
Frederick Bumble	Kenneth Connor	Paula Perkins	Valerie Leon
Peter Potter	Bernard Bresslaw	Dawn Brakes	Margaret Nolan
Augusta Prodworthy	June Whitfield	Debra	Sally Geeson
Admiral	Peter Butterworth	Miss Bangor	Angela Grant
William	Jack Douglas	Ida Downs	Wendy Richard
		Alderman Pratt	Arnold Ridley

Larry	Robin Askwith	Woman Cloakroom	
Rosemary	Patricia Franklin	Attendant	Elsie Winsor
First Citizen	Brian Osborne	Stunt Double	Nick Hobbs
Fire Chief	Bill Pertwee	Cecil Gaybody	Jimmy Logan (guest
Miss Drew	Marianne Stone		star)
Matron	Brenda Cowling		
Susan Brooks	Zena Clifton	Produced by	Peter Rogers
Francis Cake	Mavis Fyson	Directed by	Gerald Thomas
Eileen Denby	Laraine Humphrys	Screenplay by	Talbot Rothwell
Gloria Winch	Pauline Peart	Music composed and	
Mary Parker	Caroline Whitaker	conducted by	Eric Rogers
Julia Oates	Barbara Wise	Production Manager	Roy Goddard
Maureen Darcy	Carol Wyler	Art Director	Robert Jones
Constable	Billy Cornelius	Director of Photography	Alan Hume BSC
Elderly Resident	Edward Palmer	Editor	Alfred Roome
City Type	Michael Nightingale		
Second Citizen	Hugh Futcher	Made in the autumn of 1973 at Pinewood Studios and Brighton.	

Carry On Dick

In several ways this film marked the end of an era. It was Sid James' last Carry On. He appeared in nineteen of them, beginning with *Carry On Constable*, and was the leading star in all but two—*Carry On Doctor* and *Carry On Up The Jungle*, when he took second billing to Frankie Howerd. *Carry On Dick* was the last consecutive Carry On written by Talbot Rothwell. Beginning with *Carry On Cabby* he wrote twenty of them, including one (*Carry On Spying*) co-scripted by Sid Colin. After *Carry On Dick* there was also some thinking about how long Barbara Windsor, now in her late thirties, could go on portraying dolly birds and saucy, young lasses in the films.

A former Miss World, Eva Reuber-Staier and a former Miss Great Britain, Linda Hooks, played showgirls in a troupe run by MADAME DESIREE (Joan Sims). Jeremy Connor, teenage son of Carry On veteran Kenneth Connor, played a footpad. It was his second appearance in the series. The first was in *Carry On Nurse*, in 1958, in the role of his father's screen son, when he was three-and-a-half. He went on to have parts in the next two Carry Ons.

DICK TURPIN (Sid James) holds up a coach:
DICK Stand and deliver. (No reply from inside coach) Deliver I say. Deliver.
Sound of a baby being smacked, and it starts to cry.
DICK Ah well, you can't win them all.

TURPIN, disguised as a parson, approaches one of his parishioners:

DICK Don't you think it's time you came to church again?
WILLIAM What do you mean, Rector? Don't you remember? I was there last Sunday. I took the collection.
DICK I know, and next Sunday I want you to bring it back.

CAPTAIN FANCEY (Kenneth Williams) and JOCK STRAPP (Jack Douglas) of the Bow Street Runners pretend to be criminals in order to catch DICK TURPIN. TURPIN, disguised as a vicar approaches them:
DICK Have you had any luck with your investigation?
FANCEY Yes we have an important clue to his identity.
DICK You have? And what is that?
FANCEY It appears that he has a curious marking on his... If you'll pardon the expression Reverend... on his diddler.
DICK Diddler? I don't know what that is.
FANCEY Oh, well... er... perhaps a more familiar word for it would be... (whispers in Dick's ear).
DICK Ooh! But I fear that won't be much use to you.
FANCEY Why not?
DICK Well, so many folk around here keep poultry, you see.
FANCEY I don't mean that kind of c.... Oh, this is very difficult...
STRAPP If I may be permitted to speak. You see what he means Rector is that he's got a birthmark on his... (Strapp leans over table and whispers in Dick's ear).
DICK Oh!
Strapp and Fancey laugh.
FANCEY Oh! Now he's got it.
DICK Now I have got it... But I honestly don't think it's possible that Jack the woodcutter...

FANCEY Jack the woodcutter?
DICK Well he's the only one I know that has a chopper.
FANCEY A chop . . . no . . . oh . . . this is very . . . this is ridiculous . . . Mmm, Reverend, do you know the difference between a man and a woman?
DICK Oh yes, of course.
FANCEY Well, that's it. The difference . . . it's on his difference!

STRAPP takes to following men into the loo:
FANCEY I fear this is going to be a *long* job.
STRAPP Well, if it is, it'll be easier for me to see, won't it?

DICK in the pulpit giving a sermon, in his guise as a parson:
DICK What has become of the priceless gift of virginity? Gone! What has become of the promised sanctity of marriage? Gone! If there is one man . . . just one man

amongst you who could say in all truthfulness that within the past week he has not committed adultery . . . then he may leave this church now. And go with my blessings.
BODKIN, sitting in the front stands up and starts to walk out.
DICK Ah, we have at least one man with us . . . well done brother Bodkin.
BODKIN Oh, it's not that Rector, you just reminded me where I left my 'at last night.

And later: BODKIN (Bill Maynard) is in the stocks. TOM (Peter Butterworth) talks to him:
TOM Well, Bodkin, what they got you in there for, then?
BODKIN I got involved in a fight with Katie's husband. It was bad luck.
TOM What d'you mean bad luck?
BODKIN Well . . . he found my 'at before I 'ad time to get back there.

TOM You're too much of a gentleman you are . . . next time keep your 'at on.

The rector (still DICK TURPIN in disguise!) is late home. His housekeeper MARTHA (Hattie Jacques) wonders why:
DICK Well, I did drop in to see an old Mrs Giles. She is very poorly, I'm afraid.
MARTHA Oh, can it be wondered at? Her husband treats her shamefully, I hear. You'd never believe he was once a knight.
DICK Tch, Tch, Tch! It's too much for a woman of that age.

Parson DICK to curvaceous HARRIETT (Barbara Windsor):
DICK Don't tell me a nice young girl like you has gone and strayed from the primrose path.
HARRIETT Oh no, it was indoors.
DICK I hope it was only once.
HARRIETT Well, I don't know. Nobody ever taught me 'ow to count proper.
DICK Well, we'll have to do something about that, won't we?
HARRIETT Oooh! Will you teach me, sir?
DICK I'd be very happy to.
HARRIETT To count right up to one hundred?
DICK Well, up to three for a start.

Housekeeper MARTHA hears a noise late at night:
MARTHA Who's that down there?
DICK It's . . . it's all right Miss Hoggett, it's only me. You nip off to bed and don't forget to say your prayers.

Carry On Dick Hello, who's the loud-mouthed, high-handed stranger in this neck of the wood? Why, it's Captain Desmond Fancey (Kenneth Williams) of the Bow Street Runners—who has run into a tight spot. Putting the screws on is the village constable (Kenneth Connor), under the impression that Fancey is highwayman Dick Turpin. Poor Fancey! He thought he was about to capture Turpin, and now he's been left at the post. Still, he can always touch wood for luck. After all, there's plenty of it about!

MARTHA What for? I never seem to get what I ask for.

A rich wife bemoans her robbery by DICK TURPIN:
WIFE He took my most treasured possession.
FANCEY Oh come milady, surely that went long ago.

DICK'S assistant TOM (Peter Butterworth) is disguised as a woman to rescue HARRIETT:
STRAPP What's your name my little pretty one?
TOM Bridget.
STRAPP Oh, Bridget.
TOM Most of the fellows call me Bridge.
STRAPP Bridge? Why?
TOM Because I come across.

Carry on Dick **Sid James and Barbara Windsor, as Dick Turpin and his accomplice Harriett, at a time when there were rumours of a romance between them. Barbara says: 'We became very close and fond of each other, but I wasn't in love with Sid . . . I love my husband.'**

Cast:

Dick Turpin	Sidney James
Harriett	Barbara Windsor
Captain Desmond Fancey	Kenneth Williams
Martha	Hattie Jacques
Sir Roger Daley	Bernard Bresslaw
Madame Desiree	Joan Sims
Constable	Kenneth Connor
Tom	Peter Butterworth
Sergeant Jock Strapp	Jack Douglas
Mrs Giles	Patsy Rowlands
Bodkin	Bill Maynard
Lady Daley	Margaret Nolan
Isaak	John Clive
Bullock	David Lodge
Maggie	Marianne Stone
Entertainers (the Birds of Paradise)	Laraine Humphrys
	Linda Hooks
	Penny Irving
	Eva Reuber-Staier
Tough Man	Larry Taylor
Tough Man	Billy Cornelius
William	Patrick Durkin
Sir Roger's Coachman	Sam Kelly
Mr Giles	George Moon
Squire Trelawney	Michael Nightingale
Browning (Bow Street Runner)	Brian Osborne
Rider	Anthony Bailey
Highwayman (later scene)	Brian Coburn
Footpad	Jeremy Connor
Highwayman (early scenes)	Max Faulkner
Footpad	Nosher Powell
Lady	Joy Harrington
Master of horse	Gerry Wain

Produced by	Peter Rogers
Directed by	Gerald Thomas
Screenplay by	Talbot Rothwell
Based on a treatment by	Lawrie Wyman and George Evans
Music composed and conducted by	Eric Rogers
Production Manager	Roy Goddard
Art Director	Lionel Couch
Director of Photography	Ernest Steward BSC
Editor	Alfred Roome

Made in the winter–spring of 1974. Shooting began in February at Pinewood Studios and in nearby woods and countryside.

Carry On Behind

A time of change, an influx of new faces, with German actress Elke Sommer in the lead role and other important parts going to Windsor Davies of the television series *It Ain't Half Hot Mum*, Ian Lavender of *Dad's Army* and Adrienne Posta; Dave Freeman turned in his first Carry On screenplay. The film was also the last consecutive contribution by Eric Rogers who had composed and conducted the music for twenty-one Carry Ons, beginning with *Carry On Cabby*. Carol Hawkins, of the television series *The Fenn Street Gang* and *Mr Big*, who made her Carry On début in *Carry On Abroad*, returned. So did Liz Fraser—after a gap of twelve years and twenty Carry Ons. She first appeared in *Carry On Regardless*, in 1961, and completed a hat-trick with *Cruising* and *Cabby*. A name to note—actor/scriptwriter George Layton of television's *Doctor In The House* series, also *My Brother's Keeper* which he wrote and in which he starred with Jonathan Lynn. With Lynn he was later hired to write *Carry On Again Nurse*, now awaiting production. Another familiar face (and shape) for television viewers—Diana Darvey of the Benny Hill series. Despite all this, initial box office reaction for the film was not as good as for most of the Carry Ons, though it is now better overseas, possibly because of Elke Sommer.

Customer ELSE in the shop of FRED RAMSDEN (Windsor Davies), butcher:
FRED Hallo, Else.
ELSE Hallo, love (points at meat) . . . give us a bit of that for me old man.
FRED Give that to your husband and you're in for a night of romance.
ELSE Ooh! Can I do it in the oven?
FRED Do it where you like, it's your kitchen.

While on a 'stag' fishing holiday, FRED and his mate ERNIE (Jack Douglas) meet a couple of girls. ERNIE, however, talks in his sleep . . . but he has a plan to foil his wife when he gets home:
FRED What about your disability, then?
ERNIE Ah, I've thought about that. If I keep calling Carol, Charlie, I'll be all right.
FRED What good will that do?
ERNIE Well, if I talk in my sleep it won't sound so bad. The wife'll think I'm talking about a fella.
FRED Could sound a bloody sight worse.

Archaelogist ROLAND CRUMP (Kenneth Williams) and Russian archaeologist ANNA VOOSHKA (Elke Sommer) are on a dig. They find a mosaic, which includes a nude woman:
ROLAND An interesting example of Roman tessellation.
ANNA Tessellation? Is name for what they're doing, huh?
ROLAND It simply means various Roman pieces get laid . . . on cement.
ANNA Very uncomfortable for them, no?

Carry On Behind **The mud lark! When you're as sexy as actress Elke Sommer you cannot even stretch your legs without some chap wanting to lend a hand! It is, of course, Bernard Bresslaw doing a publicity shot and pretending to carry Germany's sizzling Sommer over the rain-soaked location. So much more exciting than the way Sir Walter Raleigh coped with a similar situation.**

Carry On Behind Butcher Fred Ramsden (Windsor Davies) and his pal, electrician Ernie Bragg (Jack Douglas), on a fishing holiday away from their wives, are game for a 'nibble' of another sort when they find that Carol (Sherrie Hewson) and Sandra (Carol Hawkins) are staying at the same caravan camp. Fred is already shooting a line!

And later ANNA gives her verdict on what is portrayed in the mosaic:

ANNA Is no temple. In my opinion, is place where Roman soldiers are coming for drinking and for woman . . . and for . . .

ROLAND Yes, quite. I know what you mean.

ANNA Hm! What is name for place like this in English?

ROLAND In English?

ANNA Yes, place for soldiers are coming for drinking, and for woman, and for . . .

ROLAND Yes, yes, yes . . . it's called a NAAFI.

Later, though he is only covered in tomato sauce, ANNA thinks ROLAND has suffered a serious accident:

ANNA Must be finding doctors, man is injured.

ERNIE Where? What man?

ANNA Is . . . is professor of Archaeology . . . is bleeding terrible.

FRED Never mind his qualifications. Is he hurt badly?

FRED goes to tend ROLAND who believes, himself, that he is badly injured:

FRED It's all right now, me boy. You're in good hands.

ROLAND What are you?

FRED A butcher.

ANNA encounters a randy major (Kenneth Connor):

ANNA I'm sorry, Major, but I'm not loving you.

MAJOR Yes, but . . .

ANNA You see, when I love a man I give him everything. I give it all.

MAJOR But I don't want it all. I just want a bit.

ANNA and ROLAND have made exploratory digs on the site and though her English is not good, ANNA insists on writing the report:

ANNA (dictating) We are arriving on site, making preliminary survey. Professor Crump and I are living in caravan together. We have been all over the site poking . . .

ROLAND Look, don't you think it would be better if I wrote the report?

And later:

ANNA (dictating) First we are finding remains of Roman paving . . . showing pictures of . . . a erotic nature. One of the pictures is showing . . . erm . . . erm . . . a Weenus.

ROLAND A what?

ANNA A Weenus. Certainly you must know what a Weenus is, no?

ROLAND Oh, it's neither one thing nor the other really, is it?

ANNA A Weenus, Professor Crump, is the Goddess of Love!

ROLAND Oh, you mean Venus!

ANNA Is what I am saying . . . Weenus.

DAPHNE (Joan Sims) meets her husband, HENRY BARNES (Peter Butterworth) after years and years of separation. He's working as an odd-job man, but has £20,000 in the bank:

DAPHNE Where did you get it?

BARNES Saved it.

DAPHNE What, as an odd job man?

BARNES Yeah.

DAPHNE You must've done some very odd jobs.

BARNES I've been scrimping and saving for ten years. And then, last year . . .

DAPHNE Yes?

BARNES . . . I won the football pools.

DAPHNE How much?

BARNES Nineteen thousand, nine hundred and fifty quid.

Cast:

Professor Anna Vooshka	Elke Sommer	Major Leep	Kenneth Connor
Professor Roland Crump	Kenneth Williams	Ernie Bragg	Jack Douglas
Arthur Upmore	Bernard Bresslaw	Daphne Barnes	Joan Sims

Fred Ramsden	Windsor Davies	Nudist	Helli Louise
Barnes	Peter Butterworth	Student with ice cream	Jeremy Connor
Sylvia Ramsden	Liz Fraser	Lady in low cut dress	Alexandra Dane
Linda Upmore	Patsy Rowlands	Projectionist	Sam Kelly
Joe Baxter	Ian Lavender	Plasterer	Johnny Briggs
Norma Baxter	Adrienne Posta	Lady with hat	Lucy Griffiths
Vera Bragg	Patricia Franklin	Short-sighted Man	Stanley McGeach
Dean	Donald Hewlett	Wife	Brenda Cowling
Sandra	Carol Hawkins	Man in glasses	Sidney Johnson
Carol	Sherrie Hewson	Courting Girl	Drina Pavlovic
Landlord	David Lodge	Student	Caroline Whitaker
Mrs Rowan	Marianne Stone	Man with soapy water	Ray Edwards
Doctor	George Layton		
Bob	Brian Osborne	Produced by	Peter Rogers
Clive	Larry Dann	Directed by	Gerald Thomas
Sally	Georgina Moon	Screenplay by	Dave Freeman
Maureen	Diana Darvey	Music composed and	
Veronica	Jenny Cox	conducted by	Eric Rogers
Electrician	Larry Martyn	Production manager	Roy Goddard
Nurse	Linda Hooks	Art Director	Lionel Couch
Man	Kenneth Waller	Director of Photography	Ernest Steward BSC
Man with salad	Billy Cornelius	Editor	Alfred Roome
Woman with salad	Melita Manger		
Painter	Hugh Futcher	Made in the spring of 1975 at Pinewood Studios.	

Carry On England

Another little wobble forward in the realm of permissiveness. For the first time in a Carry On film bare breasts were not only flashed but their nakedness discussed—in a scene in which Army girls, as part of a battle with their commanding officer, deliberately misconstrue an order and go on parade topless. It got the film an AA certificate from the Censor, the first in the series (in place of a U or, latterly, the more normal A) so robbing itself of some of the Carry Ons' younger and most enthusiastic fans. No child aged fourteen or under can see a film with an AA certificate. In later discussions, however, following some re-editing after the film was launched, the Censor changed the certificate to an A.

But, even apart from the topless parade, the film has a more explicit style than previous Carry Ons. The slap and tickle, the fun and giggles about sex (and then usually not getting it) have gone. There is a more realistic, contemporary, permissive attitude.

Also, some of those taking part were not comical enough, being sadly miscast. They were too physically and vocally conventional for this sort of comedy, which thrives on exaggerations, distortions and idiosyncracies of face, body and voice. Look at the characters in a seaside postcard—the mammary magnificence of young girls, the mountainous backsides of middle-aged mums, the eyes and faces and expressions of the men. Look at the best-known Carry On stars. The face and laugh of Sid James. The voices and facial distortions of Kenneth Williams. The exaggerations of voice and chest and movements put on by Barbara Windsor. The expressions and character portrayals of Joan Sims. The devilment behind spectacled innocence, the bizarre, contradictory roles of Charles Hawtrey. The bumptiousness of a Kenneth Connor little man character, hiding a will and personality of pure jelly. Alas, in *Carry On England* he appeared to be hiding nothing. The character he played was just unpleasant.

For whatever reasons, this was not one of the more immediately successful Carry Ons at the box office though, like *Carry On Behind* and all the later films in the series, it is too early to assess its success comprehensively as, over the years, different Carry Ons can be differently appreciated in different parts of the world.

Kenneth Connor had the lead role for the first time since he appeared in the opener, *Carry On Sergeant*, eighteen years previously. Windsor Davies, who made his début with *Carry On Behind*, returned, and it was also the second Carry On for Peter Jones, star and co-writer of the television series *Mr Big*, whose first was *Carry On Doctor* in 1967. Former beauty queen Linda Hooks, later a hostess of the TV quiz show *Sale Of The Century*, was back for her Carry On hat-trick. The trend for new faces continued with Judy Geeson, Patrick Mower, Melvyn Hayes and Diane Langton. There were new scriptwriters, David Pursall and Jack Seddon who, among fifty films, had worked on *The Longest Day* and *The Blue Max*. For the first time for thirteen years, there was a new Carry On head of music, Max Harris, replacing Eric Rogers. Of the long-established Carry On stars only three were included—Kenneth Connor, Joan Sims and Peter Butterworth, plus Jack Douglas, a newer member of the team who had appeared in the previous five films. There were one or two familiar Carry On faces in smaller roles, like Julian Holloway, Patricia Franklin, Michael Nightingale and Brian Osborne.

How would you fancy a problem like this? Yes, it's tough being a director. Here Gerald Thomas, on the set of Carry On England, *is attempting what he calls 'the impossible'. That is, he is trying to make an ATS uniform look provocative. With a stunner like Judy Geeson, the problem is made very much easier, of course. But it's the sort of decision a chap could muse over for hours . . . and hours . . . and . . .*

Carry On England Once more into the breech, dear friends. Gunner Shorthouse (Melvyn Hayes) and Sergeant Able (Patrick Mower) look as if they could not shell peas. But treating their anti-aircraft gun as a barrel of laughs is all part of their gunplay in a battle with the new commanding officer. Before the film is over he is the one with the look of shellshock!

Time: World War II. CAPTAIN S. MELLY (Kenneth Connor) takes command of an anti-aircraft battery and finds women troops as well as men there. SERGEANT-MAJOR 'TIGER' BLOOMER (Windsor Davies) puts him in the picture:
TIGER . . . This is one of these new mixed batteries.
MELLY So that's what the Brigadier meant when he said that this battery was an experiment.
TIGER Experiment, sir. They does not need to experiment. They gets at it right away and all the time.

Because of MELLY's strictness the troops, including SERGEANT ABLE (Patrick Mower) and Gunners

SHORTHOUSE (Melvyn Hayes) and SHAW (Larry Dann) go sick. But the medical officer is on to them:
ABLE Here, Shaw.
SHAW Yes?
ABLE What did he say to you?
SHAW He said: 'Drop your trousers.' He had a look and he gave me two asprins.
ABLE Well what sort of a doctor is he, then? Here we are, all pretending we got different complaints and he . . .
  SHORTHOUSE comes out.
ABLE Now, Shorthouse.
SHORTHOUSE Yes.
ABLE What did he say to you?
SHORTHOUSE He said 'Drop your trousers.' And he had a look . . .

ABLE And he gave you two asprins.
SHORTHOUSE No, he gave me half an asprin.

Rebellious, the troops substitute a pair of khaki bloomers for the flag during a visit by the BRIGADIER (Peter Jones):
BRIGADIER Put up a bit of a bloomer there, Melly.
MELLY I . . .
BRIGADIER Whose flag is it supposed to be? Nicaragua's?

And as the battery man their ack-ack gun during an air raid, TIGER shouts words of encouragement:
TIGER Sixpence for every one you shoot down. Two bob if it's a German.

Carry On England Dressed to kill—or dressed to thrill! Captain S. Melly (Kenneth Connor) is forced to wear an ATS skirt after members of his anti-aircraft battery play a prank on him. Before he can give them a dressing-down, however, German bombers appear and what he thought was a flat battery sparks into all-shooting action. Rather appropriately Windsor Davies is pairing the beskirted Conner as Sergeant-Major Bloomer.

Carry On England Excuse me Miss, but are you a double agent? Captain S. Melly (Kenneth Connor) may have had to give Private Alice Easy (Diane Langton) the Army order: 'Chin in!' But never: 'Chest out!' That was something nature had taken care of. Diane was playing the sort of Carry On role in which Barbara Windsor had been out in front (as it were) for twelve years. Some even talked of Diane as: 'The new Barbara Windsor'. Here Melly, the commanding officer of a rebellious mixed anti-aircraft battery during World War II, does a gasping double take as he catches sight of two of the necessary attributes for this kind of part. 'I've heard of 'at the double,' Private Easy, but this is two . . . sorry . . . too much!'

Cast:

Captain S. Melly	Kenneth Connor	Gunners	Jeremy Connor
Sergeant-Major 'Tiger'			Richard Olly
Bloomer	Windsor Davies		Peter Banks
Sergeant Tilly Willing	Judy Geeson		Richard Bartlett
Sergeant Len Able	Patrick Mower		Billy J. Mitchell
Bombadier Ready	Jack Douglas		Peter Quince
Private Sharpe	Joan Sims	ATS	Paul Tothill
Gunner Shorthouse	Melvyn Hayes		Tricia Newby
Major Carstairs	Peter Butterworth		Louise Burton
Brigadier	Peter Jones		Jeannie Collings
Private Alice Easy	Diane Langton		Barbara Hampshire
Major Butcher	Julian Holloway		Linda Regan
Captain Bull	David Lodge		Barbara Rosenblat
Gunner Shaw	Larry Dann		
Gunner Owen	Brian Osborne	Produced by	Peter Rogers
Melly's Driver	Johnny Briggs	Directed by	Gerald Thomas
Corporal Cook	Patricia Franklin	Screenplay by	David Pursall and
Officer	John Carlin		Jack Seddon
Army Nurse	Linda Hooks	Music composed and	
Officer	Michael Nightingdale	conducted by	Max Harris
Freda	Vivienne Johnson	Production Manager	Roy Goddard
		Art Director	Lionel Couch
		Director of Photography	Ernest Steward BSC
		Editor	Richard Marden

Made in the spring of 1976 at Pinewood Studios.

That's Carry On

A film omnibus of some of the favourite scenes from the Carry On series, with linking jokes, reminiscences and descriptions by Kenneth Williams and Barbara Windsor.

Scheduled for release early in 1978.

Carry On Again Nurse

Screenplay commissioned from George Layton and Jonathan Lynn who wrote and starred in the television series *My Brother's Keeper*.

Likely to mark the reuniting of members of the long-established Carry On team missing from the previous two films, and it seems possible that either this or another subject could spearhead the series into the x certificate market.

Carry On Emanuelle

Screenplay commissioned from Lance Peters, a leading television writer in Australia who has lived in London for four years. Basic aim of film: to have a beautiful young actress in the name role, supported by all the Carry On favourites, probably as members of her rich household. And, of course, it sends up sex films.

Acknowledgements

Thanks to ... Peter Rogers; Gerald Thomas; Nat Cohen (chairman and chief executive of EMI Film Distributors); Frank S. Poole (managing director of Rank Film Distributors); British Board of Film Censors; British Film Institute; Kenneth Williams; Joan Sims; Hattie Jacques; Kenneth Connor; Charles Hawtrey; Jim Dale; Barbara Windsor; Bernard Bresslaw; Peter Butterworth; Jack Douglas; Bob Monkhouse; Leslie Phillips; Terry Scott; Kenneth Cope; Patrick Cargill; Sidney Bromley; Lauri Lupino Lane, and dozens of other actors who have helped with queries and opinions; also the late Sidney James for interviews in 1969 and 1974 for other purposes than this book; writers Norman Hudis; Talbot Rothwell; John Antrobus; Dave Freeman; Sid Colin; David Pursall, and Jack Seddon; composers Eric Rogers and Bruce Montgomery; director of photography Alan Hume; Sylvia Pyke (personal assistant to Peter Rogers and Gerald Thomas); Kenneth F. Matthews (publicity and advertising manager, Rank Film Distributors); Carry On publicist Catherine O'Brien; former Carry On publicists John Troke and Tony Hill; John R. Fraser (overseas publicity manager) and Zena Courtney of EMI Film Distributors Overseas; Ethel Good, and my wife Susan.

Thanks to EMI and Peter Rogers for photographs illustrating: *Carry On Sergeant, Nurse, Teacher, Constable, Regardless, Cruising, Cabby, Jack, Spying, Cleo, Cowboy* and *Screaming*.

Thanks to Rank and Peter Rogers for photographs illustrating: *Carry On ... Don't Lose Your Head, Follow That Camel, Doctor, Up The Khyber, Camping, Again Doctor, Up The Jungle, Loving, Henry, At Your Convenience, Matron, Abroad, Girls, Dick, Behind, England*.

I am also indebted to Gerald Thomas and Bernard Bresslaw for several off-screen photographs used.